UNIVERSITIES AND LIFELONG LEARNING SERIES

Lifelong learning, the arts and community cultural engagement in the contemporary university

Manchester University Press

UNIVERSITIES AND LIFELONG LEARNING SERIES

Series editor:
Professor Michael Osborne (University of Glasgow)

Universities and lifelong learning analyses the external engagement activities of universities and third- level institutions and is concerned with the range of activity that lies beyond the traditional mission of teaching and research. This is an area that until now has seldom been explored in depth and has rarely if ever been treated in a holistic manner.

Lifelong learning, the arts and community cultural engagement in the contemporary university

International perspectives

Edited by
Darlene E. Clover and Kathy Sanford

Manchester University Press
Manchester and New York

distributed exclusively in the USA by Palgrave Macmillan

Copyright © Manchester University Press 2013

While copyright in the volume as a whole is vested in Manchester University Press, copyright in individual chapters belongs to their respective authors, and no chapter may be reproduced wholly or in part without the express permission in writing of both author and publisher.

Published by Manchester University Press
Oxford Road, Manchester M13 9NR, UK
and Room 400, 175 Fifth Avenue, New York, NY 10010, USA
www.manchesteruniversitypress.co.uk

Distributed exclusively in the USA by
Palgrave Macmillan, 175 Fifth Avenue, New York,
NY 10010, USA

Distributed exclusively in Canada by
UBC Press, University of British Columbia, 2029 West Mall,
Vancouver, BC, Canada V6T 1Z2

British Library Cataloguing-in-Publication Data
A catalogue record for this book is available from the British Library

Library of Congress Cataloging-in-Publication Data applied for

ISBN   978 0 7190 8801 8 *hardback*

First published 2013

The publisher has no responsibility for the persistence or accuracy of URLs for any external or third-party internet websites referred to in this book, and does not guarantee that any content on such websites is, or will remain, accurate or appropriate..

Typeset in Minion with Aptiva display by
Koinonia, Manchester
Printed and bound in Great Britain by
CPI, Antony Rowe Ltd, Chippenham, Wiltshire

Contents

List of contributors

JOE ALLEN has been a Lecturer in Education in the School of Education, Queen's University, Belfast, since September 2004. He teaches in the Master of Education programme and the Postgraduate Certificate in Education. He also carries out research into e-learning in higher education. Prior to joining Queen's he spent six years teaching electronic engineering, mathematics, telecommunications and computer programming in schools and colleges around Ireland. He also worked for ten years with Nortel Networks and completed a part-time doctorate in the field of microelectronics engineering. Joe is also a chartered engineer and a Fellow of the Higher Education Academy.

SHAUNA BUTTERWICK is an Associate Professor and Chair of the Adult Learning and Education Diploma and MEd Programme in the Department of Educational Studies, University of British Columbia, Vancouver, Canada. Her research explores issues of social justice and women's learning in a variety of contexts including work, welfare systems and social movements. She is also interested in how arts-based processes contribute to learning and social transformation. Recent publications include *Meaningful Training Programs for BC Welfare Recipients with Multiple Barriers: Help First, Not Work First*, published by the Canadian Centre for Policy Alternatives and 'Travels with feminist community-based research: reflections on social location, class relations, and negotiating reciprocity', in *Feminist Community Research: Negotiating Contested Relationships*.

DARLENE E. CLOVER is Professor in Leadership Studies in the Faculty of Education, University of Victoria, Canada. Her areas of research and teaching include community and cultural leadership, feminist and arts-based adult education and research. Her current study focuses on the educational philosophies of librarians and gallery and museum educators in Canada and the United Kingdom. Darlene has guest-edited special editions of journals on the arts, creativity and/or arts and cultural organisations (*Convergence, Journal of Adult and Continuing Education, Journal of Adult Learning* and *International Journal of Lifelong Education*), and a recently published book is entitled *The Arts and Social Justice: Re-crafting Adult Education and Community Cultural Leadership* (Leicester: NIACE, 2007). In 2012 she published a book on social movement learning.

PATRICIA CRANTON is a retired Professor of Adult Education from Penn State University, Harrisburg, USA. She has been Professor in Adult Education in Canada in universities such as St Francis Xavier and McGill. Patricia's books include *Planning Instruction for Adult Learners* (1989), *Understanding and Promoting Transformative Learning* (1994), *No One Way: Teaching and Learning in Higher Education* (1998), *Becoming an Authentic Teacher* (2001) and *Finding our Way: A Guide for Adult Educators* (2003). Patricia has edited five volumes, most recently *Authenticity in Teaching* (2006), and *Reaching Out across the Border: Canadian Perspectives in Adult Education* (with Leona English, 2009). She is currently working with Ed Taylor to prepare the *Handbook of Transformative Learning*.

CATHERINE ETMANSKI is an Assistant Professor in the School of Leadership Studies at Royal Roads University, Victoria, Canada. She has a passion for integrating the arts into her research and teaching. Her doctoral work employed participatory theatre as a research method with international students. Catherine's primary areas of teaching have included arts-based and environmental leadership, and action-oriented, participatory approaches to research. She has received awards for excellence in her pedagogical approach, which incorporates a range of creative elements and experiential learning strategies. Catherine is currently co-editing a book titled *Learning and Teaching Community-based Research: Linking Pedagogy to Practice*, to be published by the University of Toronto Press.

JANET GROEN is an Associate Professor of Adult Learning at the University of Calgary, Canada. Her areas of research and teaching include transformational learning and learning opportunities for marginalised non-traditional adult learners and spirituality and adult learning within various contexts such as the workplace and university. Her most recent publications include 'Humanities professors on the margins: creating the possibility for transformative learning' (with Tara Hyland-Russell), *Journal of Transformative Education* and 'An insider's view: reflections on teaching a graduate education course on spirituality in the workplace', *Journal of Management, Religion and Spirituality*.

VICTORIA HUNTER is a dance lecturer and researcher at the University of Leeds, United Kingdom. As Programme Manager for the BA dance programme in the School of Performance and Cultural Industries she has led a range of projects, working with external companies and industry professionals to develop mutually beneficial partnerships and exchange knowledge and skills. Victoria has initiated projects with Phoenix Dance Theatre, Yorkshire Dance and Dance United, supported by funding from the Higher Education Innovation Fund, West Yorkshire Lifelong Learning Network and the Centre for Knowledge Exchange. This work focuses on research and knowledge-exchange projects aimed at developing dance graduate employability and furthering professional development opportunities for practising dance artists.

MIA HUSTED is Associate Professor at Roskilde University, Denmark. A mixture of critical theory, sociology and adult education inspire her scholarship. Her main focus in teaching and research is how to address questions of workplace democracy and development. Her research is conducted as action research, inspired by critical pedagogy, and often involves music and theatre. Husted and Ditte Tofteng work extensively together on long and short-term action projects. A recent chapter with Tofteng was entitled 'The common third: the researcher, the participants and their common creation', published in *Action Research and Interactive Research: Beyond Practice and Theory* (Shaker Publishing). Husted and Tofteng also undertook a collaborative PhD.

TARA HYLAND-RUSSELL is an Associate Professor of English at St. Mary's University College, Calgary, Canada. Her areas of research and teaching include life writing, radical pedagogy and the impacts of gendered and different genre forms of literature. She is currently engaged in research on narratives of identity for marginalised adult learners in radical humanities courses. Tara's most recent co-authored publications include 'Marginalized non-traditional adult learners: beyond economics' (with J. Groen), *Canadian Journal for the Study of Adult Education*, and 'Searching for Sophia: adult educators and adult learners as wisdom seekers' (with W. Fraser) in *New Directions for Adult and Continuing Education*.

CHRISTINE JARVIS is Dean of Education and Professor of Teaching and Learning in Higher Education at the University of Huddersfield, United Kingdom. She began her career in teaching with twelve years in community, further and adult education. Christine's research, publications and teaching often concentrate on the use of popular fiction. She recently co-authored a book on the representation of education and educators in popular fiction (Routledge), and has just completed a chapter on the transformative power of film and fiction for a book to be published by Jossey-Bass. Christine was awarded a National Teaching Fellowship in 2010 in recognition of her contribution to higher education teaching.

RANDEE LIPSON LAWRENCE is an Associate Professor at National-Louis University in Chicago in the Department of Adult Education. Her research interests include extra-rational ways of knowing and learning through the arts. She is the editor of *Artistic Ways of Knowing: Expanded Opportunities for Teaching and Learning*, and the author of several publications that exemplify her practice of incorporating affective, cognitive, somatic and spiritual dimensions into her teaching. She also works with students to use these processes in their research. Additional research interests and commitments include transformative learning, feminist pedagogy, collaborative inquiry, experiential learning and non-traditional adult education.

ROB MARK is currently Head of the Centre for Lifelong Learning, University of Strathclyde, Scotland. Before joining Strathclyde in 2010, he worked at Queen's University, Belfast and at the University of Ulster, where he held posts as Director of Education and Research and Coordinator of Access and Lifelong Learning. Rob's research interests include literacy, community and lifelong learning and he has coordinated a number of European-funded projects. Before coming to the university Rob worked in vocational colleges and as an outreach worker in the adult and community education sector. He is part of a European network, Eur-Alpha and the current editor of the *Adult Learner Journal* in Ireland.

KRISTIN MIMICK recently completed her doctoral degree in Drama Education and Curriculum Studies at the University of Victoria, Canada. Her research focused on the implications of practising drama education as part of a standards-based formal education paradigm. Her background using drama education as a learning medium in schools and her considerable experience as a curriculum developer with the British Columbia Ministry of Education permitted an in-depth and critical exploration of how drama education can be used as a cross-disciplinary pedagogical approach. Kristin's current research interests include drama education as a medium for personalised learning and she also co-teaches the course at the University of Victoria on oracy.

KATHY SANFORD is a Professor in the Faculty of Education, University of Victoria, Canada. Her research interests include literacy, multi-literacies, learning in the twenty-first century and adult learning. She has worked in teacher education, previously holding the position of Associate Dean Teacher Education, and is interested in education that spans both formal and nonformal educational spaces for learners of all ages. Kathy was co-editor of two special editions of the *Journal of Adult and Continuing Education* and one of the *International Journal of Lifelong Education*. She is currently engaged in a research project exploring adult learning in museums, art galleries and libraries. Kathy has also developed research projects using new technologies for supporting learning such as electronic portfolios and Moodle.

JANET SMALL is with the Centre for Open Learning at the University of Cape Town in South Africa. She started out her working life as a development fieldworker in the rural sector and later studied adult education, ending up in continuing and public education work at a mainstream university. She now works on creating and facilitating condensed non-formal courses for a wide variety of groups from current students to working professionals. Janet's particular interests are in curriculum design, recognition of prior learning, adult access to higher education as well as using technology to enhance learning experiences.

DITTE TOFTENG is Associate Professor at Roskilde University, Denmark, and is engaged in conducting and developing democratic methods to explore and alter ways of living and working. Her research evolves around theatre-based critical-utopian action research and interdisciplinary studies of how to address and consider questions of participation, democracy and learning in work life. Tofteng, with Mia Husted, has been actively involved in a variety of action research events including 'Festival Across', a creative event that brings together caseworkers, unemployed people, disabled people and social scientists to discuss work, inclusion and special needs through the arts. Her most recent publication in the *Action Research Journal* was entitled 'Theatre and action research: how drama can empower action research processes in the field of unemployment'.

SHELLEY TRACEY is an educational consultant who coordinated a tutor education programme for adult literacy and numeracy practitioners at Queen's University, Belfast, between 2002 and 2012. This programme used a range of creative methods to support practitioners in enhancing their understanding of literacy and exploring and building on their learners' literacy practices. Shelley also designed a creative thinking and problem-solving course for PhD students, which used arts-based methods such as creative writing and collage to support the exploration of research questions. Shelley's publications include poetic inquiry, practitioner research and the use of arts-based methods in teacher education to enhance reflection and reflective practice.

WILL WEIGLER has been a community-based theatre director, teacher and playwright for over twenty-five years. He is the author of the award-wining book *Strategies for Playbuilding: Helping Groups Translate Issues into Theatre* (2001). Will recently completed his PhD in Applied Theatre at the University of Victoria, Canada, where he now teaches. For his doctoral project, Will collected descriptions by professional theatre artists, scholars and critics of their most unforgettable theatre experiences and developed a lexicon of staging strategies that can be taught to anyone to make their plays more dynamic. In 2004 Will wrote, produced and directed *Common Wealth*, a large-scale musical play created in collaboration with the community of Darrington, Washington, and members of the nearby Sauk-Suiattle nation.

SARAH WILLIAMSON is a Senior Lecturer in the School of Education and Professional Development at the University of Huddersfield, England. She specialises in the arts and teacher education for the post-compulsory sector and teaches on undergraduate, postgraduate and Masters-level courses. Sarah's main interest is in creative teaching and she contributed to a two-year 'Creativity and Innovation in Teaching in Higher Education' project, co-authoring *A Toolkit for Creative Teaching in Post-Compulsory Education* (Open University Press, 2009). Sarah has expertise in the design of creative teaching and learning materials and resources and is frequently asked to present and run workshops in this field. She is currently researching creative approaches to evaluation and reflection, and writing a textbook for teachers in a non-traditional, visual format.

ASTRID VON KOTZE has a background in theatre work and creative writing. Until recently she was Professor of Adult Education and Community Development at the University of KwaZulu-Natal, Durban, South Africa. Her research interests include popular education, livelihood studies, community-based risk reduction, women's health and performance arts. She has done extensive work developing participatory teaching/learning materials with a social justice purpose. Astrid is now a community education and development practitioner associated with the Division of Lifelong Learning at the University of the Western Cape where she oversees a popular education programme in poor communities in and around Cape Town.

GRACE WONG-SNEDDON is the Advisor to the University of Victoria Provost on Equity and Diversity. She came to the University of Victoria in 1997 from the school system. Grace's initial experience in school as a non-English speaker helped to set her on a journey towards accessible education. Following an alternate career path, she has worked at the University of Victoria Counselling Services and the Office of International Affairs, and has been the Acting Director of both the Office of Equity and the Office of Human Rights. As the Advisor to the Provost on Equity and Diversity Grace is working to advance diversity and help to create welcome and inclusive learning and working environments.

Introduction

Darlene E. Clover and Kathy Sanford

> We need to transgress boundaries and take risks with our programmes, our learners and ourselves as adult educators. (Lipson Lawrence, 2005: 81)

> Universities should be the places where we fearlessly encourage complex thinking and doing, creating and collaborating. (Burnett, 2011)

Imaginatively educate. Aesthetically elucidate. Visually illuminate. Creatively investigate. Theatrically explicate. Artistically animate. Performatively resonate. These concepts characterise the innovation, energy and courage Lipson Lawrence speaks of in the above quotation. They also reflect the work shared in this volume – *Lifelong learning, the arts and community cultural engagement in the contemporary university: international perspectives* – by adult educators from North America, Europe and Africa who, within or through their universities, engage with aesthetic pedagogical practices that aim to critically and creatively communicate, teach, make meaning, uncover and involve. We do recognise, however, that these concepts do not necessarily come readily to mind when one thinks of the arts and the university. Decades ago, Mahoney referred to the relationship between the arts and the university as 'uneasy [and] perhaps even ... unnatural' (1970: 21). Moreover, although the study of the arts was acceptable, for the inward-looking academy dominated by science, technology, rigour and rationality the ability to make music, sculpt or paint, for example, were seen as accomplishments harmless enough in themselves but definitely to be pursued 'outside' academe (Risenhoover and Blackburn, 1976). Among other things, these sentiments are grounded in complex, often contradictory discourses and understandings of the social, educational, cultural and political function and place of the arts in society.

Arts, knowledge and human and social development: some debates

> While some feel art is merely a luxury others see everything that we do as having an art component. (Mann, 1977: 4)

For centuries scholars have debated how aesthetic forms engage, undermine, elaborate on, counter or enhance 'the social, cultural, and political conditions of society' (McGregor, 2012). While no single chapter can fully capture the profundity of these debates, it is important to address some of the key social and cultural

1

theorisations around issues such as freedom, democracy, knowledge and instrumentalism that have had an impact on the university and its relationship with and to the arts.

Plato was one of the first to articulate a consistent, albeit relatively derogatory, view of the arts in human life and society. To Plato the arts were 'falsehoods', flawed or inexact imitations of the world with the potential to corrupt by stimulating irrationality and propagating immorality and associated inappropriate behaviours. This particular understanding derived from a bipartite notion in which the rational or thinking element of humanity was seen as noble and aimed towards the greater social good while the irrational side – the emotional or 'appetive' – was highly susceptible to corrupting forces, making a dangerous 'impression on suggestible people' (Belifore and Bennett, 2008: 54) by becoming their rulers rather than their subjects. Threaded through these understandings were weavings of class with artistic interpretation. While the highly educated classes were understood to have the skills necessary to assess any 'myths' portrayed in and through the arts, the 'susceptible minds' of the non-lettered classes were not. Seen to be lacking in any form of aesthetic judgement or life experience upon which to draw, the masses were unable to interpret artworks 'correctly', and discern reality from engineered situations, and they were thereby misled into believing things 'they had no grounds for believing' (Hospers, 1974: 156).

Following in Plato's footsteps, Aristotle took a somewhat different approach although one could argue that his journey terminated at the same destination. Aristotle developed a hierarchy of different forms of knowledge, separating the 'useful and necessary' from the 'beautiful and purposeless'. This distinction, McGauley argues,

> divorces art … from any purpose other than reflective enjoyment. Because the material world is governed by competing social interests and is thus unstable, messy and unreliable, the pursuit of beauty and truth has to occur within the realm of pure thought. The highest truths are the Ideal, transcending the life of exploitation and poverty of the majority, and reserved for the 'higher' level of society, those whose minds are uncluttered by distractions like cold or hunger. (2006: 11)

These sentiments of superiority formed the ethos upon which arts and cultural institutions were founded. Although private collections existed for centuries, public arts and cultural institutions such as galleries, museums and libraries only began to emerge in the 1800s. Their mandate was to provide enjoyment, enrichment and knowledge, and for the most part they attracted solely the upper classes. As an enhanced social consciousness began to seep through the cracks of this elitism, efforts to encourage the intellectual improvement of the working classes were put into place, forcing open the doors of galleries, museums and libraries. For some, greater access for the labouring classes was labelled cultural democracy; for others it was simply a means to make them more valuable to the wealthy classes or augment morality through contact with art, religious texts and literature (Lerner, 2009; Clover and Sanford, 2010). Following closely on this advancement were efforts to uplift the spirits of the poor by bringing the arts into their lives, although many cultural institutions maintained a steadfast and hearty distrust of the poor, believing they were 'incapable of becoming civilised' (Perry and Cunningham, 1999: 239). Then of course there were women, who were not yet 'persons' and were of such delicate natures that they needed to be confined 'into separate ladies' rooms' (Lerner, 2009: 133), a practice carried over into the university. In her study of the University of Toronto, Panayotidis noted two complementary natures of aesthetic contemplation: 'One for the professional man and the other, for the amateur woman homemaker' (2004: 107). Aesthetics within the academy were 'to serve to develop the taste and the appreciation of beauty' for men, while outside activities could adequately respond to women's interests in 'art and aesthetics restricted to the home sphere' (107).

Numerous scholars have been inspired to develop aesthetic conceptualisations to challenge these ingrained sentiments and practices of elitism and classism. Theorists such as Bourdieu (1993) described the artworks within these institutions, as well as elitist social and institutional practices, as 'high art', meaning particular genres or types of art –all by men who retain today the moniker of 'the old masters' – that had a reified position in the cultural hierarchy that, despite democratising efforts, or perhaps because of them, remained out of reach of the majority. Feminists such as Nochlin (1988) went further, highlighting the unrepentant sexism that shadowed both elitism as well as terms such as 'the masses' and 'the majority'. Others who denounced all separations in the aesthetic lifeworld, illustrating how they created chasms between arts and crafts and delegitimised the arts in relation to education, knowledge creation and the enrichment of citizens' everyday lives, joined in (Duvenage, 2003; Mann, 1977). Inherent in this were questions around 'use-value', giving rise to complex debates around freedom of expression and instrumentalism, central to which, and of most interest to us, is politics. On one side of the debate are scholars who argue for creative expression to be free from all politics and pre-determined use- or end-value, whether or not it is for the betterment of society (McGauley, 2006). Their primary concern was that art would become an advertising aesthetic aimed simply at selling or commodifying ideas. Moreover, political goals and messages in art, no matter how progressive, rendered them mere handmaidens to propaganda (Adorno, 2002; McGauley, 2006). There were also concerns about a tendency towards models for 'fixing' people, an insurmountable burden placed on the arts 'to transform the lives not just of individuals, but of whole community' (Belifore and Bennett, 2008: 3).

On the other side however, are those who challenge the idea that authentic expressive freedom in art only exists when it is disengaged from all interests outside of itself. While they acknowledge that the arts cannot change the world or solve 'all' the world's problems, they can contribute to an appropriately informed awareness by illuminating and naming socio-political subject matter, and encouraging active learning in ways few other methods can (Clover, 2012; Marcuse, 1978; Mullin, 2003). The problem is not the use of the arts as a political, educational or organising tool, but rather an impoverished understanding of politics, imagination and any other 'sense of the creative possibilities in human life' (Williamson, 2004: 136). For Marcuse, aesthetics was politics and working with or through an imagined reality was more than simply an oblique route towards changing the world. Arts have one of the highest potentials to rupture 'the codes and categories of how the world is seen, to imagine the world not as it is but as it might be' (Miles, 2012: 10).

These aesthetic considerations take us further along a continuum of debates around the epistemological, investigative and educational value of the arts. Some scholars argue that the arts lack any ability to supply real data or new understandings that can be judged against 'any reliable scientific standard' (Belifore and Bennett, 2008: 47). New asserts that the arts cannot 'authenticate the view [they convey]', which means they are neither factual nor reliable sources of knowledge. Although we may garner some 'truths' from the arts, 'they are not shown to be truths by virtue of being persuasively conveyed [through an artwork]' (1999: 120). Taking this further, Carroll challenges claims that the arts can educate – they simply recycle truisms that people already possess, so 'consequently, since it makes little sense to claim that people learn the truisms they already know ... there is little point in regarding the arts as education' (2002: 4). This means that the best the arts can do is to 'activate already possessed knowledge rather than its creation *ex novo*' (Belifore and Bennett, 2008: 46).

Although himself somewhat wary of truth claims, Habermas argued that aesthetic expressiveness was the 'correct way to interpret one's own and other's needs and desires; the appropriate argumentative form for revealing subjectivity' (in Duvenage, 2003: 55). On this basis alone they secured themselves a legitimate place in everyday communicative practice. However, what was recognised and valued was their 'subjective' or personal nature. Marcuse, however, lifted the arts into the realm of the cognitive/intellectual, arguing that 'imagination enables one to transcend the given, by cognitively creating the future' (in Miles, 2012: 17). For many, this was an advance against leaving the arts to languish in the affective/emotional realm where they could too easily be dismissed in a flurry of derision, scorn and condescension (Greene, 1995; Yeomans, 1995).

Other scholars, however, argued that it was this 'affective' – sensory, appetive and emotive – aspect and ability of the arts that was the most transformative. Indeed, Greene (1995) suggests that the more serious the problems in life, the more we need the arts to provide us with compassion, empathy and insight and challenge today's technically rationalised industrial culture 'whose values are brittle and whose conception of what's important [is] narrow' (Eisner in Butterwick and Dawson, 2005: 3). Wyman refers to this defying of 'the constraints of expectation of the everyday [to approach a] realm of understanding [that] lies beyond the immediate and the real' (2004: 1). Similarly, Fielder calls it 'moments of release from the ordinary burdens of everydayness and even rationality' (in Mann, 1977: 5).

Eisner, however, brings the emotional and rational together, suggesting that the mind operates at its highest level when sensory perception and emotion are understood as inseparable and integral:

To talk about thinking *and* feeling is somewhat of a misnomer, for it segregates feeling from thinking by the inclusion of the word 'and'. The ability to feel what

4

a work expresses, to participate in the emotional ride that it makes possible is a product of the way we *think* about what we see … Seeing is an accomplishment and looking is a task, and it is through seeing that experience is altered, and when altered, becomes an experience in shaping the kind of minds that people can make for themselves. (2008: 344).

It is the reuniting of the emotional and cognitive by engagement with and through the arts that will 'achieve all we hope for as a society' (Wyman, 2004: 1).

The arts on campus

Teachers of the arts argue, quite intelligently, that the understanding of art a student receives in an inter-disciplinary class is usually so superficial as to be irrelevant to the real concerns of art and a waste of everyone's time. Their colleagues in other departments argue, equally intelligently, that a little bit is better than none at all. (Roush, 1970: 73)

As one walks through the halls of academia, these complex, unresolved and unresolvable debates feel as though they are etched into the mortar and bricks. But we can with equanimity argue that matters have improved substantively vis-à-vis the arts on university campuses today. As Ransom argued in 1968, 'even when institutional organisation was unprepared to nurture it the university has had the wisdom to celebrate creative imagination' (1968: ix). Progressively, faculties, schools or departments of fine art, together with museums, arts centres, theatres and galleries located on or linked to university campuses, have become commonplace. Arts exhibitions, concerts, theatre and dance performances abound along with poets and other artist-in-residence programmes, although to suppose that all this was accomplished without murmurs or even more forceful expressions of dissent from many in the academy would be erroneous (Risenhoover and Blackburn, 1976). There is in addition the political cultural activism of students on campuses worldwide who employ a virtual carnival of arts such as community theatre, film, video, posters, poetry, music, textiles, zines, puppets and more to make statements, address social issues, challenge authority and injustice or simply have fun and celebrate.

Yet we can argue equally that improvements remain to be made. Not all of the arts (read crafts) are recognised as valid 'high' art forms; the chasm between high and low art persists, perpetuated by other elitisms on the higher education campus. Many university art museums or galleries are not actually located on campus, and few have collections of sufficient range to satisfy broad educational needs. Although technically available to everyone through public exhibitions or events such as the theatre performances and concerts as noted above, teaching and learning about, with and through the arts is still confined primarily to art history and technique 'experts' in fine arts, music conservatories, arts and cultural institutions or in adult education classes offered through continuing education programmes. These latter are themselves on the very margins of the academy, most often dismissed as 'recreational evening classes where elderly ladies and gentlemen paint pretty pictures of flowers and landscapes from their favourite postcards' (Yeomans, 1995: 219). In times of budget cuts, aesthetics lose out to the weighty teaching, learning and research of the sciences and medicine.

There is, however, another interesting or perhaps troubling point we need to raise that is connected to the above. When we began to explore the idea of producing this book, we assumed there would be a plethora of works upon which to build. We were quickly disabused of that notion. Like Jarvis and Williamson in this volume who mined the Internet looking for the concept of pop-up art schools to no avail, we came out almost empty-handed from all our 'Google scholar' combinations of 'university' or 'higher education' with 'the arts', 'fine arts', 'visual arts' and 'performance arts'. Yet faculties of fine arts and conservatories of music have been part of universities for decades. As Duke, Osborne and Wilson (in press) remind us, universities have been making major 'contributions through research, development and consultancy to heritage and cultural tourism, including sport; innovation and entrepreneurship; art and design; eco-tourism, crafts and food production; and the promotion of traditions of all ethnic groups and minority languages'.

A number of books were written in the late 1960s and 1970s, but these focused solely on fine arts faculties, schools and/or museums. Winter perhaps gives us some clue as to why there are so few publications when he writes in a edited volume entitled *The Arts on Campus* that he had never really thought of sharing his concerns about the arts in higher education with others, and instead 'brooded about them by myself' (1970: 17). In addition to this, Mahoney's query in the same volume as to whether the way the arts are taught on campuses is in fact the way all students want to learn about them is much the same question that underlies the work this volume, some forty years later. It would seem at times that with the arts and universities, *plus ça change, plus c'est la même chose.*

Lifelong learning, the arts, and community cultural engagement in the contemporary university is a response to these questions and concerns, a collective dialogue on scholarship and the arts in an interdisciplinary world, and a testament to new arts-based and informed academic and community possibilities. It is a book about change and challenge in organisation, in artistic use and value, in practice and form. It is a testament to the imagination and the courage of those who persist in creatively critiquing, educating and investigating in a world that so often violates our deepest values of justice, equity and sustainability.

This volume maps out various ways in which the arts and creative practices are manifest in contemporary university-based adult education work, be it the classroom, in research or in the community. It is written for all who work or would like to work beyond normative fine arts structures, who work or would like to work with community artists, who work or would like to work with arts and cultural institutions or to those who simply wish to augment the human aesthetic dimension in their educational and research practice or service work.

We, the authors

> A learner practices the creative act of perceiving meaning in processes, images, and environments. As those things become less familiar, he [or she] will have to become a more artful learner. (Roush, 1970: 75)

We, the authors of this volume, have differences but share similarities. We are located at universities in various parts of the world including Canada, Scotland, the United States, Northern Ireland, Denmark and South Africa. We share our stories in different formats, have distinctive foci, focus on varied genres, and work within diverse cultural, social and political contexts. Some of us have conversations about the ways in which we incorporate arts-based practices into our teaching and research. Others explore the work of arts and cultural institutions or share stories of community cultural work. Some of our projects are partnerships between our universities and community organisations while others of us carry out our practices in relative isolation. Some us respond to institutional mandates while others are more student or community responsive. Some of us teach or use creative practices ourselves, while others of us draw on the skill of community artists.

Regardless of our variances, or even perhaps as a result of them, our collective aim in this volume is to highlight imaginative practices and sites and creative voices, and problematise or provide critical insights into aesthetic pedagogical issues, tensions, potentials and challenges that we as adult educators face or have uncovered in working through and within the confines of higher education. Our mutual bias is a belief – albeit not totally through rose-tinted glasses – that not only are the arts, arts and cultural institutions and community cultural activities significant to higher education, but that they are necessary to the development of adult educators, teachers, administrators, students and/or citizens who can respond to the contemporary challenges of today's society through more imaginative approaches founded in or derived from aesthetic and critical theories. We believe in the potential of aesthetic and creative practices and methodologies to advance the common good, promote human and cultural development and change, reinvigorate research and society and provide a space and opportunity for adult learners, students or community members to creatively and critically engage with and reimagine the world as a better, fairer and more healthy and sustainable place. We also believe that the contemporary university must be a place that continually provides opportunities to open doors to larger, new worlds, and to learn to play a richer and more fulfilling role in those worlds. Universities must help people to discover who they are, who they might be and, equally importantly, offer the tools that enable students, professors and communities to reach their full potential.

We are also confounded by a number of challenges. Human life has become increasingly more quantified and administered, and neoliberal market ideology continues to be sharpened on the backs of the poor; hence universities, with the remnants of detachment and superiority still clinging tightly to their fabric, find themselves locked in a battle between active social engagement and responsiveness to community and the dictates of quality and rigour and economic competiveness. Nevertheless, we are steadfast in our belief that artistic creation and practice are effective responses, and sometimes even solutions, to the complex social, political, cultural and educational problems the world faces today.

The structure of this book

> Start with no more than a commanding notion of the sheer interestingness of the subject [then] sample, explore, revisit, choose, arrange, without claiming to have brought to the page a representative miscellany. (Sontag, 2001: 238)

This volume is divided into three sections that reflect the normative structure or 'three pillars' of the contemporary university: teaching, research and service. Section I is entitled *Arts-based teaching and learning*, section II *Arts-based research and enquiry* and section III *Community cultural engagement*. We conclude this volume with an Epilogue that sums up the messages and tensions in the book.

Although the three categories – teaching, research and service – may seem obvious, any suggestion that our choosing to use them was straightforward would be erroneous. The process was in fact a spirited engagement of Sontag's metaphoric, astigmatic dance of exploration, revisitation and reorganisation. The reason? The three pillars of separation so adamantine to the university are in fact unfixed, dynamic and cross-pollinating in the lives of its scholars. Indeed, the socially committed adult educators in this volume illustrate, although they do not necessarily name, how misrepresentative of the inextricable interrelatedness of our work, and therefore how constraining, these artificially imposed distinctions actually are. This challenge notwithstanding, as well as that of having to unfurl our circular, creative worlds of practice and research on to the linear inflexible structure of a book, the chapters provide a tapestry of aesthetic practices and strategies, imaginative learning and engagement and creative and critical reflections on new, aesthetic forms of adult education work with, in and through the medium of higher education.

Section I: arts-based teaching and learning

> Meanwhile, teachers of arts must broaden their idea of education in the arts so that they can devise pedagogies to bring an artistic sensibility to bear upon the entire gamut of human problems. (Roush, 1970: 74)

In the first chapter, entitled 'Embodied learning through story and drama: shifting values in university settings', Kathy Sanford and Kristen Mimick share their experiences of co-facilitating a graduate class on 'oracy' at the University of Victoria in Canada. Although creating a course about oral language, tenured professor Sanford was weighed down with the irony that priority would be given to written texts and essays by both the academy and the students. Mimick, however, a drama educator from the school system, carried no such burden. Working as co-instructors, co-collaborators and co-artists, the authors share how they used concepts of embodied ways of knowing and practices of storytelling and performance to refine the linguistic imagination and meld academic and creative goals into a learning community of shared ownership.

We travel to South Africa through Astrid von Kotze and Janet Small's second chapter, entitled 'Dream, believe, lead: learning citizenship playfully at university'. They focus on a programme that stems from the university's mission and commitment to encouraging its graduates to become more engaged citizens, willing to think critically and creatively about issues of global import, social justice and inequality. The arts-based popular education approach in one module of the programme demonstrates how it improves the process of building students' critical insights and abilities and deepens their sense of creative potential as a commitment to social justice. However, the authors also recognise the threat of recent financial constraints and highlight how the arts and ensuing community cultural engagement will suffer at the hands of capitalist imperatives, threatening interdisciplinary and holistic imaginations towards alternatives.

Tara Hyland-Russell and Janet Groen, in 'Crossing a cultural divide: transgressing the margins into public spaces to foster adult learning', share their work through Storefront 101, a free University of Calgary literature course for 'non-traditional' adult learners. The aim of the course is to involve students in active dialogic processes of learning and civic and cultural engagement. Using storytelling, field trips to cultural exhibits and performances, the authors speak of shifting power dynamics and enabling students to break down daunting barriers such as poverty, violence, substance abuse, negative self-perception and negative educational experiences. But students also enter a cultural world from which they have traditionally felt excluded. The authors argue, however, that by creating a trusting and respectful learning space based on an ethic of care, these cultural class barriers can give way to greater cultural agency and democracy.

Using the concept of pop-up galleries, Sarah Williamson and Christine Jarvis of the University of Huddersfield in the United Kingdom describe their work on 'Teacher education and the pop-up art school'. These pop-up art schools provide opportunities for trainee teachers to work collaboratively to plan, design and organise large-scale, inspirational art-based community-learning activities for senior citizens, members of the public, arts' enthusiasts, and children and their parents. Like Sanford and Mimick, Jarvis and Williamson provide in-depth descriptions of their collaborative development of learning communities through art and remind us of the power of the arts to teach and democratise. They also recognise how the ephemeral nature of the pop-up lacks the strong roots that community arts workers develop over time through close, sensitive engagement with groups.

A reflective, narrative approach is taken in the final chapter, entitled 'Fear of glue, fear of thread: reflections on teaching arts-based practice', by feminist adult educators Shauna Butterwick and Darlene Clover. The arts are presented as a powerful means by which to explore complexities in the university adult education classroom. However, the numerous challenges to doing this work are also discussed. They share vivid examples of teaching strategies that aim to connect mind and body and politicise the imagination through popular theatre, political fashion shows, puppet performances or quilt-making to address issues ranging from the exploitation of women to environmental degradation. The authors also remind us of the significant role played by the community artists brought into the classroom to legitimise political and activist arts against a tradition of fine arts elitism.

Section II: arts-based research and enquiry

We asked each other ... as we embarked on our investigation, questioning the place of an aesthetic within the presentation of research findings: Could [the arts] be engaging and entertaining ... and provide an authentic interpretation of our data? (Bird et al., 2010: 82)

In their chapter 'Mentoring arts-based research: a tale of two professors', Randee Lipson Lawrence from National-Louis University in the United States and Patricia Cranton, recently retired from Penn State University, engage in a spirited discussion about integrating the arts into graduate adult education research courses. Together the two feminist authors breathe imagination and life into often dull methods classes, challenge the myth of the distant researcher, and tackle issues such as the privilege of rationality and the myopia of rigour and positivism. They argue the potential of using alternative creative processes for conducting research in the academy, focusing in particular on the crucial role of the research adviser, and provide specific examples of how to incorporate music, fiction, poetry, painting, photography, theatre and more to promote more creative research in their universities.

Shelley Tracey and Joe Allen discuss the use of 'Collage-making for inter-disciplinary research training in Northern Ireland' with a group of PhD students who come from diverse disciplines and speak a number of languages, both metaphorically and literally. As adult educators and researchers at Queen's University, Tracey and Allen describe how collage-making provided a non-linguistic method for students from across disciplines to explore, express and share their research ideas in new ways. Two types of collage – paper-based and electronic – were offered as choices and although not without their challenges, these creative methods provided a compelling way for students to reimagine research practice and dissemination. While recognising the constraints of the university, the authors argue the potential of team-teaching approaches to enhance cross-disciplinarity.

In 'Theatre-based action research for health in Denmark', Mia Husted and Ditte Tofteng of Roskilde University explore the potential and the challenges of using drama as a tool of action research in the healthcare community. Embedded within the Scandinavian tradition of worklife studies and adult learning and combining the social theatre approaches of both Boal and Brecht, the authors share their programme of research entitled 'Stop Stress', which aimed, over an extended period of time and in collaboration with the community, to address issues of stress in the workplace. The authors illustrate the value of using community artists – in this case a professional theatre troupe – to conduct interviews and then create a series of vignettes that mirror the stories of workplace-related stress, because this provides a critical distance from which participants can reflect and develop collective strategies to alleviate stress in their daily working lives.

Section III: community cultural engagement

> Universities don't solve social problems, although we have an indispensible role to play in helping to understand a problem as well as frame a strategy for its resolution. (Votruba, 2010: xv)

'Weaving tales of hope and challenge: exploring diversity through narrative métissage', by Catherine Etmanski, Will Weigler and Grace Wong-Sneddon, is contextualised in the annual, campus-wide, interdisciplinary Diversity Research Forum hosted by the Office of the Provost at the University of Victoria, Canada. In this chapter, the authors document the process leading up to a métissage performance, describe its effect on the audience and reflecting on the lessons learned along the way. One aim of their artistic intervention was to advocate arts-based methods by moving beyond the traditional methods such as PowerPoint lectures and panel presentations that dominate engagement and knowledge dissemination in the university. Another, however, was to illustrate the methodological power of the arts in general and métissage in particular to foster greater understandings and empathy between people of diverse cultural backgrounds.

Set in the context of economic cutbacks resulting in structural changes and personnel reductions, Maureen Park, in her chapter 'A new "Age of Enlightenment": challenges and opportunities for museums, cultural engagement and lifelong learning at the University of Glasgow', discusses the impact that museums' changing visions as more socially responsible and responsive sites of culture and learning have had on the ways in which they operate, share knowledge and reimagine their audiences. More specifically, she focuses on how the Hunterian Gallery is meeting the challenge set by Glasgow University's *Global Vision* of embedding its activities within the heart of the university and realigning itself as a core service for the institution and for the wider community, by developing new collaborations in cultural engagement and lifelong learning.

In his chapter, 'Empowering literary educators and learners to learn together in Northern Ireland: university–community engagements for peace', Rob Mark introduces us to a Queen's University–community partnership that integrated 'creative methodologies' into adult peacebuilding literacy programmes for communities across Northern Ireland. Working within a context of decades of violence, social, political and educational exclusion and a legacy of mistrust and illiteracy, Mark takes us into a space where professors, researchers and literacy tutors work and learn together to prevent a resumption of 'the Troubles' by raising levels of literacy, empathy and cross-cultural authentic dialogue through creative practices for peacebuilding. This chapter describes training in the use of storytelling, analyses changes in the tutors' practice but also acknowledges the persistence of the idea of the arts as frivolous in the face of overwhelming proof to the contrary.

'Creative pathways: developing lifelong learning for community dance practitioners' by Victoria Hunter describes a collaborative project involving the University of Leeds and the local dance community. The problem addressed through this partnership was a lack of career possibilities for practising community dance artists and graduates of the University of Leeds dance programme. The solution was to develop an apprentice approach to mentor dancers into career opportunities. The project utilised existing partnership relationships with local arts organisations, schools and colleges. Hunter reflects upon the project in relation to lifelong learning and continuing professional development for the dance community, and discusses ways in which partnerships involving higher education can play a greater role in developing career options for people engaged in the dance industry, transitioning from school into the world of work.

Conclusion

> There is an alternative to the way things are. It begins in the imagination; the problem is how imagined worlds become material reality. (Miles, 2012: 9)

If we are, then, to educate, elucidate, illuminate, investigate, explicate, animate and resonate with and through the arts within a university setting, we must understand the power of the arts and their challenges in greater enabling all learners to engage meaningfully and mindfully in the world. The final chapter in this volume identifies key messages, weaves together common threads, and acknowledges both the challenges and the silences.

References

Adorno, T. (2002), *The Culture Industry: Selected Essays on Mass Culture*, New York: Routledge.

Belifore, E., and Bennett, O. (2008), *The Social Impact of the Arts*, London: Palgrave Macmillan.

Bird, J., Donelan, K., Sinclair C., and Wales, P. (2010), 'Alice Hoy is not a building: women in academia', in J. Ackroyd and J. O'Toole (eds), *Performing Research: Tensions, Triumphs and Trade-offs of Ethnodrama*, Stoke on Trent: Trentham Books, 81–103.

Bourdieu, P. (1993), *The Field of Cultural Production: Essays on Art and Literature*, New York: Columbia University Press.

Burnett, R. (2011), *Learning is chaotic, and that's just fine*, http://www.aucc.ca/future-avenir/author/ron-burnett/ (accessed 10 September 2012).

Butterwick, S., and Dawson, J. (2005), 'Adult education and the arts', in T. Fenwick, T. Nesbit and B. Spencer (eds), *Contexts of Adult Education: Canadian Perspectives*, Toronto: Thompson Educational Publishing, 281–89.

Clover, D.E. (2012), 'Aesthetics, society and social movement learning', in B.L. Hall, D.E. Clover, J. Crowther and E. Scandetti (eds), *Learning and Education for a Better World: The Role of Social Movements*, Rotterdam: Sense Publishing, 87–100.

Clover, D.E., and Sanford, K. (eds) (2010), 'International perspectives on adult education and arts and cultural institutions', special issue, *Journal of Adult and Continuing Education*, 16(2).

Carroll, N. (2002), 'The wheel of virtue: art, literature and moral knowledge', *The Journal of Ethics and Art Criticism*, 60(1): 3–26.

Duke, C., Osborne, M., and Wilson, B. (in press), *A New Imperative: Regions and Higher Education in Difficult Times*, Manchester: Manchester University Press.

Duvenage, P. (2003), *Habermas and Aesthetics*, Cambridge: Polity Press.

Eisner, E. (2008), 'The museum as a place for education', in proceedings of the international conference *Los Museos en la Educación: La formación de los educadores*, Madrid: Museo Thyssen-Bornesmisza, http://www.educathyssen.org/fileadmin/plantilla/recursos/Investigacion/Congreso/Actas_ICongreso_total.pdf

Greene, M. (1995), *Releasing the Imagination: Essays on Education, the Arts, and Social Change*, San Francisco: Jossey-Bass.

Hospers, J. (1974), *Meaning and Truth in the Arts*, Chapel Hill: University of North Carolina Press.

Lerner, F. (2009), *The Story of Libraries*, New York and London: Continuum.

Lipson Lawrence, R. (2005), *Artistic Ways of Knowing: Expanding Opportunities for Teaching and Learning*, San Francisco: Jossey-Bass.

Mahoney, M. (ed.) (1970), *The Arts on Campus: The Necessity for Change*, Greenwich, CT: New York Graphic Society.

Mann, D.A. (1977), *The Arts in a Democratic Society*, Bowling Green, OH: Popular Press.

Marcuse, H. (1974), *Eros and Civilization: A Philosophical Inquiry into Freud*, Boston: Beacon Press.

Marcuse, H. (1978), *The Aesthetic Dimension*, Boston: Beacon Press.

McGauley, L. (2006), 'Utopian longings: Romanticism, subversion and democracy in community arts', unpublished doctoral thesis, Laurentian University, Ontario, Canada.

McGregor, C. (2012), 'Art informed pedagogy: tools for social transformation', *International Journal of Lifelong Education*, 31(3): 309–24.

Miles, M. (2012), *Herbert Marcuse: An Aesthetic of Liberation*, London: Pluto Press.

Mullin, A. (2003), 'Feminist art and the political imagination', *Hypatia*, 18(4): 190–213.

New, C. (1999), *Philosophy of Literature: An Introduction*, London: Routledge.

Nochlin, L. (1988), *Women, Art and Power and Other Essays*, New York: Harper and Row.

Panayotidis, E.L. (2004), 'The department of Fine Art at the University of Toronto, 1926–1945', *Journal of Canadian Art History*, 25: 101–20.

Perry, G., and Cunningham, C. (1999), *Academies, Museums and Canons of Art*, London: Open University.

Ransom, H. (1968), 'Foreword', in Lawrence E. Dennis and Renate M. Jacob (eds), *The Arts in Higher Education*, San Francisco: Jossey-Bass, 1968.

Risenhoover, M., and Blackburn, R.T. (1976), *Artists as Professors: Conversations with Musicians, Painters and Sculptors*, Chicago: University of Illinois Press.

Roush, J. (1970), 'Epilogue', in M. Mahoney (ed.), *The Arts on Campus: The Necessity for Change*, Greenwich, CT: New York Graphic Society, 73–79.

Sontag, S. (2001), *Where the Stress Falls*, New York: Picador.

Thompson, J. (2002), *Bread and Roses: Arts, Culture and Lifelong Learning*, Leicester: NIACE.

Votruba, J.C. (2010), 'Foreword', in H. Fitzgerald, C. Burack and Sarena Seifer (eds), *Handbook of Engaged Scholarship: Contemporary Landscapes, Future Directions*, East Lansing: Michigan State University.

Welton, M.R. (ed.) (1995), *In Defence of the Lifeworld: Critical Perspectives on Adult Learning*, New York: State University of New York Press.

Williamson, B. (2004), *Lifeworlds and Learning*, Leicester: NIACE.

Winter, K. (1970), 'The theme: a sense of loss', in M. Mahoney (ed.), *The Arts on Campus: The Necessity for Change*, Greenwich, CT: New York Graphic Society, 1–7.

Wyman, M. (2004), *The Defiant Imagination*, Vancouver and Toronto: Douglas and McIntyre.

Yeomans, R. (1995), 'Adult art education as a subversive activity', in W. Elias, D. Jones and G. Normie (eds), *Truth without Facts, Selected Papers from the First Three International Conferences on Adult Education and the Arts*, Brussels: VUBPress, 219–28.

PART I

Arts-based teaching and learning

1

Embodied learning through story and drama: shifting values in university settings

Kathy Sanford and Kristin Mimick

Beginnings

The opportunity to teach a graduate course focused on oral language and literacy – what we call 'oracy' – came late in the year, followed soon after by the opportunity to team-teach. For both of us this was a new experience. Kathy, a faculty member in language and literacy education, was teaching the oracy course for the first time, and Kristin, having recently completed her PhD in drama education, had considerable experience with creative curriculum development. In shaping the course together we were able to explore (in Kathy's case) preconceptions about what graduate courses entail, and (for Kristin) ways to interweave expertise in drama education into the framework of the course. As a result we came to consider how we might best address issues of oral language and to imagine new ways of approaching key concepts.

As part of a graduate programme in language and literacy at the University of Victoria, this course represented foundational learning for all students, and Kathy initially felt some tension in reconceptualising the learning experiences presented. On the one hand, she was very aware through many prior teaching experiences of the importance of embodied learning – engaging the mind, body and emotions together to enable deep rich learning. On the other hand, she was aware of graduate student expectations regarding 'learning' that, although unwritten and unarticulated, included the importance of reading theoretical texts and writing papers. And while embodied, connected and collaborative work is important, tried and true academic production for future possibilities (i.e., published articles, completed theses, individual writing) continues to trump any type of engaged, creative *process* of learning. Paradoxically, while this was a course on oral language, there was a tacit expectation of using written text as the primary medium for communicating and learning. An additional tension revolved around the course's assessment framework. While it was important for us to utilise and infuse strategies for 'assessment for learning' and 'assessment as learning' (Earl and Katz, 2006) into the course dynamic, 'assessment of learning', represented as summative feedback and letter grades on transcripts, is typically privileged and expected as part of graduate courses in our university. This process of ranking, gate keeping and rewards weighed heavily on Kathy and we will revisit this later in our chapter. But fortunately for Kathy, Kristin had had no occasion to feel these tensions and pressures. For Kristin, experienced in drama education, the way forward was much more clear: to engage with and about oral language as fully and authentically, and in as whole-person centred a way as possible throughout the course. This commitment to and passion for drama education was a driving force throughout the course. The challenge, then, was for Kathy to work through her own felt tensions between the unwritten expectations of graduate teaching and her awareness of what makes significant memorable learning that would potentially transform thinking and practice. Together, we began to imagine ways of using oral language in authentic situations as much as possible to engage the students in their learning, and determine what really was of relevance to learning about oracy, while still meeting the course requirements expected by the academy.

Thus our journey as university instructors of this oracy course began. We both believed that what was most relevant to oracy was deep, rich experiences of using oral language in embodied ways, recognising that 'communicative meaning is first incarnate in the gestures by which the body spontaneously feels and responds to changes in its affective environment' (Abram, 1996: 74) and attempting to model our beliefs as much as talking about them. Because of Kristin's drama education background, and Kathy's belief in embodied ways of knowing, we saw storytelling and drama as powerful personalised approaches to introducing and exploring oral language concepts, and started using these activities from the first class. Using a team-teaching approach, we shared responsibility, ideas and successes as the course progressed. Ideas from one instructor would be shaped by the other as goals and strategies melded into a unified set of learning activities and events. As our own roles as co-instructors, co-collaborators and co-artists evolved, they informed the relationships forming among the entire class, which became a learning community sharing ownership of the ideas, activities and future directions.

Course context

The oracy course occurred during autumn 2011. This was a time in the province of British Columbia when the concept of 'personalised learning' had become central to the government's new idea of transformation for school-based education. This quickly, therefore, became a key topic of deliberation among university educators and policy makers. Awakened by the influence of globalisation, exponential knowledge expansion, rapidly advancing technology, current global economic instability, systemic health and environmental crises, as well as 'the troubling fact that industrialized, technological societies have turned out to be fundamentally unequal ones' (Greene, 1995: 170), university educators and policy makers began openly exploring how education could better meet the needs of today's learners. As part of this discussion, some educators and policy makers began reconceptualising education standards as broad 'literacies', 'competencies' and 'dispositions' that could span all curricular areas, thus challenging positivist notions of impersonal, objective knowledge and systematic control through homogenised outcomes. It seemed appropriate then that we, as instructors of this course, should also broaden our view of what it means to be 'literate' in the twenty-first century and shine light on oral language as a construct expanding beyond pure academic listening and speaking and into the realm of embodied literacies, drama and story.

With only the academic calendar course description as a rough compass, we gathered current research on oral language and envisioned a socially constructivist framework where instructors and students were both learners and teachers. We had little idea what this learning and teaching would ultimately look like; however, we did know *how* we wanted it to unfold – in emergent, contextual and responsive ways. This is our 'oracy' story.

Approaching oral language instruction

Tell me and I'll forget; show me and I may remember; involve me and I'll understand. (Chinese proverb)

In an academic educational world that is seemingly fixated on written texts, we asked ourselves what was the purpose of focusing on oral language and how we could convey the significance of oral language to our students – students who were accomplished teachers in an educational system that focused on production and assessment of written texts. We began to articulate, for ourselves and for our students, the myriad ways that oral language is vital to our learning – it is the primary mode of communicating for most people throughout their lives, and it is a significant component of the curriculum for students of all ages. We felt we simply could not engage in an oracy course without modelling multiple modes of using oral language. We were also aware of the rich background experiences and expertise of our graduate students, much of it relating to their oral language use and practices. And we were reminded of the many students for whom oral language shapes their cultural identities and learning experiences. The primacy of oral language for students of Aboriginal heritage, for additional language learners and for aural learners is paramount. Further, hearkening back to the wisdom of ancient Chinese philosophers, we believed that rich engagement with many aspects of oral language enables powerful learning through listening, speaking, feeling and imagining.

Embodied literacies and drama education

Many of our explorations in the course occurred through embodied modes of expression; the structures, strategies and skills that underpin drama education seamlessly offered media congruent with what we needed to explore. It seemed a fitting choice for us to ground much of our course work in drama education methodology because drama education enables the development of multiple literacies through its rich cross-disciplinary approaches aimed at critical and embodied exploration and expression. Such congruence would perhaps be best articulated by Gavin Bolton, an internationally renowned drama scholar and practitioner, as 'the meaning ... is, a least partially, encapsulated in its form' (1992: 19).

Drama education is a mode of learning *and* an art form in which students explore relevant issues, events and relationships within fictional contexts so they might come to make meaning about their own lives and communities. The goal of drama education is to create a way *into* understanding by engaging students in the content of fictional worlds so that the ambiguities, subtexts, assumptions and biases of the topics and issues being explored are exposed and can be reflected upon. Using voice, story, sounds, movement and our bodies as expressive and reflective media were therefore compatible pedagogical choices as we explored the complexities of language development as well as the power and privilege associated with formal and informal language and story as ways of knowing.

Through the process of integrating drama structures (e.g., story drama, role drama, choral speaking, script work, in-role reflection), strategies (e.g., improvisation, tableaux, soundscape, games) and skills (e.g., voice, movement, embodied expression) into the fabric of the course, a collective experience took shape. Our work together (as co-instructors *and* as a whole class) was possible only because everyone was willing to invest themselves in the social context of both the course (i.e., graduate students and instructors who came together each week in order to share and learn) as well as the fictional contexts within which we engaged as part of our drama education work.

As instructors, rather than following traditional pre-set lesson plans, we often found ourselves responding *in the moment* to the emergent contributions of students and the natural *flow* of where their input took us. We responded by infusing activities that permitted students to explore oracy-related concepts through embodied explorative and expressive modes. For example, we explored informal and formal language through tableaux and captioning, holistic expression through voice and movement games, story through small- and large-group storytelling, as well as ways one might privilege embodied literacies within a K-12 classroom context through story and drama. And while at times we were confronted by what we would call 'default programming' to present theoretical considerations informing current discourse on oral literacy through print-based media, we often chose to override these previously unexamined assumptions in favour of contextually responsive and embodied explorations. Indeed, despite the rich textual discussions shared each week via the course online forum, it was the in-person, participant-driven contributions that truly engaged us (instructors *and* students) in collectively creating, exploring and reflecting on our ideas and experiences with embodied literacies. In doing so, each of us came to examine our own assumptions and values, as well as those reflected by the education system, regarding the nature of 'literacy' and learning.

Emergence of a learning community

After several weeks we began to see ourselves as more of a *learning community* and less of a seminar-style graduate course with traditional instructor–student roles and responsibilities. Fuelling this growing sense of community were the sharing conversation and movement warm-up activities, facilitated by either instructor or student, which began each class. Rarely at the onset of each class did we stay in our seats for long as we quickly engaged in activities that brought new energy and trust into our learning space. We also organised a food-sharing routine in which one person brought food for everyone on a given date; 'breaking bread' together became a time to connect informally. In addition, we created ongoing opportunities for each of us to tell our own stories (formally and informally; some of personal lives, some of professional lives; some polished, some rough and exploratory). As the semester unfolded, levels of trust and emotional risk-taking increased. For example, when representing our personal experiences with informal language through tableaux and captioning, powerful images reflecting universally human vulnerabilities and insecurities emerged with little self-consciousness. A rich large-group discussion followed and then continued throughout the week via our online discussion forum. As Bolton reminds us:

> Only when you 'give yourself' to an event can you be said to be experiencing it. You let it 'happen' to you so that you can continue to make it happen. It is both active and passive ... You live spontaneously in the 'here and now' of the social event. There is an existential quality to the experiencing, where you are engaging with the social event from inside it. This concept is also critical to an understanding of classroom drama. (1992: 4)

Engaging in storytelling, role-playing and story drama provided multiple opportunities to use oral language – as excavators of our own experiences, in role as characters, in listening to stories read as impetus, and in debriefing the experiences. Reflections on our experiences in role were a key aspect of the story drama encounters, allowing for sharing in trusting, respectful environments where participants (both instructors and students) felt comfortable talking about their experiences.

As the term continued we grew into a learning community that reflected characteristics of a *community of practice*. Within such communities, suggest Wenger, McDermott and Snyder (2002), learning occurs in social and collaborative ways among those sharing a concern and/or passion and who are interested in deepening their emergent understandings through continued and shared experience. Learning evolves as the group moves collectively toward greater expertise (Lave, 1991). In essence, our 'practice' within this oracy course was focused on exploring oral literacy as comprising speaking, listening, doing, feeling, playing and collective reflecting – a literacy that ultimately acts as a medium for coming to know. These interwoven elements of oral literary all draw on embodied forms of exploration and expression.

Given the active, and trans-active, nature of knowledge construction within this learning community, it seemed fitting that traditional instructor–student power dynamics were rarely emphasised. As instructors we functioned as co-learners and co-artists yet also carried responsibilities as structural operators of the classes. We both guided and participated in activities with students. A few examples include sharing our own stories within small groups and alongside students during class discussions and reflective activities (a strategy we used several times in relation to a variety of specific foci); immersing ourselves in story drama work as participants of the fictional worlds we were creating; alternating the role of facilitator so the other could act as participant *within* the learning; and functioning as participants during the warm-up activities facilitated by students. We also noticed that students began completing their assignments in collaborative ways. Several chose to deliver their multi-modal presentations with another member of the class and a few also decided to collaborate during their 'turn' to facilitate the weekly online discussion forum. Ultimately, we, as a group of people coming to know oral literacy together, not only created a learning environment characterised by trust and respect, we also equalised the inherent power structures present in many instructor and student dynamics. Our co-constructed learning process unfolded *by and for* its participants – instructors included.

Oral and embodied expression through story drama

With the exception of Kristin, very few of us had much experience working with drama (and one student had very recently come from another country where drama education is almost never used). However, we all seemed to effortlessly engage in the collective drama experiences, particularly the story drama structures facilitated by our guest instructor Carole Miller, an internationally respected drama education scholar and practitioner. For instance, time passed quickly as we worked in role for much of a three-hour story drama structure called *A Wealth of Knowing to be Reaped* (Miller and Saxton, 2004), based on a picture book called *Josepha: A Prairie Boy's Story* (McGugan and Kimber, 1995) about an immigrant child who chooses to leave school to help support his family. It is a story about fitting in, lost opportunity and difficult decisions. The building of active ownership and collective belief in the fictional world of Josepha occurred through various expressive modes. Critical explorations and commitment to exploring oral literacy through embodied forms were represented in the following ways (to name a few):

- large group discussions (both in and out of role)
- in-role partner work (in-role interviewing; negotiating and exploring the story's foundational tension: whether or not Josepha would leave school to support his family's farm)
- speaking the thoughts of Josepha, from inside the fictional world (e.g., verbalising his inner thinking and feelings of isolation and frustration)
- in-role circle sharing (e.g., participants expressed their thoughts and feelings as well as listening to others while in role as central characters of the story)
- 'Conscience Alley' (a technique often used in drama education during which participants express [in role] their final thoughts and wishes for a character; during this story drama we offered empathic and compassionate 'goodbyes' to Josepha)
- reflective activities (e.g., participants shared thoughts about their experiences within, and responses to, the story drama; discussion of the connections between the story and real world contexts; questions were asked and observations were shared about drama education as a learning medium)

Using our bodies and voices as explorative and expressive media, we gained insights into the experiences of families who immigrated to the Canadian prairies over a century ago, critically examined the roles and responsibilities involved with being a teacher, (re)considered the value of education, as well as wrestled with complex human experiences such as belonging, acceptance and compassion.

Working *within* the story

Our explorations of Josepha's world were possible because the students trustingly engaged themselves *into* the story of Josepha – an experience that, while carefully structured by guest drama educator Carole Miller, ultimately unfolded because we powered the experience with our responses and contributions, and trusted each other enough to allow empathetic and somewhat vulnerable emotions to arise and be explored.

Through working in role we ultimately functioned within a state of *metaxis*. Metaxis is a term interpreted by Boal (1979), a Brazilian theatre director and founder of Theatre of the Oppressed, and adopted by Bolton (1985; 1992) to represent the notion of simultaneously seeing from two worlds, the real and the fictional. This is a powerful state of being because the concreteness of drama as an expressive medium helps students feel the realness of the fictional world yet 'any raw emotion of reality is also tempered by a duality of feeling' (Bolton, 1985: 155). The alternative perspectives available through metaxis coupled with the sense of investment and empathy that we experienced in relation to Josepha's decision revealed story drama to be one of the most powerful strategies we used during the oracy course. This is not surprising because, as Bruner (1986; 1990) suggests, narrative and the creation of stories are fundamental to the way people create meaning. In this view, story making is a mode of understanding – a way of knowing. According to Bruner (1990), narrative understanding is more complex than emotive expression; it is a legitimate form for reasoned knowing and, as such, is a natural part of our cognitive repertoire. He argues that people do not understand the world event by event or the text sentence by sentence (1990: 64); instead they frame their experiences in larger narrative structures such as plot, time and point of view. Story, therefore, is a common means of exploring, expressing, interpreting and reflecting on one's experience and understanding. Story, common to all cultures, is a powerful medium for connecting, sharing and co-constructing meaning.

Instructors as co-artists

Using structures, strategies and skills grounded in drama education methodology required attentive instruction that took into account students' responses as they emerged. As instructors it was our responsibility to act as the structural operators of the course, creating space for emergent and co-constructed understanding to unfold. And yet we were also contributors and learners functioning as part of the learning community that was unfolding. Fortunately, the praxis of several master drama educators (Bolton, 1992; Miller and Saxton, 2004; O'Connor, 2010; O'Neill, 1995; Taylor, 2000) offered a theoretical framework that supported us in making sense of how we might function in the dual role of structural operator and co-collaborator.

Drama practitioners often work in role alongside students, functioning as *co-artists* within the experience. This powerful mode of engagement, called 'teacher-in-role', is a way of working inside the narrative and is said by some to have transformed drama education praxis entirely (Bolton, 1992; Taylor, 2000). Instructors can use their role within the drama to engage and challenge students, develop the story of the drama, as well as build tension and integrate reflective processes. Decisions about how the drama encounter evolves are often made by the instructor, in the moment and during the action of the drama. Working in this way inherently destabilises traditional power dynamics because it shifts the role of instructor from that of 'competent technician who directs students toward pre-determined outcomes' toward 'co-constructor within a collective enterprise of knowledge creation'.

One might perceive the responsibility of using the teacher-in-role strategy as challenging because instructors must simultaneously view the encounter through two sets of eyes – that of instructor, whose is responsible for guiding the learning experience, and that of teacher-in-role, as a community member within the fictional context who is playing alongside the students. O'Neill, an internationally respected drama scholar and practitioner, suggests that the teacher-in-role strategy asks teachers to 'tolerate their own spontaneity' while bringing a 'quality of mind, the ability to think afresh, to balance impulse and restraint, and to integrate imagination, reason and intuition' (1995: 62). Indeed using the teacher-in-role strategy requires skill and practice, yet, as Bolton (1992) reminds us, it has a very similar agenda to that of an instructor's everyday purpose – to ask critical questions that engage students in their own learning. Thus, the power of the teacher-in-role strategy rests in asking genuine questions as educators work as co-artists and co-creators. O'Connor describes a genuine question as one that the educator doesn't already know the answer to. In response, students understand 'there is no right or wrong answer, whatever [they] say is right' (2010: 10). Responses then emerge through the frames of reference held by students.

As part of the oracy course students' responses to our story drama work were very positive, so much so that we decided to engage again in a new story drama structure. During our second story drama experience we explored the underlying subtext of Fox's (1985) book *Wilfrid Gordon McDonald Partridge* (an experience again facilitated by Carole Miller based on a story drama structure created by Miller and Saxton [2002]). This time, we (as instructors *and* students) paid close attention to Carole's expert use of teacher-in-role as she captured our attention with her reading of only the first few pages of the book, engaging us quickly by prompting us to share our own stories of the oldest person we know, and sustaining our emotional investment by launching us into tableau work and writing in role. She also skilfully highlighted the use of teacher-in-role, acting as Miss Nancy who had lost her memories and hoped that her memory box might be filled with treasures from her past. In response to Carole as Miss Nancy we all – instructors and students alike – came to function as participant-learners within the story drama *as well as* educators working hard to soak up Carole's craft so we might emulate it in our teaching. And while many of us could only hope that we might someday be able to replicate the ease and confidence of Carole's masterful artistry, we all gained clear insights into how functioning as co-collaborator, co-learner and co-artist serves to deconstruct traditional ownership and power dynamics – an intention that served to deepen and authenticate critical explorations of oracy during this course. Clearly these insights were not generated by Kathy and Kristin alone; a democratisation inherently occurred as we (as instructors and students) approached this learning together because we were all asking genuine questions, both within and outside the story, and none of us presumed to have the one correct answer.

Assessment and assignments

An alternative form of grading, contract grading, was used in this course to mitigate the students' concerns about taking risks and to eliminate the need to rank the students hierarchically (thus disadvantaging students who were not as comfortable using oral and multimodal formats for sharing their knowledge). The story drama and narrative activities that were central aspects of the class required the students to leave their comfort zones, working in ways that might have been difficult for them. Hence the alternative assessment process was important – students who engaged in a professional way for each of the formal assignments were assigned a professional grade, consistent with institutional standards. Students who wanted to supplement this grade were encouraged to develop extension assignments that they negotiated with the instructors. By using contract grading, we could all focus on learning together in collaborative ways, recognising the positive contributions of each member of the learning community, free from the traditional need to provide (negative) feedback in order to justify differentiated grades. We could instead acknowledge and encourage each student's ability to take risks, to contribute professional knowledge and to extend their understanding through extension assignments if they chose. The unique rich experiences of the course raised important issues regarding the types of products that would be produced to demonstrate learning and the types of assessment that would be used – this was a challenging consideration as university regulations are very structured in relation to grading. It was also challenging to think about assignments that would enable our students to capture their learning in more 'permanent' ways without defaulting to reading and writing. We had to imagine alternative ways to represent and share learning, and for that we utilised new modes of expression, such as podcasts (digital audio media), voicethreads (media using video, voice and text commenting), iMovie (video editing software) and Prezi (web-based presentation application and storytelling tool that uses a single canvas) presentations, melding voice with visual and written texts. The required course assignments included: 1) regular engagement on Moodle[1] (which became more 'oral' in nature as the class progressed) providing opportunities to debrief, reflect upon and add to the class discussion related to each activity; 2) a multimodal annotated bibliography, encouraging students to think more broadly about ways to convey ideas in formal contexts and to enable rich use of oral language; and 3) a final paper and presentation focusing on a specific issue related to oral language, encouraging elaboration of the types of modelled activities within the frame of the class. By asking the students to create their presentations in an electronic format for sharing on the Moodle site, and then asking them to share them in class, we heard their voices in multimodal ways. While a potentially risky venture, the students all rose to the occasion and experimented with modes of expression they had not previously used. As the learning community had already demonstrated its willingness to accept, share and provide feedback, the students were able to individually and collaboratively share their learning in diverse new ways. They recognised the need to explore twenty-first-century technological tools to honour the multiple uses of oral language, and to remain connected to the ways in which students are already using oral language for their own purposes. Additionally, presenting assignments in class orally served to extend and add to the conversation through their own research/exploration and reflection, which resulted in further rich conversation about their selected topics, such as drama, conversation and social media, critical conversations, storytelling, classroom discussion and additional language acquisition.

Reflecting back

As we reflect back on this course experience we can identify key elements that served to draw out students' sometimes tentative use of oral language. Early on in the course we recognised the need to provide models for this co-constructed learning experience. Rather than using oral language to convey ideas *to* the students, we attempted to create active learning opportunities through embodied forms *with* the students, providing spaces for sharing both our strengths and challenges. New learning is not always comfortable – for students or instructors – but incorporating embodied experiences requires that all step up and step out. Drawing attention to oral language in all its forms, often ubiquitous and invisible, makes it evident and observable. Using oral language in a variety of forms, drawing from drama education methodologies, enables both cognitive and affective engagement in coming to know. Drama education requires not only individual coming to know, but shared, co-constructed meaning-making, as we saw through the powerful story drama experiences that provided pivotal experiences for the students and the instructors, creating a learning community willing to immerse themselves into roles, situations and spaces new and sometimes uncomfortable. With the emergence of a learning community came the support and encouragement needed to try out new ideas in new ways, enabling deep and enduring learning. As the learning community included both students and instructors (as well as any visitors to the class), knowledge was co-created, shared and owned by the community. The equalising of power dynamics (as much as possible in a university class) encouraged a culture of inquiry in which difficult questions could be asked and multiple responses could be given using diverse forms of expression. Power dynamics were further destabilised through alternative assessment methods that encouraged collaboration, challenge and risky exploration. Utilising drama education structures, strategies and skills as compelling media for learning enabled us to shift values and expectations in this graduate class, providing (at least for the instructors) a memorable and moving experience.

Ultimately the opportunity to work as co-instructors for this oracy course challenged us to support students in developing the literacies to think and act beyond what is and towards what might be. Our overarching aim, as Miller and Saxton would describe it, was to make space for 'rich pedagogy to unfold in the midst of chaos' (2009: 548). Chaos, in this sense, was reflected in our multimodal learning encounters through which understanding was generated with authentic engagement and a sense of 'personalised' ownership. Our journey, 'personalised' for each of us as individuals as well as our collective community, took us to unfamiliar destinations where we explored, questioned and deliberated deeply about 'coming to know' through and with oral language and embodied literacies. Story and drama acted as media in this journey as they permitted us to make learning our own way, and illuminated the complexities often hidden in the subtext of human experience. Acting as the media that exposed our sometimes unexamined 'ambiguities, assumptions, perspectives, attitudes, and biases' (Saxton and Miller, 2009: 37), they were the foundational pedagogical pillars of the course. And for a short time each week, we found our emergent selves acting within and upon the world; perhaps the most 'personalised' of learning contexts one might ever expect to experience in any university graduate course. This should be, we believe, a critical goal of graduate courses and programmes, ultimately what students expect and deserve from their graduate experiences. This course has reaffirmed for us the power of artistic encounters as worth the risky business of challenging traditional educational norms and practices.

References

Abram, D. (1996), *The Spell of the Sensuous*, New York: Random House.

Boal, A. (1979), *Theatre of the Oppressed*, London: Pluto Press.

Bolton, G. (1985), 'Changes in thinking about drama', *Theory into Practice*, 24(3): 151–57.

Bolton, G. (1992), *New Perspectives on Classroom Drama*, Hemel Hempstead: Simon and Schuster Education.

Bruner, J. (1986), *Actual Minds, Possible Worlds*, Cambridge, MA: Harvard University Press.

Bruner, J. (1990), *Acts of Meaning*, Cambridge, MA: Harvard University Press.

Earl, L., and Katz, S. (2006), *Rethinking Classroom Assessment with Purpose in Mind*, Winnipeg: Manitoba Education, Citizenship and Youth.

Fox, M. (1985), *Wilfrid Gordon McDonald Partridge*, New York: Kane/Miller.

Greene, M. (1995), *Releasing the Imagination: Essays on Education, the Arts and Social Change*, San Francisco: Jossey-Bass.

Lave, J. (1991), 'Situating learning communities of practice', in L. Resnick, J. Levine and S. Teasley (eds), *Perspectives on Socially Shared Cognition*, Hyattsville, MD: American Psychological Association, 63–84.

McGugan, J., and Kimber, M. (1995), *Josepha: A Prairie Boy's Story*, Red Deer, AB: Red Deer College Press.

Miller, C., and Saxton, J. (2002), 'Wilfrid Gordon McDonald Partridge: a story drama structure', unpublished manuscript, Victoria, BC.

Miller, C., and Saxton, J. (2004), *Into the Story: Language in Action Through Drama*, Portsmouth, NH: Heinemann.

Miller, C., and Saxton, J. (2009), 'A complicated tangle of circumstances', *RIDE: The Journal of Applied Theatre and Performance*, 14(4), 545–60.

O'Connor, P. (2010), 'Talking about the way the world wags: The Garth Boomer Memorial Address 2009', *English in Australia*, 45(1): 7–15.

O'Neill, C. (1995), *Drama Worlds: A Framework for Process Drama*, Portsmouth, NH: Heinemann.

Saxton, J., and Miller, C. (2009), 'Drama: bridging the conversations between our inner selves and the outside world', *English in Australia*, 44(2), 35–42.

Taylor, P. (2000), *The Drama Classroom: Action, Reflection, Transformation*, London: RoutledgeFalmer.

Wenger, E., McDermott, R., and Snyder, W.M. (2002), *Cultivating Communities of Practice*, Cambridge, MA: Harvard University Press.

Notes

1 Moodle is an open source learning management system through which ongoing communication between students is facilitated and where artefacts (print as well as visual and aural) are shared.

2

Dream, believe, lead: learning citizenship playfully at university

Astrid von Kotze and Janet Small

Motto

Beware
what you ascribe to leaders
you take from the people.

Take from the leaders
give to the people
for leaders are colourful flags.

They wave and waver as the wind blows
as people work the bellows
and make the whirlwind's thunder. (Sitas, 1989: 61)

Creating 'development mobiles'

One wall of the Baxter dining hall at the University of Cape Town (UCT) is covered by a large mural depicting women (all Caucasian) in academic gowns ambling across lawns (higher education being for the leisure classes). Behind them are Corinthian columns (ancient Greece being the origin of knowledge and culture) populated by women whose draperies have slipped off their bodies, displaying full breasts (the Muses? sex objects?) The mural is a historic relic, at best, but in the everyday post-apartheid reality of South Africa we have become so familiar with colonial, sexist and racialised distortions, especially in art, that we barely notice. Against this background sixty of our students pick up and begin to speak about objects they have brought with them. One by one, they explain why and how this lightbulb or Bible, bank note or identity document, beaded necklace or water bottle is a sign of 'development' or not. The tables are covered in colourful paper and gluesticks, scissors and lengths of wool or string, clothes-pegs and a metal coat hanger. Beyond intellectual sparring, clarifying understanding, adding insights, they have the task of collectively constructing a mobile that will make a statement or tell a story about development / underdevelopment. The nature of a mobile itself will suggest the constant dynamics of change, and the arrangement of objects in relation to one another and lengths of string can be used to indicate relations of power. It is by finding unexpected relationships, tensions, contradictions that we can bring something new into the world (Greene, 1995a).

These students come from many parts of Africa and every faculty in the university; 'hard' scientists rub shoulders with philosophers, accountants, social anthropologists, as well as aspirant engineers and oceanographers, and right now they mostly have one thing in common. This is not what they expected university education to be like – playing with colours and sticky stuff. As leaders-in-the-making many are more comfortable with academic discourses than crayons and scissors. As long as the medium of engagement is words the process feels safe – and some clearly delay the shift towards working with their hands as long as possible.

The students procured their objects for the mobile from the 'bank': a box of equipment we supplied for the purpose. There was a brief hitch when one group challenged the resource allocation that sought to limit what each group requested on the basis of fair share principles. The group simply picked up the box and moved it to their table: 'We are the World Bank,' they declared, 'and have full control over who gets what and for what purpose.' The response was a mixture of outrage and laughter – but the point about whose interests control development was visually and, therefore, forcefully illustrated. After that, some groups commandeered additional coat hangers, claiming they had to work in a tier-system to properly represent the world, as another group ventured outside deciding their 'hanger' would best be a stick found in the gardens.

Meanwhile, some students had already fully engaged in bending and twisting their coat hangers into different shapes, clipping images from magazines and mounting them on colourful card paper. Dialogue was animated as they explored and explained, challenged and contested claims made and decisions taken. Each one contributed, drawing on her or his particular strength, and while some were more concerned with producing an aesthetically pleasing mobile, others wanted to ensure that the political message was unambiguous and strong, arguing that the world is divided and unequal and people have the responsibility to do something about it.

At the end of the session students presented their artefacts through speeches or theatrical presentations. And in the final evaluation they commented on the experience itself, expressing surprise at the task but also acknowledging that the creative collective work was a welcome extension and change from the usual individual, competitive work expected of them at university:

> The event showed creativity and different ways of tackling problems; I valued the opportunity I got to engage with debates about issues and challenges of development … I appreciate that it helped me reflect; the activities were nice because they were completely opposite to that? [lectures]and creative, again that is not really my strong side, creative side of things, so that was really cool to do. Broke the monotony of the lectures.

They also appreciated interacting actively with other people and learned much more than I expected; the task teaches you about group dynamics said one, and they learned to work under pressure to produce something.

And what of the process? Did it reflect the topic of development? Some voices linked the makeshift quality of their production process to the resource-poor base of community development. Both involve working with contingencies, making do with what is available, using the imagination to invent new ways of doing things or making statements to draw attention to issues. Thinking on the other side of the brain to imagine what we want to make is like using your imagination to make ends meet, they suggested.

The imperatives of universities say that playfulness is not enough: there has to be a tangible epistemological outcome. We wanted to know whether participants learned anything new from the 'arts and crafts' session. We discovered that the process of choosing everyday objects that have become naturalised as part of modern life and living and examining them as symbols of 'development', and the very visceral quality of practically establishing power relations with lengths of string, colour and proximity, brought very new insights from simply 'discussing' development. After all, Greene (1995a: 29) argues that 'the imagination allows us to particularise, to see and hear things in their concreteness' and students echoed this in their responses but also in their questions: What does an identity document have to do with 'modernisation'? Traditional bead works are generally considered African craft not art – how has that devalued the work? Balancing basic resources such as river water used in rural communities against water utilised by big industries raised questions about 'development' and 'modernisation' and engineering students discovered they approached issues of access to clean water very differently from medical students. Even social science students familiar with the subject matter remarked that they had come to see issues of development in a new light: 'The nuanced views it introduced to already debated issues and the avenue it provided for free academic thought, relevant issues and creating aware citizens, enabled a sense of ownership.' Moreover, the process itself was seen as very important because 'It made us think out of the box to realise sometimes when to get into another person's shoes before we can put our judgments out there.' One student later commented on his blog:

> I sometimes think that the greatest potential of development is not that we are 'doing' development in communities that need it but that, in conjunction with 'those people' we uncover the power dynamics that place them in that circumstance and place us in more privileged circumstances. That says as much about our commitment to fight injustice, inequality and oppression as it does of our 'good hearts'.

Pilot project and outline of this chapter

In the above project, entitled 'Global Citizenship: Leading for Social Justice', we had made the assumption that students who had enrolled wished to make some kind of difference in their community and/or the world. Therefore, as educators, we are obliged to help them develop the tools that facilitate change-action. What we have found is that working with the arts is one way of doing that, because it is 'a living, growing, creative process of development taking both artists and social practitioners on a journey of discovery, the fruits of which will nourish the community it is their intention to serve, in creative and unpredictable ways' (Smith, 2009). This chapter documents the creative, arts-based aspects of an interdisciplinary, non-formal initiative at the University of Cape Town. We do this because, as Clover argues, 'paying attention to the aesthetic dimension of politically-oriented pedagogies can add to knowledge and understanding of community development and social learning theory and practice' (2007: 512).

As will be clear already, 'Global Citizenship: Leading for Social Justice' is not a conventional academic project. Rather, 'it aims to engage undergraduate students as thoughtful and opinionated scholars and citizens who are keen to learn, think about, critique and respond to key contemporary issues' ('Global debates, local voices' course website, 2011). In 2011 the programme information on the website stated that this was

> a learning programme outside the formal curriculum that provides students with the opportunity to engage with current issues and debates on 'global citizenship', leadership and social justice. The programme stems from UCT's commitment to enhancing graduate attributes, by encouraging students to become engaged citizens willing to think critically about issues of global import, social justice and inequality. While voluntary and not credit-bearing, the programme is recognized on students' academic transcripts as a UCT Short Course. There are no study fees – the course is free.

The two pilot years – 2010 and 2011 – involved close collaboration between university management, an academic department in charge of teaching and learning in higher education (including internet-based/e-learning), staff from the Centre for Open Learning, academic staff members from a variety of departments, an adult education practitioner whose roots and daily activities are outside the university in popular education, an advisory panel comprising academic and non-academic staff from UCT and senior students with a disciplinary background in anthropology and sociology/labour studies. One author, Janet Small, works in the Centre for Open Learning, the other, Astrid von Kotze, is associated with the University of the Western Cape but works as a popular educator in communities in and around Cape Town in a political education programme.

While the pilot years were highly valued by participants and recognised as going a long way towards achieving their objectives, there is considerable pressure to 'go to scale', become financially sustainable and independent from funding and change the programme to increase its impact. This chapter shares our experiences as a way of asking ourselves how this may affect the quality of students' learning and hence their commitment to making a difference as socially responsible and responsive citizens. The research towards this chapter involved formative evaluation processes such as individual and collective discussion-based student activities, creative tasks performed in interim and final workshops for all students, an extensive evaluation involving three focus group interviews with students, questionnaires, interviews with staff and members of the advisory board, and journal notes written by the facilitator after each learning event.

We begin the chapter with some background information to the programme in order to situate it within the university and its mission of community outreach and social responsibility. We then focus on 'Global debates, local voices' and in particular the creative and arts-based aspects of the course designed and facilitated by Astrid. We argue that this popular education approach improved both the process of building students' critical insight and their ability to translate understanding into appropriate action with the potential to take a commitment to social justice with them into 'the world' as graduates. In the last section we ask how, given the value of arts-based education, changing the programme may threaten some of the positive outcomes recorded in the two years' evaluations. We end with some of the questions this raises for education: how can a holistic, interdisciplinary education mobilise the imagination of learners towards formulating alternatives, and lifelong moral and responsible actions?

Background

The UCT mission states: 'We aim to produce graduates whose qualifications are internationally recognised and locally applicable, underpinned by values of engaged citizenship and social justice' (UCT, 2012). And the strategic goals elaborate:

> Our mission is to educate students who will have a broad foundational knowledge that goes beyond the immediate requirements of their professional degree or major discipline; who will be equipped to compete in a globalised workplace; who will have a spirit of critical inquiry through research-led teaching; and who will have an understanding of the role they can play in addressing social justice issues. (UCT, 2012)

In 2009, following discussions in several university fora, the deputy vice-chancellor and the Centre for Higher Education Development submitted a proposal for a pilot project to stimulate a UCT Global Citizen programme. The proposed first steps leading towards a broad-based programme of learning would expose UCT students to global issues and debates, raise awareness of social justice issues and recognise the learning that happens through community engagement activities. With the support of the two deputy vice-chancellors and a senior academic involved in service learning and social responsiveness work, the programme received start-up support from a fund that was established to launch projects that would promote the university's strategic goals.

There are three key objectives of the overall Global Citizenship programme. The first is to expose students to a broad foundational knowledge on issues relating to global citizenship and social justice that go beyond the immediate requirements of their professional degree or major discipline. Secondly, the programme aims to develop students' capacity for leadership on contemporary global-political and social-justice issues through improving their active listening, critical thinking and logical argument skills. Finally, the programme promotes students' awareness of themselves as future citizens of the world with a motivation to work for social justice through involvement in community service/volunteering.

The programme pilot launched in 2010 with two modules: 'Global debates, local voices' and 'Thinking about volunteering: service, boundaries and power'. Students could elect to do either module, or both. Both modules ran over a period of 12 weeks beginning with an 'orientation' session and ending with a review and 'showcasing' and celebration. Here, as noted, we focus on course one: 'Global debates, local voices'.

Overview: 'Global debates, local voices'

This course was constructed around four themes: debating development; war and peace; climate change; and Africa in the globalised world. It set out to challenge students, who are privileged as full-time students and future leaders and graduates, to reflect critically on their own role as 'global citizens' and to consider their own responsibilities in the face of increasing social injustice and inequalities. To this end the course was designed to clearly situate students within their country, continent and world. Students asked what it means to be part of 'the developing world'; debated whether wars are ever justified and whether peace is always in the interests of all; pondered climate change and its effects especially on poor communities; and examined different notions of knowledge and how they are imbued with power.

For each topic, the emphasis was on active learning based on online activities uploaded to a university online learning platform, lectures or panel presentations/discussions, active participation in and contributions to ongoing online forum discussions, and fortnightly creative learning 'events' that required students to collectively process what they had learned and to produce an artefact as evidence. While many of the online activities demanded engagement with creative processes such as visual media, in this chapter we focus particularly on the learning events in which students had to embrace interactive processes and creative tasks that are not generally part of university curricula. Not surprisingly, as other adult educators who use the arts have found, in the beginning some felt at odds with the events and we had some dropouts and a small number of critical comments in the anonymous evaluation feedback: 'The learning events were a bit childish. This is great for opening and ending lectures but I felt guest lectures would have taught us more.'

Believing, like Greene, that ways of teaching and facilitating do make a difference we decided that our pedagogy should be 'one that dislodges fixities, resists one-dimensionality, and allows multiple personal voices to become articulate in more and more vital dialogue'(1995a: 183). The learning events drew on popular education approaches that have their roots in Augusto Boal's *Theatre of the Oppressed* and Paulo Freire's *Pedagogy of the Oppressed*. Both have argued that the arts and education should not be separated from politics and that they could in fact be powerful weapons for liberation (Boal, 1985). In each event students were tasked with extending their individual understanding of the topic and then using this to create a collective public 'voice' to communicate a message. Thus, groups constructed mobiles that depicted 'power in development', a collection of songs on 'war and peace' that were beamed with commentary through the community radio drawing attention to how words in music are often ignored, posters that called on other students on campus to respond to 'climate change', and collages that depicted how globalisation is visible/invisible in local realities.

The process of the learning events involved a number of shifts: at the start, participants engaged bodily through games or in response to provocative statements that challenged them to take a stand and experience being part of a majority or minority view or, indeed, an undecided loner/fence-sitter in the middle. Becoming physically present with the whole body (not just the mind) and in relation to one another was an important starting point for interacting creatively, and the resulting affective responses of discomfort, joy, or sometimes irritation were acknowledged as a crucial part of learning. Each opening activity was unpacked with care as a deliberate 'curtain-raiser' to the session and an invitation to both engage with the task holistically and take personal responsibility for contributing to the process. Dialogue as an act of creation (Freire, 1972) demands a commitment to other people and this necessitates relinquishing habitual ways of relating and learning. The feelings experienced in the process of opening up and becoming vulnerable may cause discomfort and insecurity – yet, as Freire asked, 'if I am tormented and weakened by the possibility of being displaced, how can there be dialogue? Self-sufficiency is incompatible with dialogue' (1972: 63). Similarly, Boal argues that changing the changers of society 'cannot lead to repose, cannot re-establish equilibrium' (1985: 105).

In groups, students then switched to add cognitive, intellectual engagement. For example, in the activity described above students began an exchange of information based on the images or objects they had brought in preparation for the session and the readings. Some strongly evocative pictures, quotes or provocative questions raised the temperature – we had selected triggers that were overtly biased in favour of excluded, oppressed, exploited people and interests, and often students followed this example. As preconceived ideas were often in contradiction with the information and views put forward participants had to shift out of their comfort zones and deliberate on new ideas and ethical dilemmas, until ready to voice a considered stand in terms of interests, agendas and social justice. Epistemologically, there were tensions as notions of what constitutes knowledge were challenged; emotionally (ethical and moral) imperatives called upon by some students provoked others and the academic endeavour was no longer simply an issue of transmitting information but became an interaction charged with values and beliefs.

Finally, when the task asked participants to switch on their creative intelligence and to produce an 'artefact', their new understandings were put to the test. Written assignments – the preferred and usual academic practice – often allow students to hide their views behind words and rhetoric. The demand to create a visual image that makes an unambiguous statement in favour of or against a principle or idea requires clarity. Creating an artefact collectively through a process of contestation and argument, imagination and craft calls on many faculties. The tasks required listening skills and practical cooperation, collective imagining and consolidated effort all under the pressures of time constraints. Writing assignments and papers had often not prepared participants for creative output and collective production of knowledge. Negotiating personal views and interpretations with those of others and then creating with minimal materials at hand an aesthetic object that would also tell a story about which all members of a group could have a sense of owner-ship was quite a challenge. It is this combination of intelligences, informed by social purpose and moral intent that underlies the creative learning events – and, we hope, social engagement, in the future.

In the end, each group had to present their work to the others, in the process finding their 'voice' and practising both presentation skills and rhetorical powers. At this moment the final switch from learning to production and action was performed as students who were informed by a common purpose moved towards rehearsing how to begin to act for change in the real world: global citizens with a sense of responsibility for others and their world.

In the second pilot the course ended with students planning and implementing a small public intervention and using social media to draw attention to the events. Some of the interventions performed by groups showed the creative turn: stringing up thousands of paper cups and 'decorating' the courtyard trees with them drew gasps from passing students: they did not know the extent to which they contrib-uted to polluting the environment every time they casually bought a cup of coffee – and yes, maybe they would bring their own cups in future, especially if this reduced the price. Another group rolled across campus on skateboards and bicycles with a colourful display of climate change messages and pamphlets. Yet another did 'guerilla theatre' performances – a form of political street theatre that uses a minimum of props and strikes suddenly and unannounced – in various places, drawing students' attention and asking them to respond to practical examples of more environmentally conscious living. Other groups used digital technology to spread messages and begin campaigns. In this small way all experienced what it might be like to translate learning into action for social justice.

Arts-based adult education at universities?: Valuing other ways of knowing and knowledge construction

Writing about arts-based educational research Willis (1998) draws on Barone and Eisler (1997) who list seven features typical of such inquiry. Among these, the presence of ambiguity, the use of expressive and contextualised, vernacular language, and the promotion of empathy were strongly present in students' work with mobiles, posters and song. Similarly, Stanley (2006) identified six social effects of culture, arts and heritage, all of which have to do with building social cohesion and fostering participation towards enhancing the capacity for action. Students were often visibly uncomfortable with the processes of creating as this involved letting go of the desire for control and certainty, and taking risks. As they learned to embrace mistakes – for example trying to construct three-dimensional collages with inappropriate materials and tools – they also learned to think of and implement contingencies. Reinterpreting or discarding original intentions in order to finish the task differently was a challenge many of them had rarely experi-enced. In plenary discussions, facilitators admitted sharing their sense of unease, frustration and fear of failure – yet all conceded that the experience of feeling vulnerable, being at the edge of control, and taking risks is very much a feature of current everyday life. There is little in academic study that prepares students to embrace and deal with these dimensions of learning. Participants on Course 2 of the programme recorded similar feelings; as McMillan et al. (2011: 16) recorded:

> Being forced out of your comfort zone was a theme that came up at multiple places in our review of the course. As the student below attests, it is not often in their academic careers that they are challenged in this way: 'We can live so easily in our own little comfort zones but it could help society a lot if we were forced out of our own views and I don't think you're going to get that out of a lot of courses here.'

The role of songs and music in social movements as mobilising and sustaining forces is well known to anyone who has participated in protest marches. Adult educators Martin and Shaw have written about songs for learning and yearning because

> songs of protest and struggle can be both aspirational and inspirational, lifting our sights from the seeming inevitability and intractability of things as they are. They help to turn things round, renewing our confidence in our collective capacity to act as agents of change – to make a difference. (2003: 214)

The learning event around 'war and peace' asked students to search for, bring to the event and share songs about war and peace. They had dialogues around the use of music and songs for raising consciousness, and they compiled/created new songs and performed these for each other. The subject matter and many of the examples raised emotions and tensions, creating an opportunity for building insights and understanding that required empathy and affective effort. When students moved into the recording studio of the campus community radio in the second pilot, they experienced another mode of public action and the potential for using media to pass on the message.

Creative processes as opportunities towards change

In the final session of the Global Citizenship course in 2010 students were asked how one might recognise 'social justice'. We took down the comments made, such as 'people stand up for everyone's rights'; 'when the root of injustice has been identified and is being addressed'. And what about global citizenship? A global citizen 'knows his/her personal contribution in the world; s/he feels a sense of responsibility to others regardless of artificial borders.' Such feelings need to translate into action and students suggested they felt better equipped to take on the role of active citizen: 'This programme has made me an active citizen, making me socially aware of my surrounding with issues such as poverty and development, and, I have come to understand the world I live in and how to be a more socially responsible citizen.' Looking into the future one said: 'We will be part of the decision makers of tomorrow. This course surely should influence the decisions we make and I hope what we have contributed to and learned from each other does make a difference some day.'

In 2011, when we asked the students why they might recommend this programme to other students, one responded by saying: *Dream, believe, lead.* We thought this sums up rather well what the programme is trying to do: first, to get students to imagine an alternative socially just world; secondly, to believe that change is possible and achievable if people work together; and thirdly, to lead the process, thereby contributing as people who have had the privilege to study and hence the obligation to try and make a difference beyond advancing personal advantages.

University education is a preparation for the future; this programme is meant to further 'graduateness' as a practice imbued with values of justice and equality. Arts-based education asks participants to look beyond what is, to play with imaginative possibilities, to engage with the not-yet. Crucially, collective arts-based academic work such as that described here can also be an inspiration and rehearsal for relationships of understanding between citizens in everyday life. Such relationships 'are suggestive of new, more flexible, negotiated, cosmopolitan and popular forms of citizenship, with the emphasis on inclusion, conviviality and the celebration of difference' (Nyamnjoh, 2007: 74). These are all qualities that are crucial for working towards an-other future, for using education to make a difference in the lives of those who did not have the chance to study. Feedback received indicated clearly that the creative art-based activities made learning for social purpose leadership possible in ways that went beyond the usual academic teaching. Here, we propose five epistemological arguments for this pedagogy.

First, shifting students from an exclusively cognitive process to thinking by 'doing' and 'relating' provided an alternative vision of being an intellectual. One student suggested that the course 'challenge[d] typical UCT theoretical thinking'. Liberating learning from books, paper and writing to become a playful experience offering a lived challenge to the notion that intellectual endeavours should eliminate and exclude anything to do with the affective, the physical or the creative.

Secondly, the course exposed students to the views and knowledge of their peers. One student wrote in his/her evaluation that 'meeting people with different opinions helps change perspectives of different things happening'. Working together cooperatively on one project and learning to listen, tolerate, negotiate others' disciplinary positions and viewpoints is useful in order to recognise the relativity and boundedness of one's own views and interpretations. The collective as a source of building understanding rather than relations of transmission and competition opened the perspective towards interdependence and interrelationship of knowledges and the values of more holistic approaches. In addition, 'an ethical disposition' (von Kotze, 2009: 155) towards other people, learned through productive joyful work together, is a crucial cornerstone for becoming a global citizen who is respectful of other cultures and peoples.

Thirdly, different group members drew on a variety of sources and roots for their contributions and the gendered and cultured nature of knowledge became visible as some contributions threatened to dominate others. When groups are composed of cross-sections of languages, cultures and academic disciplines students can also begin to recognise that curricula are an exercise of power as they exclude so much knowledge. This may give rise to questions about how canons are constituted, and in whose interests this happens. The privileging of one (Western/ male) knowledge over others and the contested nature of knowledge itself became the subject matter under the microscope both in the creative learning events and in the 'Africa in a globalised world' theme. A mere juxtaposition of information would not highlight these tensions as much as a process that demands the employment of multiple knowledges and skills in order to create something tangible.

Fourthly, ideas and new imaginings required pushing beyond the familiar already-known and daring to experiment, taking risks, making mistakes. Participants expressed anxiety about getting it right rather than allowing the process itself to become the learning. Creativity is something we all have but academia rarely rewards it in favour of following and fulfilling 'correct' conventions. The very playfulness which the learning events set up allowed students to test their own ideas about the key social challenges and try out taking a stand on a controversial issue, with limited risk and no assessment.

Lastly, participants engaged with hope and anticipation as they worked on their tasks. The emerging quality of arts-based activities encouraged the imagination to push beyond the what-is towards the not-yet. This utopian dimension is crucial for all change-work.

Towards the future

It is significant that the university has been willing to fund the programme and provide public support for three years. There has also been growing support from senior academic leadership in the faculties who are identifying the importance of equipping students to be able to engage social problems directly, whatever their major discipline. However, there is pressure to increase the reach and impact of the programme on the one hand, and to make it financially sustainable on the other. The pressure comes in part from the university management's desire to see greater returns on the investment, given that it has been aligned to the graduate qualities. To claim effectiveness as a 'graduate' programme, it needs to show a greater proportion of graduating students moving through the experience.

Hence, despite the successes of the pilot years, organisers have been asked to embed the programme firmly within the core of the institution. This means looking for innovative ways of fitting Global Citizenship into the mainstream by making it part of the 'core business' of academic teaching and learning, and increasing opportunities for participation of larger numbers of students through mass events and online activities. This has raised difficult questions about accreditation and assessment, and about the arts-based component of Course 1.

One direct result may be the danger that the programme will lose key elements of the pilot's success: first, the epistemological dimensions rooted in the understanding that we learn with the whole body and in relation to one another; secondly, that learning should lead to action and that such action at best would also address social, economic, political injustices and abuse/misuse of the world's resources.

In a place that is so dominated by the notion that the only knowledge worth acquiring is cognitive this emphasis on multiple knowledges and ways of knowing is crucial. Furthermore, reducing the creative aspects that make this programme so different and exciting undermines the essential playfulness that allowed students to take risks. Clover has rightly claimed that risk is not often talked about in depth yet it is 'a key aspect of any transformative or feminist social learning and community development practice' (2007: 519). Embracing vulnerability and experimentation, recognising that 'less can be more' (in the sense that resources should be used sparingly), and becoming more reliant on the imagination in our work with communities – these are elements under threat when the programme grows large and more reliant on technology.

Finally, given the popular education principles underlying this course, the processes and activities of the course were carefully designed towards action – not just for individual competitive advancement but for the collective good. Learning to work together with a sense of common purpose is important for all change-action, as is the ability and practice of imagining things as they could be otherwise. The arts and creative playful activity can generate orientations and dispositions (Willis, 2001) towards wanting to move beyond what is. Where might such orientations and dispositions come from in a mass-based programme?

And so, as we are poised at the end of the first phase of this innovation, we hold our breath. The Global Citizenship programme is one practice that goes beyond the normalised Western way of 'doing' academic study. Is this to be sacrificed at the altar of rationalisation and massification – whatever claims otherwise may be made?

Conclusion

Assessment, financial sustainability, global competitiveness and ratings – these are the concepts that have currency in contemporary higher education institutions. Yet there also seems to be an awakening in the university to the urgent need to equip students to face huge problems both locally and globally. The Global Citizenship programme's interpretation of most effective learning methodologies arises from the practitioner biases as adult educators and popular educators. Will this focus on animation and creative learning spaces remain as the GC programme moves to a greater extent into the mainstream? Can other approaches produce the same kinds of outcomes? Can the small successes of the GC of activating students as citizens be sustained as it tries to increase impact, formalise learning for credit and integrate with more traditional academic practices?

> The questions remain open. The dissonances remain. Those of us who are serious about art and the future will have to continue struggling against the determinates of the technical and economic world, the world of inattentiveness and violence and lack of care ... But we will be untrue to the message of the arts if we accede to thoughtlessness, conventionality, petrification, mystification. (Greene 1995b: 72)

Indeed, it is time, as Greene (1995b: 72) suggests, for us to 'educate in such a way that more people, standing up against the banal and the everyday, can make spaces for themselves'.

References

Barone, T., and Eisler, E. (1997), 'Arts-based educational research', in R.M. Jaeger (ed.), *Complementary Methods for Research in Education*, Washington DC: American Education Research Association, 73–94.

Boal, A. (1985 [1979]), *Theatre of the Oppressed*, New York: Theatre Communications Group.

Clover, D.E. (2007), 'Feminist aesthetic practice of commnity development: the case of Myths and Mirrors Community Arts', *Community Development Journal*, 42(4): 512–22.

Freire, P. (1972 [1970]), *Pedagogy of the Oppressed*, Harmondsworth: Penguin Books.

Greene, M. (1995a), *Releasing the Imagination. Essays on Education, the Arts and Social Change*, San Francisco: Jossey-Bass.

Greene, M. (1995b), 'The arts, aesthetics and values in adult education', in W. Elias, D. Jones and G. Normie (eds), *Truth Without Facts. Selected Papers from the First Three International Conferences on Adult Education and the Arts*, Brussels: VUBPress, 61–72.

Martin, I., and Shaw, M. (2003), 'Songs for learning, songs for yearning', in Peter Willis (ed.), *Lifelong Learning and the Democratic Imagination: Revisioning Justice, Freedom and Community*, Adelaide: Centre for Research, Equity and Work, 209–33.

McMillan, J., van Heerden, J., and Small, J. (2011), 'New ways of "being" in the academy: service, context and social justice', paper presented at the Community Engagement Conference: The Changing Role of South African Universities in Development, East London, Fort Hare University, 8–10 November 2011.

Nyamnjoh, F.B. (2007), 'From bounded to flexible citizenship: lessons from Africa', *Citizenship Studies*, 11(1): 73–82.

Sitas, A. (1989), *Tropical Scars*, Johannesburg: Congress of South African Writers.

Smith, L. (2009), *So What does Art have to do with Development?*, Cape Town: Community Development Resource Agency, www.cdra.org.za (accessed 12 January 2012).

Stanley, D. (2006), 'Introduction: the social effects of culture', *Canadian Journal of Communication*, 31: 7–15.

UCT Global Citizenship (2011), 'Programme overview', closed site https://vula.uct.ac.za/portal/site/7e62e117–bd4e–48bd-9738–65f21b81ab00 (accessed 17 February 2012).

University of Cape Town (2012), 'UCT mission and strategic goals', http://www.uct.ac.za/about/intro (accessed 12 February 2012).

Von Kotze, A. (2009), 'Zebra crossings: public participation to remake the city', in Emilio Lucio-Villegas (ed.), *Citizenships as Politics. International Perspectives from Adult Education*, Rotterdam: Sense Publishers, 145–61.

Willis, P. (1998), 'Inviting learning: an exhibition of risk and enrichment in adult education practice', unpublished PhD thesis, University of Technology, Sydney.

Willis, P. (2001), 'Tales from Zorba: orienting to adult learning', *Adult Learning Commentary*, 16.

3

Crossing a cultural divide: transgressing the margins into public spaces to foster adult learning

Tara Hyland-Russell and Janet Groen

> You already know about the ability of language to oppress. This course is about the power of literature to liberate, transform, and give hope. You have been silenced and hurt through language. But language can also help us to understand the forces of power and longing. It can lead us to apprehend ourselves and the world around us in a new way, and can give shape to our voices and aspirations. Master storyteller Brother Blue once said 'enough fleas can stop an elephant'. Storytelling can change the world.

So began Tara's introduction to her first class as instructor of Storefront 101, a free university-level literature course for marginalised non-traditional adult learners. Tara observed the mingled responses of eagerness and resistance from the students. She sensed from the ways they held their bodies tight to themselves that there was a powerful sense of isolation in the students that needed to be overcome if the class was to be able to cohere into a community of learning and access the potential of literature. She realised that, in addition to her painstakingly crafted syllabus for the course, she also needed to help these students overcome their isolation. Though her academic skills were required, the persona of the 'expert' professor was less needed, connected as it often is to the discourse and practices of elite learning and power differentials that separated these adult learners from the opportunity to learn. What these learners needed was a storyteller.

It had been many years since Tara had practised the art of storytelling and she had never brought that craft into her university teaching. Yet in that initial moment of Storefront 101, her instincts told her that she must help the students find a way to inhabit the learning space comfortably and begin to participate in the active dialogic process that marks both learning and civic engagement. From her storytelling repertoire, Tara recalled a tale grounded in the communal story-telling practice of Haiti that offers a model of belonging and dialogue as listeners are invited into a shared community space. In Haiti, when people are gathered and someone wants to tell a story, they stand up and say 'cric'. If listeners want that particular teller to tell a story at that time they respond with 'crac'. If the community does not respond or if the reply is weak, the teller does not have permission to bring a story into that space. By relating this form of exchange to the students and giving them permission to determine whether or not she was allowed to speak, Tara shifted the power dynamics in the class and instructor and students embarked on a dialogic journey of co-learning. Without a 'crac', Tara told the class, she did not have their permission to offer a story. 'Would they like a tale? Cric,' she said. 'Crac!' came the spirited response from the class, and she began the Haitian tale of 'The Magic Orange Tree'.[1]

What began as an intuitive response was followed up by a desire to more fully understand how and why certain modes of teaching work with marginalised non-traditional adult learners and how disciplinary knowledge can be effectively utilised in a non-threatening way. Tara joined forces with Janet Groen, an educator and researcher in adult learning who was a member of the Storefront 101 working committee. Together we researched Radical Humanities[2] programmes across Canada. This chapter explores the insights gained from Tara's experience as instructor in Storefront 101, Janet's experience as long-time working committee member of the programme, and our joint research to explore how access to the arts and such cultural spaces as art galleries, museums, theatres and universities affects the lives of marginalised adult learners.

To capture the multiple layers of barriers experienced by the students, particularly the impact of living in poverty, we introduced the term, 'marginalised non-traditional adult learner' (Groen and Hyland-Russell, 2009) which draws on Schuetze and Slowey's definition of non-traditional adult learners as:

> socially or educationally disadvantaged sections of the population … those from working class backgrounds, particular ethnic minority groups, immigrants, and, in the past, frequently women … older or adult students with a vocational training and work experience background, or other students with unconventional educational biographies. (2002: 312–13)

The term 'marginalised' points towards the barriers such as poverty, violence, substance abuse, negative educational experiences and self talk that reinforced their perceptions of self as inadequate learner. Deliberately choosing the term 'marginalised' highlights the systemic and institutional effects of racism, violence, discrimination and oppression on the basis of gender, age, sexuality, and/or life experience that mark those who have been in many ways the 'left out people' of our society (Groen and Hyland-Russell, 2009).

Using data from a case study of three Canadian Radical Humanities programmes, this chapter takes up Taylor's (2007) call for research on transformative learning to focus on the role of public environments as we explore the symbolic and pedagogic processes initiated by crossing cultural divides. Transformational learning has been described as being a fundamental change in how learners see themselves and the world around them (Clark, 1993). Radical Humanities programmes deliberately transgress invisible boundaries that consign marginalised people to the edges of society and invite them into universities and other cultural spaces. For most students in these programmes, it is the first time they have set foot on university grounds, seen a live performance, or entered a public cultural space with a sense of entitled access to that place.

Two examples of the impact of the arts on students in the programme spring to mind. In Storefront 101 we attended a play at a downtown theatre. When we arrived at the venue an hour before the evening performance, one of the students exuberantly greeted us. She had been up since dawn and waiting on an outdoor bench near the theatre for three hours, unable to contain her excitement and anticipation of attending her first-ever live theatre. She was 45 years old and never imagined that she would be permitted to pass through the doors of the theatre, a doorway in which she had huddled more than once during her days of homelessness. In Humanities 101, the course highlight for one student was the class trip to the art gallery. She was reluctant to leave the gallery, she said, because the art had struck her to her core. Here was beauty and a passage into an imaginative world that lifted her out of her current life of fear and deprivation in which her abusive partner banned her from attending public events. While she did not claim to understand what the art was saying, walking through rooms of abstract art opened up vistas of hope for this woman – hope that there could be a better life for her.

Approximately ten Radical Humanities programmes operate across Canada, all inspired to varying degrees by the work of Earl Shorris and his Clemente programme founded in 1995. Socrates' oft-repeated dictum that the unexamined life is not a fit life 'exemplif[ies] the connection between the political world and the humanities' (Shorris, 2000: 5). Shorris made the connection between the humanities and an active civic life through his research into intergenerational poverty in the United States and the barriers excluding people from fully participating in civic life. Shorris asked Viniece Walker, who was 19 years old when she became an inmate of Bedford Hills Correctional Facility, 'why do you think people are poor?' Her reply was that poor people required 'a moral alternative to the street' (Shorris, 2000: 97). What she meant was that poor people needed the ability to reflect and this critical reflection was a necessary prerequisite to any kind of civic engagement or life change. To Shorris, this meant 'taking them downtown to plays, museums, concerts, lectures, where they could learn the moral life of downtown', and he began to offer the education usually reserved for the elite to marginalised people: free, university-level humanities education, with a strong grounding in the arts.

Core to this education was not only the curriculum normally associated with a quality liberal arts education modelled on the Renaissance idea of the humanities but also access to the cultural institutions and spaces that are taken for granted by more privileged members of society but rarely accessed by those on society's margins. For Shorris, helping poor people become fully engaged, civic members of society entailed providing them access to the public spaces and stories that inform their individual and communal identities. At the heart of the programme was dialogue: both the *maiuetic* dialogue of the Socratic method and ongoing dialogue between individual and public spheres. 'As Socrates would have it, nothing about the operation of the course is fixed, dead; it exists in dialogue, which begins with the idea that the poor are human and that the proper celebration of their humanity is in the public world, as citizens' (Shorris, 2000: 11).

The Canadian programmes share Shorris's curricular structure of philosophy, literature, art, history and critical thinking, though they extend beyond his classical or 'great books' emphasis to include contemporary texts and approaches. Each of the three programmes we studied – Storefront 101 in Calgary, Humanities 101 in Thunder Bay and Discovery University in Ottawa – shaped its curriculum according to the social and cultural contexts in which the students lived, the academic institutions and community agencies in which the programmes were housed, and the particular cultural and institutional spaces with which the programme coordinators were engaged. In this chapter, we focus on two of the programmes, Storefront 101 and Humanities 101, for their richness and depth of examples.

Universities as ivory towers: trespassing on sacred ground

A common perception held by Radical Humanities students before they began their first course was that academics were a special, elite breed. Professors were 'scary', 'aliens', 'privileged' (Groen and Hyland-Russell, 2010: 40). In each of the programmes we visited, we heard students' awe and fear of inhabiting the public grounds of the university, what to them was a sacred and inaccessible place of deeply desired but remote learning. It is no accident, then, that most Radical Humanities programmes locate at least some of their activities in the physical space of the university. Students report that when they first entered university grounds they felt a tremendous sense of liberation, privilege and possibility opening up before them. They began to feel a sense of belonging to a realm of academic dialogue that encouraged them to think about who they are in the world around them. One student says the programme was important to her because 'I wanted to be a real university student ... I wanted to be in a building that said university on it.'[3] Another says she has spent her whole life in the same city and not once had set foot on the public university grounds because 'they weren't meant for me'. She felt immense pride at attending classes at the university and now brings her granddaughter to the university library to do research for her high-school assignments.

Programme coordinators recognise the transgressive nature of the Radical Humanities programmes within the framework of their respective universities and often deliberately engage with the symbols associated with the academy. In Thunder Bay, graduates of Humanities 101 are invested with scarves in Lakehead University's colours to evoke the hooding ceremony. Storefront 101's graduates process in black academic gowns with the university's instructors and administrators in their academic regalia. One woman said she felt she could go on from the Storefront programme to a university degree programme when the president of St Mary's University College, the programme's accrediting body, explained the significance of the academic regalia during the graduation, the 'strange cap' he wore and the symbolism of the garb that originated in the medieval university. 'As he welcomed us to celebrate our achievements in the programme,' she recalls, 'he was giving us permission to be academics, to join that exalted group in a lineage that stretches all the way back to the middle ages. I was blown away.' No longer were universities the sacred preserve of the academic elite.

As one of the Humanities 101 instructors framed it, 'It is a kind of de-familiarisation, if you like, of the institution and the institutional structures and the disciplinary lines and all of the assumptions and invisible walls and structures that we just traverse through every day and don't even think about, suddenly becoming visible and potentially changed.' In a similar way, Wilson spoke of the symbolic power of place and in particular the university setting. His reference is to another programme but is applicable to Radical Humanities courses: 'In terms of seeing this place as a site for constituting certain social practices, the college campus represented certain significant connotations and values. We collectively presumed that by meeting physically in this place we would then become deliberately associated with the putative authority and legitimacy of academic enterprises' (2001: 234). However, as one of the Radical Humanities instructors clarified, hosting the programme at universities is not a refusal to cede the ivory tower but rather a way of being intentional about how the university regards itself and being committed to changing itself as it becomes more open to social justice. The programme thus reflects a broad notion of transformative learning that aspires to change society, mirroring Friere's (1970) notion of emancipatory education.

A critical pedagogy of the imagination: finding the words to speak

Simply trespassing on the physical space of the university was not enough to transform the lives of students in these programmes, however. *What* they study and *how* they encounter subject matter is just as important. Rautins and Ibrahim call for a 'critical pedagogy of imagination, humanism and belonging' (2011: 25) that facilitates what Greene calls 'wide-awakeness', an 'awareness of what it is to be in the world' (25). Drawing upon Richard Rorty's notion of the 'strong poet', Rautins and Ibrahim expand the notion of a poet beyond the writer of verses to 'someone who not only has the language but also the vision to tell us something new, or invent the known in an unknown language' (25) and assert that 'the arts are a kernel space' (28) in a critical pedagogy of imagination.

One of the core constraints pushing people to the margins of society is not only the financial impoverishment that circumscribes daily choices but the social, intellectual, moral and spiritual impoverishment that is often the result of long-term economic deprivation. Life becomes a perpetual battle waged against holding back the boulder of crushing despair that looms when there is no sustained access to safe, affordable housing; nutritious food; timely and effective medical care; counselling and support services. The immensity of the struggle is exacerbated when social services are not coordinated and when days are spent standing in queues to access available services or to fulfil prerequisites before services will be offered. Shorris (2000) offered the image of the 'surround' as a metaphor for the forces constraining poor people. The surround refers to the manoeuvre used by armies to create a pincer around the enemy or the movement by wolves and other predators to capture game. The function of the surround is to isolate prey and eliminate the possibility of escape: it radically changes the behaviour of those held immobile.

For marginalised adult learners, access to privileged imaginative and intellectual cultural spaces in the face of the surround seems remote indeed, if not impossible. Yet arts-based educators contend that it is possible for the arts to help prevail against the forces of the surround: 'Arts-based adult education and learning opportunities enlarge people's creative capacities, enhance cultural community leadership and encourage new aesthetic forms of civic engagement' (Clover and Stalker, 2007: 4). Certainly it has been our experience that students in the Radical Humanities programmes, when able to access humanities education and cultural spaces, are able to engage in transformative learning and to begin to see beyond the constraints that govern their lives. This does not mean that they are able to move out of positions of economic poverty into prosperity but rather that they begin to perceive the nature of the forces surrounding them, their position within those systems, and to negotiate new ways of being and behaving within social systems (Hyland-Russell and Groen, 2011). A key aspect to enlarging people's capacities and facilitating civic engagement is their ability to learn to reflect, to understand the discourses surrounding them and to engage critically with those discourses. Perhaps it is the arts' capacity to engage people in critical self-reflection that is behind Clover's assertion of a 'steadfast belief in the arts as a tool or catalyst for change' (2010: 235).

The concept of 'community literacy' (Moneyhun, 1997; Peck et al., 1995) is useful here as a 'liberatory' pedagogy serving marginalised, under-represented people and is 'explicitly aimed at empowering them to understand and have some degree of control over the worlds they live in' (Moneyhun, 1997: 2). Gillian Siddall teaches modules on figurative language in Humanities 101 and sees the significance of teaching marginalised adults to understand how to decode the symbolic and semiotic nuances of language. Her reflections about teaching in Humanities 101 are worth quoting at length:

> figurative language is very interesting to me because it looks at … the complexities of language and the idea that one thing is always standing in for another, in language … I thought I would start with that and throw out some examples of figurative language that we use regularly and get them to … unravel that and think about, 'Oh, yeah, that's not literally true. That doesn't make any sense.' So why has that developed, that kind of shorthand for saying something else? … we went from that to talking about figures. We talked about what a simile is and what a metaphor is. I got them to write a simile and to write a metaphor. We put those together to write a poem together … And then we looked at a poem and then a song by Sam Roberts … It is quite densely figurative. It was actually more difficult than the poem because I talked about tenors and vehicles and metaphors and about implicit metaphors. I played it for them and gave them a copy of the lyrics. We analyzed it and they were fabulous. They came up with the most amazing, wonderful ideas for how one might interpret these figures.

Siddall was able, in a step-by-step process, to take students through the process of understanding figurative language and decoding its literal and symbolic meanings. She connected the meaning-making process beyond poetic, academic content to the lyrics of a contemporary song-maker. Throughout, she was teaching students how to decode the world around them.

Arts and 'turning the gaze outward': from isolation to civic engagement

Making change both individually and on a broader social plane requires more than understanding how language works, however much that process may illuminate the functioning of the broader world. Colleen Wiessner suggests that 'Adults with stalled educational histories require alternative approaches to unlock their educational potential' (2005: 101). In her work with middle-school students in the Bronx and Harlem, Amanda Gulla noted that 'the lack of exposure to the arts became a self-perpetuating problem as students matured with the sense that art forms and genres were not a part of their world' (2009: 52). When poor people are caught in the forces of the surround, there is no capacity to look beyond the immediacy of their situation and no way to imagine a different world. 'The wordlessness of isolation, which also leaves no middle ground in which to exercise human manoeuvres, may be one of the most dreadful of all the many forces people use against each other' (Shorris, 2000: 42). If, as in Gulla's experience, people are not exposed to art that offers a space of imaginative possibility, they may remain caught in the surround. 'Profound social change comes not from simply staying at the level of the individual but from turning the gaze outward,' asserts Clover (2010: 243). To this end, Radical Humanities programmes expand the classroom learning space to turn students' vision outward by incorporating field trips to community cultural spaces: museums, theatres, art galleries and public lectures.

Storefront 101 classes have visited Calgary's Glenbow Museum to explore immigrant experiences, lives of the Aboriginal Blackfoot peoples who occupied this territory before European colonisers, settlers and immigrants, and the artistic legacy of modernist painters. Van Fossen Stott argues 'the actual social ambiance and traditional reputation of museums can be daunting, as well as appealing. Some people will feel "at home" in a museum and others will not. Association of class and race are obvious, and subtler feelings may also lead audiences and individuals to self-select themselves in ways that are not predictable' (in Humes, 1996: 11).

Curators helped students navigate their layered responses to the museum space itself as well as to the content. In addition to touring the museum and listening to interpretive commentary, the students were invited to reflect on their experience and the experience of the peoples represented through the museum exhibits by regular ten-minute writing exercises. Sharing their creative writing responses elicited lively dialogue from the students on their personal backgrounds and how their history had affected the people they had become and how they understood their sense of belonging or not belonging in the world. For one student, the visit to the Glenbow evoked mixed feelings. She was proud of her Aboriginal heritage and felt the museum represented the Blackfoot accurately but some of that knowledge had come from elders like her grandfather who had freely shared their stories, only to find them appropriated without credit.

Other Storefront 101 classes have attended *When Women Rule the World: Judy Chicago in Thread* at the Calgary Art Gallery; the Paget-Hoy lecture 'Why Literature?' by literary theorist and deconstructionist J. Hillis Miller at the Nickle Arts Museum; and Theatre Calgary's performance of Canadian author W.O. Mitchell's

Jake and the Kid. Invited guests to classes have included Theatre Calgary's director, who addressed the practical aspects of theatrical production and the role of theatre in society, and Haida manga artist Michael Nicoll Yahgulanaas, who explored through visual images the genesis and evolution of his hybrid artistic style (2008; 2010). These cultural events were not randomly chosen; rather, they were selected to resonate with or reflect themes or trajectories of inquiry that were threaded through the course. In some cases they offered a counterpoint or juxtaposition to texts studied in class, while in other cases they offered an interpretation of a text students had studied, as in the case of the dramatisation of W.O. Mitchell's novel.

Student responses to these cultural exhibits and performances were keen and engaged. They responded aesthetically, intellectually and morally, offering perceptive comments and questions relating to their personal experience as well as to broader concepts of social construction and negotiation. For instance, in the conversation following the rather dense Miller lecture, students noted with appreciation the acceptance they were offered by the academic audience, even though they held a different view of the relevance of literature than the noted theorist. Students drily wondered if the academic audience would have quite the same appreciation of Miller's literary deconstructionist theories if they had ever spent a night sleeping on the streets! The range of art forms students accessed over several courses offered them diverse exposure to aesthetic genres and media and generated conversations about the relationship between form and content. Such was the case when students compared the dramatic forms of Sophocles' *Antigone*, studied in class, with the live performance of *Stones in His Pocket*. Concepts of audience, textual reception and individual versus state responsibility arose as students considered the function of literary texts and the choices made by the characters within those texts.

Decoding the symbolic meaning behind figurative language is not important solely to understand formal literary texts. English language is replete with symbolic language and is used daily to represent social constructions and values. An unexpected example arose during Tara's Storefront class. Alberta premier Ralph Klein had publicly derided the province's programme for the severely disabled, saying 'severely normal' people don't want to talk about the Assured Income for Severely Handicapped (AISH) programme and suggesting that many people on AISH weren't really handicapped. Klein related a story about two AISH recipients who approached him at a sod-turning, 'yipping and saying their AISH allotment wasn't sufficient to live on. They didn't look severely handicapped to me. I'll tell you that for sure. Both had cigarettes dangling from their mouths, and cowboy hats' (CBC News, 2004).

When Tara walked into class the day after Klein's remarks hit the news, the atmosphere was electric. Students on AISH were trying to subsist on incomes of $850 monthly when even a substandard apartment could not be found for under $600 a month. Nor was income the only issue. The students were infuriated by the personal nature of the attacks on vulnerable people. 'The students had shut down,' Tara recalls. 'They were angry and fearful and totally unable to focus on the literary texts we were studying. So we examined the language of Klein's speech instead.' Putting the full text of Klein's speech on the board, Tara went through it line by line, prompting the class to analyse *why* Klein's words were having such a powerfully negative effect on them: 'The first thing we did was look to the figurative language and say OK, what does this mean? What is he getting at? How does it make you feel?' Once the students evaluated Klein's comments about two women 'yipping' at him they understood he was dehumanising the women – and other vulnerable people by association – through words used to characterise dogs. 'Once they understood *how* Klein was utilising language to oppress them, the students could see their way out of allowing themselves to be trapped by his words. Their economic reality had not changed, but their understanding of how language can function to oppress and surround had.' Some of the students in the class were anti-poverty activists who suggested that letter-writing campaigns could be an effective tool in working towards social change. The class ended with a consideration of different ways to respond to Klein's speech: 'What if we were going to write to Premier Klein, what would you say? And if you were going to just write an emotional sort of knee jerk letter, what effect would that have? If you wanted to write a more powerful letter that might make some change, how could you do that?'

A note of caution: the need for an 'ethics of care'

Elizabeth Kinsella advocates for what she calls an 'ethics of care', attentiveness to the way the learning relationship unfolds and to learners' needs. She notes that 'although literature and stories have the potential to transform, it is certainly not a given that growth or transformation will occur as a result of engagement with literary texts. In a sense it depends on the quality of the relationship between the subjectivity of the individual and the text at hand' (2007: 53). In another strand of our research into the Radical Humanities programmes, we have located a key element of the programme's effectiveness in the 'mature authenticity' of the instructors (Groen and Hyland-Russell, 2011), a capacity to cultivate mutually respectful and trusting relationships with the learners, the use of dialogue as an essential praxis in the classroom, and a willingness to break down barriers of exclusion. Part of this mature authenticity is the willingness to be attuned to the learners and the flexibility to adapt to learners' needs. Such an ethics of care extends to both the content and the process of Radical Humanities courses.

Experience has demonstrated that, while the texts chosen for course syllabuses should be resonant with students' experience, too much proximity to the grittiness of their daily lives may overwhelm students or trigger traumatic responses. Such was the case with one student who began a course early in addiction treatment. He was unable to read James Baldwin's short story 'Sonny's Blues' without being overwhelmed by the knowledge that he had caused the same kind of pain in his family through his addictive behaviour as did the story's main character. The instructor substituted another text. Similarly, Charlotte Perkin Gilman's 'The Yellow Wallpaper' initially upset a student who had experienced psychic disintegration similar to the story's main character. However, after discussing her reactions in the class tutorial group and learning more about the enforced 'rest cure' that histori-cally informed the text, the student was able to integrate the troubling experience of the text with her own personal experience. 'The Yellow Wallpaper' became a touchstone text for her as validating her experience of mental illness and recovery. These examples highlight that, as poet Dionne Brand contends in her poem of the same name, 'no language is neutral'. If stories and other artistic productions have the power to move us, they can do so in many ways. An ethics of care prompts instructors to be attentive to students' responses to the texts they employ and to support students within a community of empathic dialogue.

Donald Smith, director of the Scottish Storytelling Centre, which is located in the liberal arts ethos of Newbattle Abbey College, asserts that 'storytelling has a close connection with adult education and real relevance to the work adult educators do today ... that is about fulfillment of people's potential and enriching society' (Stanistreet, 2009: 20, 25). Drama, literature, the visual and performing arts are all forms of storytelling. Helping marginalised adult learners recognise, name and push back the force of surround will not only facilitate individual growth but also civic engagement and community development. The arts help us name reality but also envision a world of possibility that opposes isolation and deprivation. As we recall the beginning of this chapter, the most illustrative way we can end is to let a student reflect about the power of pedagogy and transforma-tive learning in his life.

At the age of 11 this young man was put into what he thought was a boarding school in the Sudan, but turned out to be a camp for training child soldiers. His formal education stopped until years later he enrolled in the Radical Humanities programme. As he relates, the several courses he took in the programme helped him reconnect with his love of learning, touched him in a deeply personal way, and helped him regain confidence in his abilities and himself as a person. We conclude with how he began to refigure his traumatic history into a way of helping others:

> Taking English 105: Literature was to me an unforgettable experience. For the first time ever, since leaving my extended family including my grandmother, parents and the rest in thirteen years, that I hear a story similar to the ones my grandmother used to tell me after supper. It was the story of an Orange Tree. I became homesick. During presentations I told my favourite story from my grandmother's collection. It was 'The tale of a talking skull.' I used to press her to tell it over and over again—almost daily. Whole in all, the stories we discussed and read in class impacted my life immensely. Storefront 101 courses rebuilt my life and shaped it to the direction of my dreams. They helped me gain a profound self-esteem—enough to make the judge at Queen's Court tell a prosecutor to keep me in the courts to interpret whenever possible.

This man's experience speaks powerfully to the way the arts can help give voice to and translate marginalised students' experiences. Through an oral storytelling experience in Storefront 101 that resonated with his life story, he was empowered to voice portions of his own educational and life journey in class. He took part in Literacy Alberta presentations and began to offer his wisdom to others as a court interpreter and cultural mediator in domestic violence incidents. Within a framework of an 'ethics of care' and 'wide-awakeness' in Radical Humanities programmes and in the context of universities committed to social justice, the arts can catalyse critical changes in learners' perspectives and actions. Access to public and cultural spaces for marginalised learners transgresses invisible boundaries and can facilitate transformative learning not only for the learners, but society itself.

References

CBC News (2004), '"Severely normal" people don't want to talk about AISH: Klein', CBC News, www.cbc.ca/news/canada/story/2004/10/28/aish041028.html (accessed 13 September 2012).

Clark, M. (1993), 'Transformational learning', New Directions for Adult and Continuing Education, 57: 47–58.

Clover, D. (2010), 'A contemporary review of feminist aesthetic practices in selective adult education journals and conference proceedings', Adult Education Quarterly, 60(3): 233–48.

Clover, D., and Stalker, J. (2005), 'Social justice, arts and adult education: guest editorial', Convergence, 38(4): 3–7.

Clover, D., and Stalker, J. (2007), The Arts and Social Justice: Re-crafting Adult Education and Community Cultural Leadership, Leicester: NIACE.

Cranton, P., and Roy, M. (2003), 'When the bottom falls out of the bucket: toward a holistic perspective on transformative learning', Journal of Transformative Education, 1(2): 86–98.

Freire, P. (1970), Pedagogy of the Oppressed, New York: Continuum.

Groen, J., and Hyland-Russell, T. (2009), 'Radical humanities: a pathway toward transformational learning for marginalised non-traditional adult learners', http://www.ccl-cca.ca/ccl/Research/FundedResearch/201009GroenHyland-RussellRadicalHumanities.html (accessed 13 September 2012).

Groen, J., and Hyland-Russell, T. (2010), 'Riches from the poor: teaching humanities in the margins', in M. Alfred (ed.), Learning for Economic Self-Sufficiency: Constructing Pedagogies of Hope Among Low-Income, Low Literate Adults, Charlotte, NC: Information Age Publishing, 29–47.

Groen, J., and Hyland-Russell, T. (2011), 'Humanities professors on the margins: creating the possibility for transformative leaning', Journal of Transformative Education, 8(4): 223–45.

Gulla, A. (2009), 'Changing things as they are: promoting social justice through encounters with the arts', Perspectives on Urban Education, 6(2): 51–57.

Humes, B. (1996), 'Public libraries and community-based education: making the connections for lifelong learning', summary of the proceedings of a conference sponsored by the National Institute on Postsecondary Education, Libraries, and Lifelong Learning. Office of Educational Research and Improvement, US Department of Education.

Hyland-Russell, T., and Groen, J. (2011), 'Marginalized non-traditional adult learners: beyond economics', Canadian Journal for the Study of Adult Education, 24(1): 59–77.

Kinsella, E. (2007), 'Educating socially-responsive practitioners: what can the literary arts offer health professional education?', in D. E. Clover and J. Stalker (eds), The Arts and Social Justice: Re-crafting Adult Education and Community Cultural Leadership, Leicester: NIACE, 39–58.

Moneyhun, C. (1997), '"Work to be done": community literacy as a new model of social action for literacy educators', unpublished paper presented at the annual meeting of the conference on college composition and communication, Phoenix, AZ, 12–15 March.

Peck, W., Flower, L., and Higgins, L. (1995), 'Community literacy', *College Composition and Communication*, 46(2): 199–223.

Rautins, C., and Ibrahim, A. (2011), 'Wide-awakeness: toward a critical pedagogy of imagination, humanism, agency, and becoming', *International Journal of Critical Pedagogy*, 3(3): 24–36.

Schuetze, H., and M. Slowey (2002), 'Participation and exclusion: a comparative analysis of non-traditional students and lifelong learners in higher education', *Higher Education*, 4: 309–27.

Shorris, E. (2000), *Riches for the Poor: The Clemente Course in the Humanities*, New York: W.W. Norton.

Stanistreet, P. (2009), 'Mind to mind, heart to heart', *Adults Learning*, November: 19–25.

Taylor, E. (2007), 'An update of transformative learning theory: a critical review of the empirical research (1999–2005)', *International Journal of Lifelong Education*, 26(2): 173–91.

Weissner, C. (2005), 'Storytellers: women crafting new knowing and better worlds', *Convergence*, 38(4): 101–19.

Wilson, A. (2001), 'The politics of place: producing power and identity in continuing education', in R. Cervero and A. Wilson (eds), *Power in Practice: Adult Education and the Struggle for Knowledge and Power in Society*, San Francisco: Jossey-Bass, 226–46.

Wolkstein, D. (1978), *The Magic Orange Tree and Other Haitian Folktales*, New York: Schocken.

Yahgulanaas, M. (2008), *Flight of the Hummingbird: A Parable for the Environment*, Vancouver, Greystone Books.

Yahgulanaas, M. (2010), *Red: A Haida Manga*, Vancouver: Douglas and McIntyre.

Notes

1 Both the tale and knowledge of the cric-crac practice were drawn from Diane Wolkstein's book *The Magic Orange Tree and Other Haitian Folktales*, which contains transcribed and translated tales gathered from oral Haitian storytellers, a source Tara credited in class when she offered the tale.

2 We coined the term 'Radical Humanities' to mark and name this radical education that is rooted in social justice (Groen and Hyland-Russell, 2009)

3 This and all other student or instructor quotations are from interviews conducted as part of our research study 'Providing access to transformational learning for non-traditional adult learners: a study of the Clemente programme as a model for lifelong learning', funded by the Canadian Council of Learning (2006–09).

4

University teacher education and the pop-up art school

Christine Jarvis and Sarah Williamson

Genesis

Johnson (2010: 26) argues that most ideas 'do not happen in a flash' but rather form as a result of the 'adjacent possible', a term coined to describe the notion that ideas are only 'built out of a collection of existing parts' at a certain time. The pop-up art schools (PUAS) at the University of Huddersfield, the focus of this chapter, resulted from an eclectic collection of temporary and alternative cultural, social and retail events at a particular time. Pop-up shops began opening in unexpected places; pop-up restaurants and bars offered new experiences in unusual locations; and art galleries inhabited disused shops. These 'pop-ups' seemed fresh and exciting, and were portrayed by the media as creative 'go now or miss it' opportunities. They brought *zeitgeist*, something 'in the air'. Many pop-ups offered the chance to form an instant community through shared 'real-life' experiences and connection with others. They provided an antidote to the impersonal, the corporate and the slick. They had more of a soul. Their popularity attests to an attraction to their fleeting and ephemeral nature, combined with a desire to experience something unusual and memorable, if only for the moment.

Reading about a pop-up art gallery was the inspiration behind the pop-up art schools that we developed and discuss in this chapter. These textual introductions coincided with a radio programme we heard entitled 'For One Night Only' featuring seminal shows such as the 1969 'comeback performance' of Elvis. As arts-based adult educators with interest and excitement mounting, we combed the Internet using the term pop-up art school and ... nothing! 'No results found.' Although one-off art events and arts festivals were commonplace, it seemed no one had organised something called a pop-up art school, so we decided to harness the attraction and the appeal of the pop-up concept by organising an instant one ourselves.

We are adult educators in the University of Huddersfield's Professional Graduate Certificate in Education (PGCE) programme in the United Kingdom. The aim of our programme is to train students to be art and design teachers in the further and adult education sector. The 'pop-up' presented an opportunity for students to work collaboratively to plan, design and organise a large-scale, informal, community-learning event. The trainee teachers had been actively studying creativity theories and it was now time to experience collaborative creativity. The course tutor, Sarah Williamson, had become increasingly interested in the potential of the arts to reach out through collaboration and shared participatory experience. The PUAS provided the opportunity to explore this with trainee teachers and to model the risk-taking and challenge to oneself and others that arts-based scholars such as Clover (2007) argue can lead to transformative and critical learning. Christine Jarvis is Sarah's colleague, and has overall responsibility for the university school in which teacher training takes place. She has a long-standing interest in the impact of the arts in education and there seemed to be many connections between the PUAS and her research and reading in this area. Her specific role in this project was the analysis of the feedback from participants and the examination of the relevance of the literature on the arts and the professions and art in the community to the PUAS.

A total of three PUAS were held, each in a different community setting. This chapter describes these and the way they enabled the School of Education to engage with the wider public, with a music festival, an art gallery and a community school. It sets out the university's position with respect to the arts in broad terms and tries to situate the PUAS within the literature relating to arts and professional education and the arts and community education. Finally, we discuss the feedback from the art schools and reflect on the impact they clearly had on the professional training of teachers in the university.

Three events; three communities

The first pop-up art school was held on university premises. Inspired by a lecture on sustainability in education, the trainee teachers focused on recycling, using found, discarded and unwanted materials. A 'campus call' put out for unwanted paper, fabric, buttons, beads, ribbon and wool yielded a great response. This was the first indication of a strong desire to be part of something creative on the part of the wider university community. Many people were looking forward to being involved and being part of the event.

The university's largest function room was booked. Transforming a corporate space into an instantly welcoming and appealing creative environment was a major challenge. Temporary 'walls', created by hanging a variety of things such as exhibition posters, drawings, photographs and some sculptural objects from washing lines fixed around the perimeter and across the room, were simple and surprisingly effective. On one length of washing line an instant exhibition of 'paper dresses' made from road maps, wallpaper, atlas pages and paper doilies, commissioned from students studying fashion design at a local college, caught the eye.

At the event each trainee teacher set up a large table as an activity base like a stall at a fair. Participants could wander around, join in, or just watch. Activities included making 'junk jewellery' from bottle tops and crisp packets, fashioning delicate accessories from newspaper and buttons and using origami techniques to make gift boxes from unwanted wallpaper. Shredded paper was used for decorative weaving, and art postcards made from magazines. 'Newspaper couture' (pleating pages from newspaper and old telephone directories to make paper dresses and ballgowns) was very popular, as were the opportunities to practise drawing techniques and construct collaborative pieces of artwork. Learning to knit with 'Auntie Barbara' was an unexpected success, seeming to reveal a desire to learn a traditional skill once handed down through generations. Guerilla knitting and yarn-storming activities linked to the growing popularity of using knitting and yarn (rather than paint) as a form of graffiti or street art, and to groups such as London's Knit the City and the Canadian-based protest group 'The Revolutionary Knitters' (Robertson, 2007).

A programme of 'pick and mix' mini-lectures was devised for a specially created classroom area. These included talks from the trainee teachers who gave insights into their careers as arts professionals, for example in television set design. Some talks were more fine-art based – discussing performance and installation – and one talk invited the audience to contribute to a growing patchwork piece which captured stories of 'first love'. Refreshments were served in vintage china cups and saucers that formed a decorative display in their own right. Visitors were encouraged to select their cup and saucer, promoting a visual sensibility. The china had been collected from charity shops and car boot sales to reuse in keeping with the sustainable ethos of the event. It was noticeable that while the 'tea room' provided a sociable area where people could have a break and relax, it also provided a 'safe' area where people could just watch the art school around them. French music from an 'Age of Couture' exhibition at the Victoria & Albert Museum in London enhanced the vintage atmosphere. The day closed with a live performance from a jazz funk band whose style and improvisation added to the creative ambience. The event was summarised by trainee teacher Ellie who said 'there's been a great aura about the place seeing people get creative'.

The second PUAS was held in conjunction with the internationally acclaimed Huddersfield Contemporary Music Festival (HCMF) and Huddersfield Art Gallery. The festival featured work by the avant-garde composer John Cage and coincided with the hosting of a prestigious national touring exhibition of his artwork, 'Every Day is a Good Day', at the art gallery. The PUAS 'popped up' to run alongside a performance of Cage's music being held in the gallery itself. The timing of the event coincided with renewed media interest in Cage and his controversial piece of music entitled 4'33" (consisting of four minutes and thirty-three seconds of silence). At the event, the ensemble Apartment House performed Cage's 'Atlas Eclipticalis' and 'Winter Music'. These pieces, described as 'illuminating space with constellations of sound' (HCMF, 2010: 34) were performed and amplified in the gallery space using various instruments including two grand pianos, cello, harp and voice. The music performance was non-seated which promoted accessibility and the opportunity to experience both the music and the art school. Participants could wander freely around the gallery spaces, and many of the art activities involved making responses to the exhibition and music.

Cage commonly explored text and mark-making in his art and many of his compositions were inspired by numerical combinations and notions of 'chance'. These provided a theme and starting point for the PUAS activities. For example, participants created a 10-metre floor painting, which involved painting or collaging a particular word selected from a 1920s encyclopaedic 'Book of Knowledge'. The page, line and word were selected through techniques of chance, with the results eclectic and intriguing. A 'memory quilt' of chance events was collaboratively assembled, and for this people were asked to remember and write down an event or occurrence in their lives which had happened by chance. These memories were written on to randomly found pieces of paper such as bus tickets, receipts and shopping lists, then decoratively stitched on to fabric and quilted together. Still-life drawing was dictated by the roll of a dice to determine the media to be used, distance and viewpoint. Postcards and bags were made using printing techniques inspired by Cage, and a 'John Cage Video Booth' was set up to make a collaboratively constructed piece of video poetry from randomly selected words. Simple concertina journals with lino-printed covers were made together with handcrafted bookmarks to capture responses to the music and art on display. One activity also asked participants to respond in the form of a haiku (a three-line Japanese poem) and this became a film installation when the poem was typed using a vintage typewriter, filmed and projected.

Over two hundred participants came to the event, including students studying contemporary music at high school and university level, art students, senior citizens, a supported women's group, members of the public, supporters of HCMF, John Cage enthusiasts and trainee teachers studying to teach in different sectors. It was fascinating to see the successful fusion and overlap of these people in a shared cultural and learning experience. Indeed, the atmosphere was seen as positively vibrant: in the words of one member of gallery staff, the gallery had 'come alive'. Participants were encouraged to write feedback on PUAS postcards and to 'peg' their completed postcards on to washing lines hung in the gallery entrance.

Following the success of the previous PUAS, Sarah wanted to see if the university could use this to work with other communities, both adults and children. A primary school headteacher inspired by the university PUAS asked if we would be willing to 'pop up' at her school. In collaboration with the school, a day of original and exciting art activities was planned with the aim of inspiring teachers, parents and children to be creative, in particular through the use of recycled, reused and discarded materials. The trainee teachers worked with 120 children aged between 7 and 11 and their teachers, and then with 50 parents and carers who came into the school for an afternoon of family learning.

Art and the University of Huddersfield

The origin of the PUAS within a teacher-training course in the University of Huddersfield is important to us, because of the challenges involved in introducing the arts into teacher training, even in a university that values the arts highly. Huddersfield is an industrial town in the north of England. It is home to a world-famous choral society and to the Huddersfield Contemporary Music Festival and the arts are integral to the life of the university. There is a strong focus on the creative industries in its portfolio. Its School of Art, Design and Architecture develops artists, architects and designers working in a wide range of media and works closely with local arts organisations and businesses, as well as with prestigious international organisations such as Saatchi and Saatchi. For example, students recently held textile workshops for local young people and ran pop-up art shops in local towns. It has great strengths in textiles and fashion design, in keeping with the history of the area. Huddersfield was an important centre for the textile industry in the nineteenth and early twentieth centuries, and many of its buildings are imaginatively converted textile mills; the university is one of only six to be invited into membership of the Worshipful Company of Woolmen, one of England's ancient craft guilds. Fashion students from the university worked on the Oscar-winning film, *The King's Speech*. The university has a formal partnership with the Yorkshire Sculpture Park, which is home to a superb collection by internationally renowned sculptors; Huddersfield's research students based there use its national arts education archive, the park's staff use the university library, university staff have exhibited at the park and students make regular visits to draw and for inspiration and work as guides at exhibitions.

The School of Music, Humanities and Media also develops arts practitioners: writers, actors, directors, multimedia specialists and musicians. It provides concerts and performances on the university's town centre campus, but uses neighbourhood venues too, so that it is fully integrated within the community. Its professor, Richard Steinitz, established the Huddersfield Contemporary Music Festival in 1978. The university hosts this festival, which emphasizes innovation and pushing musical boundaries and has welcomed virtually every major living composer since its inception. The university has a formal agreement with the Royal Armouries Museum, which enables students to study the design of weapons and jewellery from an extensive historical period (the museum holds the crown jewels). The university's chancellor, Sir Patrick Stewart, a theatre, television and film actor, is very involved in university life, for example giving master classes to drama students. In essence the relationship between the university and the local arts community is symbiotic. The university benefits the creative life of the local community by acting as a focus for activity, hosting international events and drawing in major artists, as well as training people to work in the creative industries; the local community provides opportunities for student placements, advises on curriculum content, and engages staff and students in projects and research.

But while the arts have an important role within the university and the region, finding space for creativity in the professional training of teachers is often challenging. We consider this to be related to the nature of nationally specified teacher-training standards. Government specified teacher-training requirements are highly prescriptive. The trainee teachers involved in this project were preparing to teach in the lifelong learning sector; standards for teaching in that sector require the students to evidence 37 separate pieces of knowledge and understanding, and 37 skills in professional practice (http://webarchive.national-archives.gov.uk). Inevitably, most of their time is spent developing portfolios with evidence (from mentors, lesson plans and teaching observations) that they have met these standards. They also have to undertake extensive teaching practice in colleges over a 36-week period, so time for open-ended, creative thinking is fairly limited. For these reasons, trainee teachers can feel isolated from the subjects that led them to wish to teach in the first place and rarely have the opportunity to participate in wider aspects of university life. One of the positive side-effects of the PUAS was that it involved trainee teachers with the wider university community through participation in the HCMF. Participation of this kind is rare because of the demanding and prescriptive nature of the curriculum.

Arts and professional education

The PUAS provided a rare opportunity for teacher-educators to do something different. They enabled them to stretch the thinking of their trainee teachers, by giving them the chance to think about the educational potential of the arts for working in the wider community. The first PUAS was used to educate two groups of professionals simultaneously; the trainee art teachers themselves, and other trainee teachers, working with different age groups and subjects who participated in the day. There are good and well-theorised examples of professional education in which the arts are used to enhance professional practice. Many come from outside the UK, particularly with respect to adult education. Manigaulte, Yorks and Kasl, for example, use 'various art activities – drawing, making collages, and using clay', while working with student interns learning about community health education, to improve their reflective practice by supporting the process of 'surfacing our underlying thinking' (2006: 29). Kinsella (2008: 48) describes using literary arts in the education of health professionals as a transformative process. She argues that this enables them to 'reawaken attention to the lived experience of those with whom we work' by engaging them with texts that present them with the experience of care from the perspective of those who are vulnerable. Gelo's (2008) work demonstrates how the visual arts can be used to develop empathy in medical students. At the PUAS the arts were used to show trainee teachers, who were not art specialists or intending to teach arts, that they could be highly creative and that the arts could readily be used by those who were not art specialists to promote all kinds of learning. It helped them understand instantaneously and experientially how they could integrate these methods into their professional practice.

The trainee teachers who specialised in art and design were also influenced as professionals, but in their case this had a different dimension. They experienced arts education's wider remit. There is an extensive literature on community arts that analyses a wide range of practice and comes from diverse political and theoretical perspectives and in this section we reflect on the relationship between the PUAS and this literature. Many of these writers have noted the capacity that participation in the creative arts offers to people to construct and express the world for themselves and to transform their perception of themselves. This democratising process has strong roots in adult and community education. For example, Clover (2006) demonstrates the empowering impact of a photography project in which women from disadvantaged communities were able to express their realities through their camera work; Sandlin (2007) discusses how adults take part in creative protests outside formal educational institutions, through the process of 'culture jamming', a form of cultural resistance in which activists create alternative forms of popular culture that subvert consumerism. Further, Muterspaw and Fenwick (2007) discuss multiple ways in which educators have used music, particularly community choirs, to inspire and energise communities and Tett et al. (2011) have outlined the dramatic potential of arts work in prisons. Other kinds of programmes reach out in order to bring more people into an existing, more elite community. Rademaker (2007) describes the role of an arts advocacy group that produces an extensive programme of outreach activities in schools and communities, in order to encourage wider consumption of art in that region.

If we try to situate the PUAS in the context of these kinds of work, it seems that its ephemeral, eclectic and serendipitous character is also reflected in its theoretical orientation. It is not a mechanism for teaching people about the elite arts, but it does start to overcome some of the barriers people may have felt regarding art, and introduces them directly to practising artists. The location of the second school as part of the HCMF meant it brought people closer to some elite performances, as well as offering cross-fertilisation between different artistic communities. Nor can the activities be construed as community activism or conscientisation, in the sense of focusing on community issues, injustice or restorative action. The trainees do not start by focusing on 'generative themes' (Freire, 1970) of concern to specific groups and communities; nor do they develop the kinds of sustained relationships with participants that could lead to further work; nor do participants themselves operate as any kind of cohesive community, with the possible exception of some aspects of the primary school. Rather, the PUAS is a kind of sampler for the trainee teachers of the possibilities for further work, including more sustained community activities. There are many aspects of the curriculum in schools and colleges in England that, albeit not intentionally, militate against encouraging and exploiting this more general and democratic approach to creativity. Schools and colleges are judged by grades that students achieve in public examinations, which form a central part of league tables and inspections by Ofsted (the Office for Standards in Education). In recent years, schools have of necessity focused more heavily on teaching to the examination and ensuring as many children as possible achieve the required grades. This leaves teachers with less time for developing children's wider interests, experimental work and broader social purpose. The intense focus, especially in colleges and universities, on employability and vocationalism has also meant that the development of industry-ready skills and an orientation towards a consumer rather than a community market is likely. This has had a direct impact on the way that the university is able to train its art and design teachers. The PUAS did indeed develop some very practical organisational, marketing and administrative skills in our trainees, which enhanced their employability as teachers, but it also reinforced the potential that art has to reach out and have a powerful impact on the lives of many people for whom art will never be a career.

An interesting comparison can be made with the University of Lapland's programme as part of its work to 'familiarise art educators with the strategy of place-specific art, community art and environmental art' (Jokela, 2007: 239). It supports arts educators to develop the ability to work in communities to carry

60

out winter arts projects, through its 'Winter Art Education Project', which also involved individuals in temporary art work. The Winter Project includes specific training in snow- and ice-making techniques, and has a much more specific focus (on the cultural heritage of winter, snow and ice) than the more eclectic PUAS. What it does have in common with it, is the desire to democratise art-making within communities rather than within elite groups and to evaluate the impact of *process* rather than to prioritise aesthetic judgements about products.

The PUAS also created empathic moments for trainee teachers by creating a setting in which they came face-to-face with those who did not self-identify as artists, with those who in many cases had been excluded from arts by poor experiences of schooling, or by internalising beliefs about art that made them question their own worthiness to participate. The trainee teachers running the PUAS developed a sharp understanding of the potential for participation and creative expression that so many people keep relatively hidden.

Pleasure and possibilities

Feedback from the PUAS was captured using creative processes in keeping with the events. Responses mirrored the instantaneous nature of the event, and captured immediate feelings. They have the value of being relatively unmediated and uninfluenced by any researcher, or by a desire to please a specific teacher. The disadvantage is that we cannot know how much more participants might have been able to say if they had been questioned in more depth or subject to follow-up to see whether the art school had changed their behaviour or thinking.

For the first event, feedback was collected on recycled wallpaper cut into squares and formed into a 'patchwork quilt'. This grew during the day, forming a piece of artwork in its own right from people's personal responses. The quilt format was in keeping with the ethos of creative collaboration, and captured both individual and collective experience. The PUAS held in conjunction with the HCMF and a local art gallery collected feedback on specially designed postcards, pegged on to a washing line in the gallery entrance. This created a visually attractive display and playfully suggested the idea of a postcard being sent from the event. Feedback from all the PUAS also suggested that an appreciated sense of creative community had been created, although temporary, through a shared creative experience. One postcard stated how the event 'reached out' to people and brought all ages together.

When we read and analysed the feedback, three themes emerged. The most dominant was a strong, enthusiastic assertion of sheer pleasure, often combined with gratitude towards the organisers and an awareness of the therapeutic value of participation. This sense of delight was evident in almost every piece of feedback across all participants: 'amazing event'; 'really enjoyed myself today'; 'wouldn't have missed it for anything. Fascinating experience, all the senses involved.' In some cases this was explained more fully: 'loved the paper dresses'; 'enjoyed making the flower bracelet'; 'I didn't realise it was so easy to create a piece of art work from everyday items'; 'would love more time to play'. These comments showed the satisfaction people got from the way the PUAS tapped into suppressed artistic needs. It would seem that participants valued equally the dimensions of 'art as process' and 'art as product', described by Butterwick and Dawson (2005: 286) as 'the act of making' and 'the result of work', in that they were thrilled by the things they made as well as loving taking part. The conclusion we drew was that the PUAS can demonstrate very quickly that everyone can take intense pleasure in arts practice and that teachers can be confident that everyone has a creative aspect to their character.

The second most prominent theme was the quality of the ideas and their applicability for people's professional practice. Phrases such as 'very inspirational', 'excellent ideas for us to use in our classrooms', 'the idea is sooooooo exciting', 'leave brimming with ideas', 'fantastic ideas for primary teaching' confirmed that professional educators do not always know how arts can be readily adapted by non-specialists as tools for learning. They saw applications for specific contexts that had nothing to do with art teaching. 'Brilliant literacy and numeracy ideas.' One participant wrote:

> Dear daughters and sons of the future of teaching. I had an inspirational couple of hours today and dearly hope you will spread these ideas like viruses in your own practice. It's time for change and Art is the way to make it happen.

The third theme was that of 'creativity' more generally. Participants repeated this word, and also stressed the value of the creative work itself and a creative environment: 'We had forgotten how to express ourselves via art or doing something. Very inspiring'; 'place looks lovely, great ambience'; 'the dresses looked wicked'; 'love the paper dresses, want one'. Cutting across all three themes were other responses around prompting deeper thinking about the nature of art and how everyone 'should have a chance to do it'. There were also comments about the nature of the organisation and the attitude of the trainees running the session that indicated that the open, caring and uncritical approach that underpins the PUAS was important; 'the teachers were really friendly and helpful'; 'very friendly and approachable staff'; 'had a go at everything!'; 'the organization is second to none'. The openness and accessibility to all ages and backgrounds was acknowledged: 'Something that reaches out to all people, let's have more ways of bringing people together.'

Trainee benefits

The experience of designing, planning, marketing and running the PUAS benefited the trainee teachers tremendously. The art schools gave the trainees the chance to see at first hand the benefits of community outreach work. They developed the confidence to plan and deliver a large-scale arts event, working within constraints of limited budgets, resources and facilities. One trainee reflected that it had been useful to be placed in a situation that required creativity in 'adapting and improvising within available space'. The trainees also noticed how working within constraints actually generated creative ideas and solutions, linking their experience to theories that suggest that 'too much freedom' can inhibit creativity (Stokes, 2006: 5).

Trainees study the subject of creativity in order to become creative teachers who can teach creatively but also teach *for* creativity. Working collaboratively on the PUAS gave the opportunity to reflect on the extent to which they were experiencing aspects of different creativity theories as individuals and as a group. Interesting discussions took place in which theory 'came to life' and the trainees could make connections between theory and practice, such as the notion of 'unconscious incubation' as a stage in the creative process (Robinson, 2010: 29) and moments of 'flow' (Csikszentmihalyi, 1996: 110).

Taking part in the events increased the trainees' 'cultural capital'. In addition to working alongside gallery professionals, festival organisers and professional musicians at the HCMF, trainees studied the art, music and creative working methods of John Cage and were introduced to the world of international classical contemporary music. The benefit of this and of continuing to increase their cultural capital as arts practitioners was highlighted by one trainee who stated that 'as somebody who grew up without culture, or even religion, I was never exposed to real culture until I was an adult – it is still difficult for me to actively seek it as a result'. Art can be seen as an elitist and exclusive club populated by a 'professional field of experts and elites, who carefully police the borders of their practice' (Gauntlett, 2011: 218). Trainees realised how their practice had played a part in starting to build cultural capital for many of the participants at the PUAS, by breaking down some barriers of an exclusive field, promoting accessibility and a 'way in' to the arts.

Conclusion

Williamson (1998: 136) felt that for many adults 'creativity has been thoroughly tamed and disenchanted'. This was echoed in comments made by many in the lead-up to the PUAS. It seemed they had enjoyed art, design and craft at school and then lost their connection to, and participation in, the subject. The feedback from the PUAS experience suggests that they were looking for re-enchantment, to reconnect with remembered enjoyment and what Clover called 'recapturing the creative sense of self and being acknowledged as creative beings' (2007: 92).

This particular use of the arts in the university enabled Sarah to introduce trainees to their wider role as adult educators. It gave them an insight into the untapped creative potential of groups and communities who would not normally enrol on or participate in arts classes or art schools. It also helped them understand the kinds of activities that enable those who do not self-identify as artists to overcome their self-consciousness and liberate that creative potential. They also learned how to organise a large-scale event for public consumption. The trainee teachers were able to compare and contrast the success of pedagogical approaches and art activities across different age groups, sectors and locations. They responded to the challenge of designing inclusive art and craft activities for differing age groups, levels of ability and experience and gained real insight from doing this. Wix and John-Steiner (2008: 225) suggest that 'higher education students emerge from experiences of facilitating and participating in creative collaborations richer for having practised a variety of ways of knowing and being' and indeed trainees expressed elation from the positive experience and success of the PUAS, reflected in the following comment: 'I came away from the experience feeling that I had really achieved something, and I felt very fulfilled.'

Our reflections on the relationship between these pop-up events and the wider literature on the arts and professional education and arts and community engagement brought home to us the limitations as well as the value of the PUAS. The buzz and excitement and the awareness of individual and collective creative and expressive potential were powerful but momentary. They do not have the strong roots that community arts workers develop through close, sensitive and developmental engagement with groups. Nor do they have obvious shoots and branches reaching into the future for the participants. Follow-up work is done with the teachers organising the events, to consolidate their learning and build strategies for the future. For example, they reflected on the status of craft in society and considered strategies for minimising perceived gender-related barriers to some activities. However, there is no follow-up work with participants. The experience demonstrated the huge potential that well-organised one-off arts events can have for stimulating creativity and promoting a desire for creativity. In order to take advantage of this as a trigger for sustained change, a logical next step would be to link these events to a wider context, offering participants the opportunity for appropriate follow-through. This would strengthen existing links between the university and a range of community arts groups that might offer that kind of support. For now we recall the intensity of the experience and continue to reflect on the potential it offers.

References

Butterwick, S., and Dawson, J. (2005), 'Adult education and the arts', in T. Fenwick, T. Nesbit and B. Spencer (eds), *Contexts of Adult Education: Canadian Perspectives*, Toronto: Thompson Educational Publishing, 281–89.

Clover, D.E. (2006), 'Out of the dark room: participatory photography as a critical, imaginative and public aesthetic practice of transformative education', *Journal of Transformative Education*, 4(3): 275–90.

Clover, D.E. (2007), 'Tapestries through the making. Quilting as a valuable medium of feminist adult education and arts-based inquiry', in D.E. Clover and J. Stalker (eds), *The Arts and Social Justice: Re-crafting Adult Education and Community Cultural Leadership*, Leicester: NIACE, 83–104.

Csikzentmihalyi, M. (1996), *Creativity: Flow and the Psychology of Discovery and Invention*, New York: Harper Perennial.

Freire, P. (1970), *Pedagogy of the Oppressed*, Harmondsworth: Penguin Books.

Gauntlett, D. (2011), *Making is Connecting*, Cambridge: Polity Press.

Gelo, F. (2008), *The Heart of Empathy. Using the Visual Arts in Medical Education* (DVD), George Washington Institute for Spirituality and Health.

Greene, M. (1995), *Releasing the Imagination: Essays on Education, the Arts, and Social Change*, San Francisco: Jossey-Bass.

HCMF (2010), *Festival Programme 2010*, http://www.hcmf.co.uk/event/show/196 (accessed 1 July 2011).

Johnson, S. (2010), *Where Good Ideas Come From*, London: Allen Lane.

Jokela, T. (2007), 'Winter art education project', *International Journal of Art and Design Education*, 26(3): 238–50.

Kinsella, E. (2008), 'Educating socially-responsive practitioners: What can the literary arts offer health professional education?', in D.E. Clover and J. Stalker (eds), *The Arts and Social Justice: Re-crafting Adult Education and Community Cultural Leadership*, Leicester: NIACE, 39–60.

Muterspaw, F., and Fenwick, T. (2007), 'Passion and politics through song: recalling music to the art-based debates in adult education', in D.E. Clover and J. Stalker (eds), *The Arts and Social Justice: Re-crafting Adult Education and Community Cultural Leadership*, Leicester: NIACE, 147–65.

Rademaker, L. (2007), 'An arts advocacy group performs community arts education', *Arts Education Policy Review*, 108(3): 25–33.

Robertson, K. (2007), 'The revolution will wear a sweater: knitting and activism', in D. Graeber and S. Shukaitis (eds), *Constituent Imagination: Militant Investigations, Collective Theorization*, London: AK Press, 209–23.

Robinson, A. (2010), *Sudden Genius? The Gradual Path to Creative Breakthroughs*, Oxford: Oxford University Press.

Sandlin, J. (2007), 'Popular culture, cultural resistance and anticonsumption activism: an exploration of culture jamming as critical adult education', in E. Tisdell and P. Thompson (eds), *Popular Culture and Entertainment Media in Adult Education*, San Francisco: Jossey-Bass, 73–83.

Stokes, P. (2006), *Creativity from Constraints: The Psychology of Breakthrough*, New York: Springer Publishing Company.

Tett, L., Anderson, K., Colvin, S., McNiell, F., Overy, K., and Sparks, R. (2011), 'Literacy, education policies, arts and prisons', in A. Houghton (ed.), *Creating and Sustaining International Connections: Proceedings of the 41st Annual SCUTREA Conference*, University of Lancaster, 5–7 July.

Williamson, B. (1998), *Lifeworlds and Learning*, Leicester: NIACE.

Wix, L., and John-Steiner, V. (2008), 'Peer inquiry: discovering what you know through dialogue', *Thinking Skills and Creativity*, 3: 217–25.

5

Fear of glue, fear of thread: reflections on teaching arts-based practice

Shauna Butterwick and Darlene E. Clover

> Creativity is both the impetus and the result of cultural activity. Music, poetry, dance and other forms of cultural expression are valuable methodologies of adult education. (Macleod, 1989: 122)

Decades ago, J. Roby Kidd, founder of the International Council for Adult Education, suggested that the arts and adult education were old and familiar partners. And as feminist adult educators and activist-scholars we have for many years woven the arts into our community practice and university teaching. However, in the hectic act of doing so we have sometimes neglected 'the constant interplay of action and reflection' (Brookfield, 2005: 504) or praxis that helps to transform and inform. This chapter provides us with a space to critically reflect on how and why we integrate the arts into our adult education work at the university. Using a narrative approach, we discuss our backgrounds in/to the arts; our understandings of the potential of the arts; methods and activities we have used; challenges we faced; and constructive things we, and our students, have learned from our intentional emphasis on the human aesthetic dimension in our classrooms.

Although our backgrounds and practices sometimes differ, we share two common assumptions. First, no university – and certainly no adult education programme – should claim to be educating people unless it exposes them to the complexities and problems of society and incites a passionate desire to explore, to change oneself as well as the world and, particularly, to create and imagine. We believe the arts are powerful means to achieve these aims. Secondly, art and culture exist in, and are fundamental to, all cultures worldwide and should have a place across the university curriculum, both within and beyond the confines of faculties and schools of fine arts or literature. We believe compartmentalising aesthetic experience simply reinforces problematic preconceived or elitist notions about the arts and limits their capacity as instruments of critical, social and creative education.

Over the years we have worked within adult education and community organisations where the arts were not regarded as peripheral. In the International Council for Adult Education, for example, the arts – from photography, theatre, music, poetry and dance to collage, murals, basket-weaving and knitting – were seen as powerful instruments to enable new understandings of a complex and rapidly changing society. But we have also noticed the seriousness of scholarship in adult education and how it seemed to preclude any use or even discussion of the arts. The message is often that the arts are fine in the affective world of community work, but simply have no place in the serious 'cognitive' space of the university classroom. In the classroom we analysed, discussed, debated, challenged and read but we did not render these discussions visual through imagery nor did we enact or embody them. We query whether adult educators in the academy do this to vie for legitimacy within a rigid, normative university structure. We challenge whether this need be the course of learning and teaching. We acknowledge that we began cautiously to bring the arts into our scholarship. But we have found students' responses to be often overwhelmingly positive and this has motivated us to use arts-based educational and research practices. Our motivations for bringing arts-based activities into the classroom also include a desire to interrupt the domination of academia by hyper-abstract or rational discussions of concepts and theories and the tendency for these discussions to leave women or students of non-European ancestry on the margins. This is some of our story.

Antecedents of/in the arts

> To exercise our imagination [through the arts] is part of our search for significance within the greater cycle of being, our investigation of our relationship with the wondrous. (Wyman, 2004: 2)

Shauna: My current engagement with the arts and its transformative, illuminating and pedagogical possibilities feels like a second childhood. Indeed in the past few years I've been taking continuing education classes in various art forms (poetry, collage, music, jewellery making). I'm fortunate to have had a partner and teachers in these courses who encouraged me and welcomed my somewhat tentative efforts. I was not blessed by such enthusiastic responses during my early schooling. I recall my last art class in grade nine where I was harshly admonished for my poor use of colours. I was not, however, badly injured by this critique and cannot lay claim to a lifelong fear of art-making as a result. Instead, I took my creative desire elsewhere; my sewing projects were often about making something new or different out of something old that had a previous function. Home economics was the space where this transformation took place. I also found space for my creative passions in high school English literature class where I wrote some (rather bad) poetry.

Post high school, however, I turned my mind to getting trained in an area in which I could find work anywhere in the world. And so I entered a three-year, hospital-based nursing programme in which my sewing and poetry writing activities happened only occasionally. I found myself in a science-oriented world where learning the basics was valued over creative alternatives. Hospital nursing was a tough place to bring in art-making; however, I did witness how some patients who engaged in art-making, particularly music, seemed to heal faster. I shifted from the hospital to community health nursing where I had more room to bring in art-making and invited participants in my community-health drop-in clinics to dance, draw and sketch their ideas. In my thirties I made a career change and began working in a women's centre, counselling and running programmes; in all of these activities I continued to bring art-making into my teaching practice. In one career-planning course I invited participants to use colours to paint the past, present and future in relation to their vision of work or career. In graduate school I had further opportunities to teach and develop curriculum, which I found to be a very creative process. I have been fortunate to teach in institutions where my creative quirks, while regarded as different, have not been suppressed.

My arts-based pedagogical desires were greatly enhanced when I collaborated with Jan Selman, a community-theatre specialist, to conduct a research project using popular-theatre processes and activities to explore the politics of feminist coalitions. While I had witnessed and read about the power of popular theatre, I had no theatre background. That collaborative project deepened my skills and appreciation for how aesthetic and embodied processes, so much a part of expressive arts, were central to transformation. My research into women's social movement learning continues and I am now exploring how Filipino feminist activists use arts (theatre, dance, visual art) in their participatory action research, community organising and civic engagement. I occupy a hugely privileged position in which I can continue to bring art-making processes to my teaching and forms of inquiry and examine its power through my research. As I grow older I find myself drawn to making things again. I don't sew much, but I feel like a kid again when I dabble with my paints, glue, beads, beach glass, found objects and so on and find new ways for self-expression.

Darlene: My relationship with the arts is a web of contradictory thoughts and experiences so let me begin with two of these from my youth to set the scene. In one sixth-grade art class I drew from a postcard the typical western Canadian image of a mountain in the distance foregrounded by a winding river lined with trees and rocks. When I stepped back to marvel at my artistic prowess – I had managed to integrate every single one of the pastel colours from the box into the drawing – the teacher appeared at my elbow and sighed, 'Well you will never be an artist.' Later, in grade eight, I was assigned a minor part in a play that captivated the audience during its public performance and earned me an acting award. So one could say that my forays into 'serious' or fine arts was marked by both wretchedness and exhilaration, out of which a seed began to sprout. I realised I enjoyed honing my dramatic skills but I was aware that the satisfaction depended upon hearing applause! But more importantly, the intrinsic value of art – the joy of simply making art for the sake of making it – was not going to be an integral part of my make-up.

I joined the International Council for Adult Education in Toronto in the mid-1980s. I also decided to undertake an undergraduate degree at the same time. As a voracious reader I enrolled in English Literature. While I recognise that literature can be a moral anarchy of stereotyping and contempt for the poor, it is also powerful, with an ability to be ostensibly about one thing when in fact it is really about something else. For example, a mystery novel can be a provocative commentary on class inequality or violence against women. One comment in particular made during a lecture given by Northrop Frye, a professor at the University of Toronto, has stayed with me: 'You do not read Macbeth for a history of Scotland but to learn what it is like to lose your soul.' I was somewhat naive when I joined the ICAE and struggled to understand what adult education in that global, social justice and non-formal context actually meant. It was in fact the more understated, even subversive, focus on socio-political issues and the human condition articulated so artfully in the novels I was reading that was, more than anything else, the catalyst to my comprehension of the depth and breadth of what actually constituted radical, popular and feminist adult education and learning.

Potentials of the arts

Is the revival of community art merely a perverted side effect of ongoing neoliber-alisation and the dismantling of the welfare state or does [it] now offer a powerful alternative to hyper-individualisation and endless flexibility? Will art always remain a fiction, or can it, in fact, generate social change? (De Bruyne and Gielen, 2011: 3).

Shauna: I have been moved by art forms and have seen others, both creators and observers, undergo a shift in thinking and world-view through their engagement with art-making and creative expression. In the late 1980s I was involved with the local chapter of Status of Women (SoW); we were protesting against cuts to women's centres by the federal government, which provided most of the funding. We learned that the cost of supporting these centres was the same as the cost of refurbishing some government offices, which included new framed photographs of the current minister. We were outraged that money could be spent on these things while the vital services provided by women's centres was so readily dismissed. This fuelled protest strategies which I call 'the politics of embarrassment'. We were not the only group fighting this battle; other SoW groups across Canada were also engaged; we kept in touch, sharing strategies, successes and problems.

At one point in the debate, a government official suggested we have a bake sale to raise the money. We were initially shocked by this sexist comment, but then quickly seized on the idea and made it into a protest theme. A bake sale was organised and held in the entrance of the Vancouver-based federal government offices. We wore aprons and set up several tables with breads, cakes and cookies, pricing these items according to the level of skill and knowledge required and the hours of labour given, basing the final price on the hourly wage a chef would make. Loaves of bread were thus priced at several hundred dollars and the other items reflected similar pricing.

We sent out news releases that outlined how the government had suggested we have a bake sale to raise funds. We invited the media, politicians and bureaucrats; there was an amazing turnout, I think because of the creativity of this protest. We spoke at the event about the costs of running women's centres, the services provided and the volunteer hours given by women to keep them running; we broke down the various services, priced them based on professional work and indicated that government funding was not a 'hand out'; it was a bargain given the services provided. We also compared the costs to the money being spent on refurbishing government offices. The media ate it up. Other protests occurred across the country, each using different tactics. Videos of these events were made and couriered to different groups so that we could see and learn from each other's initiatives. The government eventually returned funding to women's centres. Another example of the 'politics of embarrassment' is the use of political fashion shows by Filipino activists. In the Philippines (and elsewhere), fashion shows and beauty contests are popular events. The early days of feminist activism saw protests against these events. In Canada and the United States, Filipino activists have built upon the idea of the fashion show and politicised it; many shows have been produced. The fashion shows often build on participatory action research which has explored topics such as the trafficking of women, their exploitation as migrant workers and Philippine independence. Each outfit modelled was designed to symbolise a particular story or theme.

In one political fashion show a shiny, red cocktail dress had been created; it was beautiful. However, the woman wearing it was taking small steps and holding herself rather rigidly. Upon closer inspection, I saw that the material was actually constructed from over 1,000 plastic phone cards, each linked to the other with small metal rings. The phone cards had been collected by one Filipino domestic worker who used them to keep in touch with her family in the Philippines. She had come to Canada through the Live-in Caregiver Programme (LCP). In this programme, women cannot bring their children and must live with their employers (sometimes in very poor conditions); many are exploited, working long hours for minimal pay, sometimes seven days a week. Their domestic location means they are hidden from public view. This 'phone card dress' brilliantly captured these restrictions and the efforts made by this domestic worker to maintain communication with her family and children.

The beauty of the dress spoke to the way in which programmes like the LCP are seen as desirable to both Canadian families looking for affordable child and elder care and to Filipino women seeking a way to survive economically. These women are required to have professional credentials and many are university educated, but they cannot find jobs in their home country and so leave to work elsewhere, sending their pay home through remittances. While the dress is attractive, it is also a prison, for once women enter this migrant labour market most cannot break free of their economic marginalisation. Even when they have finished their required 24 months of employment and succeed in their application for landed immigrant status, they often end up working in the low-waged service sector.

Darlene: I have spoken of literature in terms of how it enabled my own learning about adult education, so let me speak about two other experiences that illuminated the fascinating potential of the arts for me. I had read scholars such as Griffiths (1997) who noted the ability of the arts to attract positive but, equally importantly, negative public or 'official' attention because of their potential to imaginatively disrupt, visually critique, performatively illuminate and creatively educate. I understood this theoretically or abstractly, but I had never really experienced it empirically, the volatile clash of public art and public opinion so often captured in the newspapers notwithstanding. But that changed in 1995 at a women's march in Ottawa. A group of 30,000 women were marching through the streets calling for the elimination of everything from violence against women to the predatory practices of global capital. If you have ever attended a women's march you cannot fail to have noticed the plethora of small children, squeaky toys, balloons, prams, sticky foodstuffs and strollers, making it perhaps *the most* non-threatening gathering possible. Nevertheless, as we marched along I observed the streets lined with police dressed in full riot gear, leaning lethargically against motorcycles. All remained calm until someone announced a puppet show. I was some distance from the actors on stilts moving through the sea of women and children calling us to the makeshift stage, so I was not at first totally sure what I had heard, but the police were sure and they were instantly on their feet, checking for truncheons and grasping for helmets and shields amid furtive gasps into walkie-talkies of 'puppets, puppets, puppets, move!' My first thought was that either they, or I, had gone mad until it dawned on me that women circulating pamphlets, carrying banners and shouting slogans were run of the mill; however, a creative, dynamic and engaging piece of culture, combining the potency of satire, irony, imagery, metaphor, fact and feeling was decidedly not. Indeed, the women and children were moving rapidly towards the actors and electricity was in the air. But was this 'artful' activity actually going to provoke the 'crowd' to uncontrollable flights of enthusiasm, which would need to be subdued by force? Were, as Griffiths (1997: 31) argued, the arts 'the most vigorously effective' in terms of mobilising dissent and encouraging action? I watched in fascination – and I will never get this image out of my mind – as some officers closed in on the puppeteers while others positioned themselves to impede the flow of women and children.

In 2000 I was invited by the Laidlaw Foundation to evaluate cultural animation projects facilitated by community artists in three underprivileged communities in Toronto. As I listened to the stories of the artists, community members, project administrators and numerous others connected to the project, a portrait formed of a powerful aesthetic process of community development and a potent, cultural, social and educational combination. One of the things I began to see was that the arts, but also the artists, had the ability to bring people together – or perhaps better out of their homes, although I use this word with misgivings as so many lived in substandard accommodation – in ways that these communities, nor I for that matter, had not witnessed previously. Whether or not the people involved, who came from all walks of life and all cultural backgrounds, saw themselves as artists, they were attending the art-making workshops in droves. Community members spoke passionately of hope, caring and nurturing, of safety and inspiration and of feeling less isolated and alone. This latter in particular reminded me of a comment by the cultural theorist Theodor Adorno that I found in an article by Farkas: 'while art could not completely solve all social dilemmas, it could solve one problem: the loneliness of spirit' (2000: 15). The art workshops were powerful because they invited people to tell their stories and to listen to the stories of others, often for the first time, since, although they lived next door to one another, they were still so very isolated. This speaking and listening process cut across socio-economic, gender, age and race barriers, enabling people to celebrate who they were and what they knew. The arts are really a function of life itself, and the process of making art – both the creative and re-creative – was providing people with insights and weaving them historically, culturally and even aesthetically into the fabric of the community. People spoke of new understandings and visions of their 'neighbours', many of whom they admitted to fearing, such as groups of teenage boys. I believe it was Marshall McLuhan who suggested that we do not create art as much as it creates us by changing the way we see and act upon the world. Further, the arts serve as a catalyst or vehicle for fun; they instigate deep laughter, something that Illeris (2003) argues is essential to the process of adult learning about difficult issues.

Yet there was also risk and challenge in the work. People 'risked' making art, showing real courage to create in front of and with others. And this is where the community artists enter the frame. The ICAE firmly believed that visual artists, poets, musicians, muralists and theatre performers were mediators of critical social learning and creators of knowledge. These projects were the application of this belief; the artists acted as agents and instigators of transformation. They played the roles of critical friends, mentors and guides who challenged people to engage in a processes of discovery and rediscovery and to move towards new creative possibilities, which in turn built an individual and collective sense of cultural and social agency. Cultural expression was their means to democratise culture and demystify 'art'. I watched as the artists actively encouraged people to add colour for emphasis, to centre an image to find balance and so forth. The artists paid equal attention to context and purpose, and form and artistry, placing equal value on the educative-community building process and the product – the artwork. And the pride in their work, when it went on public display, was so apparent in the faces of the community. The artistry was also noticed by outsiders, as this comment from one woman that I captured in my journal illustrates: 'I was surprised at how artistic the piece was. The artist paid attention to the art itself and not just the issue. It was the most beautiful and the most thought-provoking piece.'

But as I mentioned above, the arts are not always about celebration and beauty, camaraderie and collaboration. They can arouse what Overton (1994) called feelings of righteous anger and indignation as they tackle stereotypes and inequalities or illuminate structures and practices that pollute and endanger or stifle democracy and citizen participation. One of the Toronto community animation projects I spoke of earlier that dared to address a particularly explosive environmental issue resulted in a media maelstrom, with city councillors screaming for retribution. While this was difficult at the time because I had been hired by the funder, and had to explain how this was not 'really' political and that they need not worry that they would lose their charitable status (since foundations cannot engage in political activities in Canada), this only deepened my resolve to use the arts and my respect for the community artists who risked much to engage in creative practices of direct action.

Arts-based activities and student response

> Play is not action. Action can be playful, but it should remain action: a political
> activity, gesture or statement. (De Cauter, 2011: 14)

Shauna: The arts-based activities I have used in my teaching include collage,
zines, scrapbooks (reading journals that include drawings and visual artefacts),
theatre-based exercises, dance and poetry, among others. I will begin with a story
of poetry. I often invite students to use poetic form when they are writing. I find
poetry is a form that allows thoughts to be expressed that might not be included
in narrative structures. I have used haiku and have also directed students to write
free form poetry when we are working through issues and concepts in which
there is tension or contradiction. Poetry seems to hold the notion of opposites in
a different kind of relationship. In one class on ethnography as methodology, we
were exploring the location, role and responsibility of the researcher. One student,
Indy Batth, wrote a poem in response; here is part of that poem (included with
permission).

> Identity in motion: Racism and assimilation
> I once had an accent and then I assimilated.
> My point of entry towards assimilation,
> began with giving up my accent, my British accent, that is.
> Fitting in; disassociating, I was made to feel shame
> Shame about my dress, food, values, and beliefs.
> I became racist about/towards my own cultural heritage.
> Running away from my India/ness;
> How does one run away from one's self?
> I've stopped running.

It was truly a turning point in her thinking about her identity and experiences of
racism as an Indo-Canadian woman.

I also use collage, and one summer I was teaching an intensive course on
community-based adult education. I invited Barbara Bickel, a painter and collage
artist, to lead the class in creating a collage about the meaning of community.
Using ¾-inch pieces of plywood cut into small rectangles, together with all kinds
of paints, beautiful handmade paper, magazines, glue and scissors, Barbara invited
the class to explore, indicating that everyone had the basic skill: glueing. The class
then engaged with great enthusiasm using the glorious array of paper, magazines,
ribbons, paints and other objects that Barbara had brought. A hive of activity
followed, sounds of rustling paper, cutting and tearing, heads bent in concen-
tration and laughter. I worked on my collage alongside the students as Barbara
moved around the room, responding to questions, admiring the work, cheering
them on. Three hours later we finished our activities and displayed an amazing
collection of images outside on the grass. Each artist spoke about their collage
and what emerged were stories about community, of feeling at home, connected
and understood. There were also stories of struggle and exclusion. The ease with
which the class told their stories, listened intently and delighted in each other's
creativity was striking. I learned so much from this artist and educator about

setting the stage for such work by honouring it and creating access to a creative form of expression. This was serious play, playful seriousness. The creative expression created a space for sharing experiences and respectful listening. Students indicated that this process tapped into long-held stories and experiences that they had not thought about for some time. As Leland and Williams note, collage is an inclusive process that has 'something for everyone [and offers] enormous creative potential. Unlike painting and drawing mediums, where a stroke of the brush or pencil is a commitment, collage is a constant metamorphosis' (1994: ix).

Student responses to my invitations to make art include enthusiasm, fear and resistance. Most students, although hesitant at first, welcome these activities, often commenting about how long it has been since they have engaged in such activities. Some are surprised to find such activities in a graduate classroom. Many students are uncomfortable and sometimes fearful, with memories of being told by parents, peers and teachers that they had no creative or artistic talent. These students, after watching others and seeing that there is no critical judgement about their creations, join in and find it fun and helpful to their learning. There are those who actively resist arts-based processes and simply do not see their value, although some eventually grudgingly participate and indicate that they had enjoyed it. However, in both cases they remain unconvinced of any pedagogical value. Some are even angry with me for including such processes.

Students often grasp the meaning of rather abstract concepts through various art processes; creating a visual image captures in some way the meaning of theories and ideas. Sometimes the process includes showing these creations to an audience who then comment on what they see. There is often a wide range of meanings attributed to an image, illustrating the diversity of interpretations present in the group and highlighting how the hermeneutic cycle, that is, the process of generating interpretations of others' interpretations, is core to the creation of knowledge and understanding. The arts create a pathway to sharing diverse views that are often constrained in traditional 'rational' academic discussions. Art-making can also equalise the risk-taking as students speak their 'truths'. Some might call this creating a safe classroom, but what is safe for one person can be risky for another. Foregrounding the risk attached to learning instead of emphasising safety challenges the way declarations of safety can render invisible the dangers that some learning environments hold for some students. It is important to be ready for the unknown when using the arts in one's pedagogical practice.

Darlene: I will focus on three approaches that I use in my teaching. One is individual artistic practice and often takes the form of a learning journal. Although students are given the 'safety net' of simply typing up reflections on the readings or other activities in the class, such as guest speakers, I encourage them to aesthetically problematise and explore the ideas in the literature through, for example, 'altered books' – the remaking of an existing hard-cover book using magazine images, poetry, their own writings and so forth. They can produce any type of creative reflective piece and often do really imaginative things. One student carved a paddle covered in reflections while another created a room out of cardboard. In her room she had herself in a chair, a bookshelf, windows, coloured rugs and so forth. It spoke metaphorically of opening up to new ideas, learning as a kaleidoscope of colour.

This individual focus allows students to explore their own place as a creator of culture, their own sense of artistic agency, identity and meaning-making. But I am also wary of reinforcing academic and aesthetic theory that prioritises individualised learning and art-making (e.g. Eschle and Maiguashca, 2006; Felshin, 1995), and therefore the majority of activities are collective. Students report back from small-group discussions on theories of power, citizenship, feminism or social movements using poetry, skits or songs. There are few things more inspirational, revealing, and hilarious for that matter, than watching a group of students perform Foucauldian power discourses or sing Habermas' notions of the lifeworld to the tune of 'Auld Lang Syne' and relating these to aesthetic theory and arts-based practice. The adult education, social and aesthetic theories I use in my classes allow us to problematise, reflect, go beyond the personal and the immediate and reframe practice. Engaging with theory through the arts, conversely, refracts them through a creative prism, making them more human, personal and accessible. In other words, art-making makes theory an art, in an extraordinary way, and students truly grasp and retain the power and complexity of the ideas they perform or re-visualise.

Thirdly, I use community artists. They attend the class as guest speakers and share their arts-based educational work in the community. Following this they facilitate a six-hour workshop with the students. Before the workshops students choose a genre from a list I have generated based on available community artists, and also a theme or social issue – examples include violence against women, multiple perspectives, environmental issues or isolation and marginalisation – around which they wish to work. The genres to date have been photography, quilts, mosaics and shadow puppetry. You will notice here that I call all these forms 'art' as I take up Shiner's (2001: 9) challenge 'to heal the fracture' between arts and crafts by holding together imagination and skill, pleasure and use, freedom and service.

The students work with the artist to develop the artwork and then make a one-hour presentation to class on the experience. Last year, my students used photography to explore the theme of seeing the world through multiple perspectives. What was most interesting was that they did not use PowerPoint to display their photos but rather hung their striking images from a tree and engaged us in a series of creative activities around 'seeing'. In one of his writings, Walter Benjamin argued that a work of art could be politically correct only if it was also correct in an aesthetic or artistic sense. While I do not agree that non-artist-driven artworks are illegitimate or meaningless, I have come to realise that artists bring and, therefore, demand from us a more technical artistic ability that both students and I crave. The workshops are an opportunity to learn 'a craft' they would not encounter outside fine arts or teacher training. I have actually learned to sew, something I was morbidly afraid of until the quilting workshops. You now know that I am the fear of thread in the title, while Shauna is the glue!

Challenges, tensions and lessons learned

It is, perhaps, no coincidence that liberalism, with its strong belief in the beneficence of the market, embraces the individual as protagonist. (De Bruyne and Gielen, 2011: 5)

Through our narratives, we have touched upon a number of different challenges, tensions and lessons learned. But to conclude, we add others that are central to our calling, for perhaps in may ways a calling is what it has become – a calling to integrate art-making and various expressive forms into the academy beyond the fine arts. One challenge comes from the ever-persistent, 'taken-for-granted and highly problematic ontological dichotomies, including mind/body, theory/practice, reason/emotion, abstract/concrete and "ivory tower"/"real world"' (Eschle and Maiguashca, 2006: 119). Challenging these dichotomies through theorising and reflecting, creating a culture and space for doing and acting, enables emotional or affective practice. This attention to the affective and emotional is important, as it has been neglected in adult education theorising. However, if we defend the arts in higher education by emphasising only these dimensions, we are in danger of suggesting that their primary role is to provide libidinal release, and they could be, and in fact often are, justifiably kept apart in a class as entertaining, trivial activities as a result. Creating art, as we have witnessed, is a very conscious intellectual activity of reflection and reasoning, but also of imagination. As Murray argued, 'human beings live in concepts of the imagination even before reason has had the opportunity to establish them' (1986: 2). If the imagination is suspect in terms of 'thinking', we would suggest that, given the state of the world, reason makes many questionable deals with itself as well! In our classes we evoke the aesthetic imagination to make or construct meaning; through and from art we analyse and theorise. Moreover, as Mullin (2003: 189) argues, the imagination is 'simultaneously artistic and political', critical to us but also leading to another tension or challenge.

Felshin titled her 1995 book, *But is it Art?* We will not enter the abyss of this aesthetic debate but this question has resonated in our experience. Darlene in particular has come to realise that while some professors in the Faculty of Fine Arts are open to her courses, many are not. Each term, she receives two or three requests from students from Fine Arts to register. They are always extremely excited to have found an activist arts-based course that offers an admixture of art-making and critical social learning. The students request a copy of the syllabus to share with their supervisors in order to obtain permission to participate. However, few actually acquire permission. When questioned, students say such things as, 'Well, my professor says this is nothing more than "activist" art and not "real" art', by which we assume they mean 'art for art's sake'. Mullin (2003) goes a long way to challenge the dismissal of activist and political art from the 'non-real' category, but myopia remains.

We live in a world awash with visual images, 'where knowledge as well as many forms of entertainment are visually constructed, and where what we see is important' (Rose, 2001: 1). Yet few of us are taught to critically interpret or read these visuals. Although narratives that accompany or explain imagery or symbols in art are vital in terms of subjectivity, control and voice, another service is to engage our students not only in making art but also in interpreting images from other works of art and society for themselves. As Hall (1997: 9) argues, there is no law or guarantee that 'things will have one true meaning', and it need not be a debate between who is right or wrong but an analysis of 'equally plausible though sometimes competing and contesting, meanings and interpretations'. Interpretation and analysis would develop better visual learners, but also provoke deeper reflections on the specific social practices and power relations within which the images were made or to which they were responding.

Arts processes aim to reconnect mind with body. Moreover, arts-based activities can lessen the anxiety of many graduate students as they encounter a new language of academia which can include dense theoretical texts to which they struggle to relate, at least initially, since we show how this process works. Thus arts-based activities create alternative spaces for engagement by more students. And perhaps most importantly, they interrupt the ingrained power/knowledge discourse – the Kantian mind over body dynamic we spoke of in the introduction – and help students to ground theory and concepts in relation to their own lived experience.

Finally, we have learned much about the complexity of imagination and its valuable place in encouraging critical social and cultural learning. We give the last word to Canadian literary artist Max Wyman, who argues so eloquently,

> A defiant imagination ... defies the constraints of expectation and the everyday ... because the imagination – liberated by engagement with cultural expression – is necessary to the achievement of all we hope for as a society. (2004: 1)

References

Brookfield, S. (2005), 'Praxis', in L. English (ed.), *International Encyclopaedia of Adult Education*, London: Palgrave Macmillan, 504–08.

De Bruyne, P., and Gielen, P. (eds) (2011), *Community Arts: The Politics of Trespassing*, Amsterdam: Valiz.

De Cauter, L. (2011), 'Notes on subversions/theses on activism', in L. De Cauter, R. De Roo and K. Vanhaesebrouck (eds), *Art and Activism in the Age of Globalization*, Rotterdam. NAi Publishers, 8–19.

Eschle, C., and Maiguashca, B. (2006), 'Bridging the academic/activist divide: feminist activism and the teaching of global politics', *Millennium: Journal of International Studies*, 35(1): 119–37.

Farkas, S. (2000), 'Women artists creating space for health communities', *WE International*, 48/49: 15–18.

Felshin, N. (ed.) (1995), *But is it Art? The Spirit of Art as Activism*, Seattle: Bay Press.

Griffiths, J. (1997), 'Art as weapon of protest', *Resurgence*, 180: 35–37.

Hall, S. (1997), 'Introduction', in S. Hall (ed.), *Representations: Cultural Representation and Signifying Practices*, London: Sage, 1–12.

Illeris, K. (2003), 'Adult education as experienced by the learners', *International Journal of Lifelong Learning*, 22(1): 13–23.

Leland, N., and Williams, V. (1994), *Creative Collage Techniques*, Cincinnati, OH: North Light Books.

Macleod, C. (1989), 'Exchanging the heart of the Huapango with the soul of Africa', *Convergence*, 22(2–3): 120–31.

Mullin, A. (2003), 'Feminist art and the political imagination', *Hypatia*, 18(4): 190–213.

Murray, E. (1986), *Imaginative Thinking in Human Existence*, Pittsburgh, PA: Duquesne University Press.

Overton, P. (1994), 'The role of community arts development in nurturing the invisible culture of rural genius', in *From Artspeak to Artaction: Proceedings of a Community Arts Development Conference*, Saskatoon: University of Saskatchewan, 87–97.

Rose, G. (2001), *Visual Methodologies*, London: Sage.

Shiner, L. (2001), *The Invention of Art: A Cultural History*, Chicago: University of Chicago Press.

Wyman, M. (2004), *The Defiant Imagination*, Vancouver and Toronto: Douglas and McIntyre.

PART II

Arts-based research and enquiry

6

Mentoring arts-based research: a tale of two professors

Randee Lipson Lawrence and Patricia Cranton

A rts-based research has tremendous potential to foster human creativity and bring about cultural and social change. Unfortunately, in our experience, graduate programmes in mainstream academic cultures may not always seek to foster creativity. Bringing the arts into graduate adult education research has the potential to breathe new life into what has become a fixed and often rather dull process. This chapter discusses this practice as it critiques and challenges the myth of the researcher as a distant outsider, debunking the researcher's privilege of rationality and positivism. We argue the potential of using alternative creative processes for conducting research in the academy, focusing in particular on the crucial role of the research adviser. We also believe arts-based qualitative research can engage all of our senses and bring forth extra-rational knowledge that has the capacity to bridge cultural differences and promote transformation and social justice, in agreement with Finley (2008: 72) who argues 'at the heart of arts-based inquiry is a radical, politically grounded statement about social justice and control over the production of and dissemination of knowledge'.

Just as qualitative research once struggled for legitimacy in a quantitative world and is now quite common in education and the social sciences, arts-based research, while still on the margins in mainstream institutions, is nonetheless gaining popularity as a legitimate and rigorous form of research (see Knowles and Cole, 2008).

We have both worked in adult education where we have mentored doctoral students writing dissertations. In recent years we have become intrigued with the potential for arts-based research to open up new possibilities, expanding opportunities for students to bring their creative talents to the world of research. Over the last three years we have been dialoguing over email, sharing both our excitement when students come up with new and creative ways to conduct research as well as our struggles when this research is misunderstood or not taken seriously by the institution. Following a brief introduction to arts-based research, we present this chapter as a dialogue so as to invite others into the conversation. We describe how research can incorporate music, fiction, poetry, painting, photography, theatre and more and provide specific examples from our practice and experience with arts-based research. We also review some of the challenges and obstacles encountered in promoting creative research in our universities.

Arts-based research is any research that makes use of the arts in the collection, analysis and/or dissemination of data (Lawrence, 2008). The researcher may create art such as writing poems based on interview transcripts or performing participants' stories. He or she may analyse artworks such as movies, fictional literature or paintings as part of the research data. Alternatively the researcher could engage the research participants in the creating of art. For example, participants may be directed to create photographic images or engage in collage-making to express their understanding of a phenomenon. As Leavy (2009: 11) stated, 'The arts simply provide qualitative researchers a broader palette of investigative and communication tools with which to garner and relay a range of social meanings.'

Arts-based research is real research

Randee Lipson Lawence: There is a common assumption that arts-based research is somehow not as rigorous or scholarly as other forms of research. For example, I had a student who was at the beginning stages of her doctoral thesis approach me with what she perceived as a major dilemma. 'I'm really intrigued by the possibilities of doing research in some of the more creative ways that you shared with us Randee, but I want to do real research, the kind that is serious and scholarly. So I can't decide. Should I do arts-based research or real research?'

Patricia Cranton: How did you respond?

RLL: I asked her what she hoped to do with her research. Did she want it to sit on a library shelf or did she want it to be accessible to a wider community? I then explained that she didn't need to make a choice. Research need not be either creative or scholarly; it can be both. We've both mentored students whose work was incredibly rigorous, by which we mean that it paid the same attention to literature review, data collection and analysis as in other methodologies. Their methods of collecting data and presenting their findings made use of arts-based processes. Arts-based research actually extended the possibilities for how research was conducted.

PC: For me this issue is very much tied to institutional requirements and constraints. When working at a traditional university, I can still support arts-based research, but I disguise it in some way; that is, the student uses an arts-based approach to collecting data, but still follows the standard format for describing and presenting the research. For example, one of my students studied how individuals with diabetes viewed their disease and their identity as a 'diabetic person'. She used photography as a means of helping participants describe their perspective on diabetes, but she presented her dissertation in the traditional format.

RLL: That sounds interesting! Did she share photos with the participants or did they create their own photos? Were the photos included in the document?

PC: The whole group of participants went out together to take photographs, including Heather Stuckey, the doctoral researcher. They then held a focus group in which they discussed the meaning of the photographs to each participant. Heather did include some of the photographs in her dissertation.

RLL: It sounds like the exploration of the photographs helped to deepen their understanding of living with diabetes and contributed to what scholars call 'thick rich description', a cornerstone in qualitative research. When you say that students follow the 'standard format', I assume you mean that they uphold the same standards of rigour as in more traditional dissertations.

PC: By 'standard format' I mean following fairly detailed outlines for what should go in each of six chapters. This creates an artificial distinction between 'results' and 'discussion', as well as artificial distinctions between other aspects of research, for example, theory and method, which does not work well with arts-based research.

RLL: Our university is a bit less restrictive in that students can present their research in non-traditional ways; however, they are required to complete a literature review and write up their methodology to submit to their advising faculty even if it does not appear in the final document. Rigour is just as important in arts-based research projects, maybe more so because of the controversial nature of this method. For example, I worked with a student, Yolanda Nieves, who presented her research findings as a play. Yolanda's EdD dissertation was a performance inquiry based on narrative interviews with second-generation Puerto Rican women regarding their identity issues. The study was situated in Latino critical race theory and critical race feminism in which Yolanda conducted a meticulous and exhaustive literature review. Her analysis had the same rigour as any other research; however, the presentation was an ensemble play that was performed in the community where the research participants resided, reaching a wider audience, and thus connecting in deeper ways than possible with a written academic paper. Yolanda's research won the Arts-Based Research Dissertation award at the American Education Research Association Conference in 2010.[1]

Arts-based research as a methodology

PC: Randee, I was intrigued to find that arts-based research can be a methodology on its own, a methodology combined with other methodologies, a data collection technique, or a data presentation technique (e.g. McNiff, 2008). I think these different ways of understanding arts-based research are important. If we view arts-based research as a separate methodology, what do you think would be the unique characteristics of that methodology?

RLL: It seems to me that art would have to be the primary unit of analysis, that is, everything would be mediated through art. Leavy (2009) sees arts-based research as a holistic interdisciplinary process that bridges both art and science. Moreover, the main features of arts-based research that she contrasts with quantitative and traditional qualitative research include stories, images, sounds, scenes and sensory data. It is evocative, it is often represented as opposed to written, it is often political and emancipatory with the intent to raise consciousness. It is authentic, its purpose is to compel rather than to convince or persuade and it is transdisciplinary in nature.

PC: Thank you. That is helpful. So the underlying assumptions of the methodology would be emancipatory in nature?

RLL: Yes, arts-based research is an inherently political process as it shakes us out of complacency, tapping into our emotions and provoking us to interact with the research not just as passive consumers but, rather, as active participants.

PC: In my practice, I have seen arts-based research combined with narrative inquiry (using poetry, theatre, photography or collage to tell stories), phenomenology (creating drawings or writing stories to explore the essence of a phenomenon), case studies (creating a photographic journal of the environment of a specific case) and ethnography (using art to depict a cultural context). I'm thinking about one example and wondering if it qualifies as arts-based research. Michele Mont, in her dissertation, did a narrative inquiry interviewing five professors who draw on arts-based processes and nine African American students to determine what engages their learning when they have been exposed to arts-based ways of knowing. One part of the rationale behind the study was that African American students engage with the arts more in their learning. Would you say this is arts-based research or is it research about arts-based learning?

RLL: That's an important distinction. It seems there could have been many opportunities for Michele to use the arts in her research as she was working with people who already valued the arts. If she didn't, I would say this is not necessarily arts-based research. Since I work in adult education rather than art education, most of the arts-based research I see is on topics not related to art at all. So it is about the methodology or method as opposed to the subject matter.

PC: What other combinations have you encountered?

RLL: Similar to you I have worked with many students who combined arts-based research with other methodologies. For example, one woman who was from Guyana and currently living in New York did a narrative inquiry about the experiences of Caribbean women who had emigrated to the USA and were currently in university programmes. She analysed her data using found poetry. Found poetry is a technique I learned from my colleague Anne Sullivan (2004). The researcher works with transcript data and creates poetry with the participants' original words by distilling the main concepts and then making decisions about what to express. In this case the poems were used to introduce each research participant.

PC: Found poetry is very interesting. It works well with narrative inquiry, since found poetry tells a story using existing words and phrases.

RLL: Another student, Rick, was interested in the experiences of black men who had been mentored by other black men, not so much in the workplace but in life. Looking through the lenses of black identity development and critical race theory he used narrative inquiry to listen to the stories of five young men. Rick wrote his entire dissertation as a story, which was a conversation between himself and his alter ego, whom he referred to as 'You'. Within the conversation he made sense of what he was learning in the literature as well as his research findings. Rick could have written his narrative inquiry as a traditional thesis but instead chose an arts-based approach. It read more like a good novel.

Action research also works well with arts-based processes. Roslind, an executive director of a non-profit organisation, conducted an action research study to create a collaborative and participatory leadership model. Roslind would never consider herself an artist, in fact she was terrified of art due to negative child-hood experiences. Nonetheless she engaged her research participants in creating 'journey maps' which were drawings of how they saw the organisation. Of course, it would not be fair to ask the participants to do something she was not willing to do as well so Roslind completed her drawing using stick figures. She later acknow-ledged how powerful the exercise was in engaging people in a meaningful way.

PC: Heather Stuckey's research on diabetes was also action research. She used the arts in her action cycle beyond taking photos; for example, she used medita-tion and imagery in the initial action research cycle. Heather was interested in helping people see and relate to their bodies in a new way.

RLL: What a wonderful way to help people reframe what it means to be a diabetic! I've also had a few students using collaborative inquiry as their research methodology. The arts are an integral part of collaborative inquiry. Heron (1996) advocates presentational methods (art, theatre, poetry, etc.) as a complement to more rational or propositional methods of engaging in research.

PC: It wouldn't be collaboration alone that would make it arts-based research, right? It would have to involve collaboration using presentational methods?

RLL: Right. I suppose one could do collaborative research without using presentational methods but for Heron they are essential. We've been talking about infusing the arts into dissertations but they can also be used in informal classroom inquiries. I know you've been experimenting with using fiction in your classroom.

PC: Yes, I have. I would call this arts-based learning rather than arts-based research. In a sense my work with fiction in my classroom has been informal research, as we all worked together to understand how to use fiction in our class. Everyone contributed to the process. The course was on transformative learning, and we read short stories. For each class, we read two or three short stories, then during class we worked with those short stories in a variety of ways – putting ourselves into the shoes of a character in the story, rewriting the story from the perspective of a minor character, engaging in a debate with a character in the story, deconstructing the story line, creating a new ending for the story, and so on. We did something different with the stories in each class, and then we discussed the ways in which our activities encouraged transformative learning.

RLL: I can see the distinction you are making between learning and research but maybe they are more connected than we think. I can see possibilities for including fiction as part of research data. One of my current students is interested in informal learning to be a 'strong BBlack woman' despite adversarial life experi-ences, and I've been encouraging her to explore some fictional literature such as Alice's Walker's *The Color Purple* as data along with her interviews.

PC: It seems that learning and research are closely intertwined here since we are really facilitating or 'pulling out' something that already exists within the student. This reminds me of Belenky and Stanton's (2000) chapter in which they use a metaphor of being midwife for the role of adult educators. I have heard you use this metaphor as well.

Research advisors as midwives

RLL: I find that many of my students are already practising artists. They are poets or painters or have backgrounds in theatre or music. It would seem like a natural process for them to incorporate art into their research; however, many are reluctant to do so. They don't know how or think it is not a possibility or, as we discussed above, may be afraid it would not be considered 'scholarly'. It helps me to see the advisor role as similar to a midwife helping with the birth of a baby. We assist in bringing forth that which is already happening. We give 'permission' to students to use their creative talents in the research process. By encouraging but not directing the research or getting in the way of the process (akin to giving drugs or inducing labour) the student researcher brings more of who they are into the research process.

For example, I worked with Bette, a student who had been a drama major as an undergraduate some years prior to working on her doctorate. She was at this time in her mid-fifties. She and I attended a workshop by Augusto Boal at the 'Pedagogy and Theatre of the Oppressed' conference in 2001. On the plane ride home she talked excitedly about the workshop and how she longed to somehow reclaim her roots in theatre. I asked her to consider using theatre in her research. Her eyes widened as she had not considered that a possibility. When Bette got home she searched for a group involved in theatre for social change and found Scrap Mettle S.O.U.L. (Stories of Urban Life) in a Chicago neighbourhood. This group collected stories about community issues and then wrote scripts, inviting people from the community to create a dramatic performance. Bette joined the show as a participant and her research became a case study of the production. She attended all of the rehearsals as a participant observer and then interviewed several of the other cast members. Bette's research brought her back to her passion for theatre that had been lying dormant for thirty years.

PC: What did you do as Bette's advisor beyond suggesting that she incorporate theatre into her research? It sounds like she didn't need much convincing. She took the idea and ran with it.

RLL: That's true. She was ripe for the idea and just needed permission to get started and a little coaching along the way. I did feel very much like a midwife in this sense. Childbirth is a naturally occurring process. Babies come when they are ready and women's bodies seem to know what they need to do to get ready for the birth. Midwives are there to monitor the process, offer suggestions to facilitate the birthing and catch the baby when it comes. Once Bette got involved in her process I just stepped out of the way and let it evolve. The main coaching came in the writing up of the study. And what a proud moment witnessing the play performed!

PC: I haven't had very many students who see themselves primarily as artists. But I am thinking of Sandy Reed's dissertation. Sandy was a musician and had taught music for many years. She was a musician first and an adult educator second. She used phenomenology as a methodology, and she worked with performing musicians to help them make meaning of ageing and life as an older person through their music.

RLL: So Sandy *was* an artist. I like how she brought the musician part of herself into her research. What of the students with no formal art background?

PC: Any student who is drawn to arts-based research has some connection to art – either as a consumer of art or as a self-defined 'amateur' artist – but I don't think people have to be artists to do arts-based research.

RLL: I agree. Anyone who has a passion or connection to the arts can do arts-based research. And it doesn't require full immersion into the process as in Bette's research. For example, another student, Charlene, was doing a phenomenological study on the meaning of intercultural competence for corporate trainers. Charlene had no art background but was intrigued by the examples of arts-based research I shared in class. She gave each of her research participants a set of four coloured markers and sheets of paper, asking them to create a metaphorical drawing of intercultural competence. Creating the drawings allowed the participants to tap into a way of knowing that may not have surfaced in spoken language alone. The drawings were used as a jumping-off point for the interview and many appeared in her written document.

PC: Oh really? I would not have thought of that as arts-based research. I guess I am still struggling with the boundaries of this.

RLL: Maybe we are getting caught up in the language. Gary Knowles and Ardra Cole at Ontario Institute of Studies in Education in Toronto use the term 'arts-informed research' and in a chapter on using arts-based methodology in dissertations, Knowles and Promislow (2008) talk about 'infusing' art into the process. So in Charlene's case, art was not the main focus of the dissertation but a component of her data collection and analysis. Does this make sense?

PC: Yes, I understand. So, to stay with your metaphor of advisors as midwives, we bring out their interest in using arts in students' research in whatever way is suitable for the particular student. This could be 'arts-informed research' or 'arts-infused research' instead of the arts being the main focus of the work. In this case, I would go back to Michele Mont's dissertation and suggest that her work falls into the same category as Charlene's. Michele was studying how people engage in arts-based learning from the point of view of both the educator and the learner. As a part of her interview process, she did include symbols, images and drawings, but these methods were not central.

RLL: Right.

PC: The participants in Michele's research were African American, and a part of Michele's rationale was that African American learners are marginalised in the text-based, cognitive, rational approaches used in white higher education environments. Let's talk about how arts-based research is concerned with creativity in relation to social change and social justice. The metaphor of midwife is a very gendered one, and most of the researchers seem to be women. Is this a coincidence, or are their connections between gender and arts-based research or is it just adult education?

Human creativity and social change

PC: Jarvis (2012), in writing about using fiction and film in adult education, proposes that such strategies are often concerned with social justice. They draw on the concepts of hegemony and resistance, focusing on the development of a critical consciousness that heightens awareness of the power structures that maintain inequalities. It strikes me that this is just as relevant to arts-based research as it is to teaching practice. As you said earlier, arts-based research disrupts mainstream assumptions about the research as being objective and distant, or, in other words, it re-humanises the process of research. However, Jarvis says that working towards social change can occur through empathy (identifying with the art form in a personal way) or by 'standing back' and looking at art as a representation of 'other'.

RLL: I'm not sure I understand the part about standing back but I definitely agree with the empathy part. When I watched Yolanda's play I was riveted. It didn't matter that I'd read and reacted to several iterations of her script and even watched some rehearsals. The subject matter was very graphic and at times painful to watch as it dealt with the real lived experience of the research participants, including poverty, racism, incarceration, negative body image and silenced voices. It didn't matter that I was not Puerto Rican. The impact was even more profound on the largely Puerto Rican audience. For many of the younger members it was a chance to learn their own history and the injustices experienced by their people. Having a question and answer session with the cast members after the performance helped them to connect with the subject matter, collaboratively continuing to make meaning of the research findings.

PC: Let me see if I can explain Jarvis's thinking on 'standing back'. It seems to me to be an equally important way of understanding how art can be associated with social change and research on oppression. She suggests that film and fiction can serve to distance the reader by drawing attention to the fictionality. Standing back allows the reader/viewer to see the world with its 'values assumptions and ways of being laid bare' and this can shake up our assumptions (Jarvis, 2012). The use of narrators, for example, who address the reader or viewer directly draws attention to the fictionality and allows for critical commentary on the characters. Similarly, using multiple perspectives shows the same story through different lenses, breaking up the reality of there being one perspective. Manipulating time and space in fiction and film is another way of 'standing back' in order to see more clearly.

RLL: Oh, I think I see what you mean. Stepping back also allows a person to see his or her own experience in new ways.

Bridging cultural differences through transformation and social justice

RLL: You've written a lot about transformative learning. Do you think arts-based research has the potential to promote transformation?

PC: That's a big open question. The first thing that comes to mind is that arts-based research leads us to question our assumptions about what research is, and that is potentially transformative. Often students come into a graduate programme with the understanding of research as experiments conducted by objective scientists in laboratories or well-controlled environments. Our adult education students, who often have been out of school for many years, hold a point of view on what research is that comes from earlier decades and understandings of knowledge. For them, moving to an acceptance of qualitative research is a paradigm shift, and introducing arts-based methods into that is, again, quite a shift in thinking.

RLL: So true. I encounter this all the time with students who come from a positivisitic paradigm.

PC: Beyond that, I can also see that conducting arts-based research can be potentially transformative for the researcher, as participants express themselves in ways that allow a deeper and richer way of making meaning out of the phenomenon or experience being studied. And I suspect that this is similarly potentially transformative for the participants in the research. One of my current advisees is using storytelling to help understand the experience of recovering from cocaine addiction; another is using storytelling with terminally ill people to help make meaning of their lives and death. Both of these researchers report that some of the participants in their study feel changed by the process itself. Whether it is transformative or not, I am not sure, but I imagine it could be. It is really the participants who best determine what is transformative.

RLL: This is powerful. So the transformative potential is there for the researcher as well as the research participants.

PC: We were talking earlier about standing back from fiction in order to see multiple perspectives and to separate one's self from the fiction. I suspect that this also applies to the ability for arts-based research to bridge cultural differences. You have said that art is a universal language and that all cultures have some kind of art. Is there a parallel here? If participants in arts-based research feel changed by their participation in the process, would this also be the case when the research is focused on cultural differences?

RLL: I would think so. Consider the fact that communication is often culturally grounded. Some cultures communicate more naturally through their art than through written prose. We can relate to the artwork even if we speak a different language or know little about the culture. So to incorporate the arts into research is to consider extra-rational knowledge as valid as rational knowledge.

Engaging the senses and honouring the extra-rational

RLL: It seems to me that mainstream research, even many forms of qualitative research, simply privileges rationality as the only way of knowing. I like the concept of extra-rationality which I understand as beyond rational or incorporating other ways of knowing, including affective, embodied and spiritual knowing. Boyd and Myers (1988) talk about the extra-rational being expressed through symbol and imagery as contrasted with more rational processes which have to do more with judgements and decisions based upon objective facts. The arts engage all of our senses, relying on our emotions to help make sense of our experiences.

PC: Yes, indeed. Sandy Reed, whom I mentioned earlier, used the Jungian concept of individuation to frame her research with older performing musicians. I also want to recognise Dirkx's (2000) contributions in this area. The arts help us to see learning through emotions, embodiment and relations. On the other hand, I would not want to dismiss rationality in research!

RLL: I see extra-rationality as a complement to rather than a replacement for rationality in arts-based research. Yorks and Kasl (2002) advance a theory of 'whole-person learning', meaning learning that is experiential as well as cognitive and happens within an empathic connection with others. The arts encourage this level of interaction.

I also want to emphasise the relational nature of arts-based research. Whether one is doing art with the research participants as part of the data collection or presenting the research to others through story, visual art or performative processes, the relationship aspect is paramount. Arts-based research engages the researcher, research participant and audience at a deeper level than reading a report can do. We experience the message at an emotional and visceral level and often at a spiritual level as well. It is this connection that helps to deepen our understanding.

PC: This is very much the point I was making earlier when you asked me about arts-based research being transformative. I think we have come to see that relationships play a central role in transformative learning. And here, with arts-based research, relationships are also an integral part of the process. As you say, people are engaged at a deeper level.

We haven't really talked about 'engaging the senses' so far. I see a difference between this and extra-rational learning. I am reminded of Jim's Spaulding's doctoral thesis. Jim teaches boating safety and he was interested in finding a way to make such a topic interesting. He chose to use embodied learning and experiential learning as a strategy in an action research project. Jim designed a 'boat' that participants wore around their waist. The boat had lights and a horn. Jim then set up a harbour in the classroom, using desks. Jim's participants 'became' the boat. They moved around the classroom, obeying the 'rules of the road', using their lights and horns appropriately to get to the dock. Jim took videos of the process, and it was amazing how the participants became energised by this activity. They truly did 'become the boat'. Jim found that they learned more and they transferred the learning to the boating season in a way that did not happen in the traditional course format.

RLL: I love it! Was this totally Jim's idea or did you give him suggestions?

PC: It was completely Jim's idea. He had taught boating safety for decades, always with a lecture and PowerPoint strategy. He felt that the students retained the information only long enough to pass the test required for certification as a boat operator, and then promptly forgot the material. I thought his 'become the boat' idea was a bit silly and adult boat operators would feel foolish 'becoming the boat'. So Jim built the boats, did a pilot study and demonstrated that the idea got learners involved and having fun. In his dissertation, he even demonstrated six-month retention of the learning, which was something he cared about very much.

RLL: How did you shift from thinking the idea 'a bit silly' to embracing his artistry? It seems to me that one of the challenges students who consider arts-based research face is finding faculty who support and believe in what they are doing. I suspect that many faculty advisors are just not comfortable deviating from the norm or challenging the 'powers that be' to advocate for these students. This is just one of the many challenges involved in doing arts-based research.

PC: Good point. I am generally open to what students want to do, and Jim's pilot study was very convincing. Jim demonstrated to me, through his pilot project, that the idea wasn't silly at all. But I can see that this could be a challenge.

Challenges

PC: One thing that has been problematic for me has been a combination of university policy and colleagues' discomfort with arts-based research. At the university where I worked most recently, a doctoral student's committee has four members: two from adult education and two outside adult education, but from within the university graduate faculty (for example, psychology, nursing, business). There are a variety of levels of expectation within this structure. The graduate school formally reviews the format of all dissertations; the adult education programme adheres to graduate school requirements and also has its own standard format within that; the outside committee members come to the table with their own idea of what a dissertation should be (and this rarely includes art-based strategies). Do you share this kind of challenge?

RLL: Fortunately we are a small university and we don't have a graduate school. Our department has full authority to decide what counts as research. Not all of my colleagues are fully on board, however. I teach a seminar on arts-based research for the doctoral students. It used to be required, as I argued that arts-based research cuts across all methodologies; however, at some point it got relegated to an elective as some felt it would not be of interest to everyone. I still get a large percentage attending, however.

PC: You are fortunate to have that freedom with determining what counts as research for your students.

RLL: I find it somewhat challenging as an advisor when working with students doing creative research. I want to help stretch them as scholars but also want to honour their creative process. At times students conducting arts-based research get so carried away with their creative process that they lose sight of the fact that they are still conducting a study. For example, when I worked with Rick on the black male mentoring study he would sometimes go off on tangents or side trails, telling stories from his own experience that were only peripherally related to the research. When I suggested he pull back and stay more focused he sometimes became a bit resentful. So it is a balancing act.

PC: Yes, I can imagine it would be. I don't think I have encountered this. Students in our doctoral programme come in with Masters degrees in disciplines other than adult education, and it has always seemed to me that they have learned 'compliance' in their previous education experiences. They want to stay within 'traditional norms'. My problem is most often more related to helping them to step outside those boundaries rather reining them in.

RLL: Well yes, students like Rick, Yolanda, Bette and Jim who need little encouragement to incorporate their art into their research are unusual, but I like to think that is changing.

Conclusions and recommendations

By inviting readers into our conversation we hope to have conveyed a sense of the wonderful, messy, creative world of arts-based research in the academy and to have shared some of our success stories as well as our struggles with mentoring students. Arts-based research is real research that is as rigorous and scholarly as any other methodology. As can be seen in our conversation, the newness of arts-based research in education leads to it being a somewhat elusive concept. It does not have a given structure and form as do methodologies such as phenomenology and narrative inquiry. Is it important that arts-based research has a given structure? Or can each project have a unique structure? How can guidance be given to researchers wanting to try arts-based methodologies? This can be problematic for advisors and students who want guidance in what to do. But, it can also be freeing, as we hope to have conveyed in this chapter.

Arts-based research can be combined with most research paradigms and methodologies or it can stand on its own. Arts-based research is a political process that can bridge cultural differences and promote social justice. It is often transformative for both the researcher and research participants. Arts-based research engages all of our senses and taps into extra-rational ways of knowing. Advisors can encourage arts-based research by helping to bring out students' natural creativity like midwives who help bring babies into the world. Challenges for students conducting arts-based research exist both internally and institutionally; however, research advisors can help navigate the challenges.

For those considering arts-based research in theses and dissertations we offer the following recommendations.

For students:

- If you have a strong interest, talent or passion for the arts, consider incorporating it into your research.
- Talk to your faculty advisor about your ideas early in the process. Try to locate advisors who are open to creative research.
- Play with ideas; let go of preconceived notions of what research 'should be' and dream about what is possible.
- Find like-minded others among your peers and consider setting up an arts-based research discussion and support group.
- Read as many arts-based research studies in your area of interest as you can find, even if they are not directly related to your research question. Some are included at the end of this chapter.
- Think about whether you want your research to have arts-based strategies as

central to the research, used in data collection, used in data interpretation, and/or used in data presentation, and why.

- Consider your research participants as co-researchers on the journey to discover how to use art-based techniques.

For faculty advisors:

- Listen to students' ideas with an open mind. Just because it hasn't been done doesn't mean it can't be done.
- Find supportive colleagues who are experienced mentors of arts-based research.
- Experiment, play and be flexible. Work with your advisee to try things out.
- Be prepared to advocate for students to governing bodies in the university.
- Be prepared to be amazed! Your students may surprise you and open you up to new possibilities.

Faculty advisors and students who are interested in innovative and interesting ways to conduct graduate theses and dissertations will find the incorporation of arts-based research to be a freeing and creative experience. This can be done at several levels, including using arts-based data collection techniques, interpreting data through an artistic lens, presenting results in an artistic form or creating art work with the research participants as a way of understanding a phenomenon or experience or telling a story. The possibilities are limited only by one's imagination.

References

Belenky, M., and Stanton, A. (2000), 'Inequality, development, and connected knowing', in J. Mezirow and Associates (eds), *Learning as Transformation: Critical Perspectives on a Theory in Progress*, San Francisco: Jossey-Bass, 71–102.

Boyd, R.D., and Myers, J.G. (1988), 'Transformative education', *International Journal of Lifelong Education*, 7(4): 261–84.

Dirkx, J. (2000), 'Images, transformative learning and the work of soul', *Adult Learning*, 12(3), 15–16.

Finley, S. (2008), 'Arts-based research', in J.G. Knowles and A.L. Cole (eds), *Handbook of the Arts in Qualitative Research: Perspectives, Methodologies, Examples, and Issues*, Thousand Oaks, CA: Sage, 71–82.

Heron, J. (1996), *Co-operative Inquiry: Research into the Human Condition*, Thousand Oaks, CA: Sage.

Jarvis, C. (2012), 'Fiction and film and transformative learning', in E.W. Taylor and P. Cranton (eds), *The Handbook of Transformative Learning: Theory, Research and Practice*, San Francisco: Jossey-Bass, 486–502.

Knowles, J.G., and Cole, A.L. (eds), *Handbook of the Arts in Qualitative Research: Perspectives, Methodologies, Examples, and Issues*, Thousand Oaks, CA: Sage.

Knowles, J.G., and Promislow, S. (2008), 'Using an arts methodology to create a thesis or dissertation', in J.G. Knowles and A.L. Cole (eds), *Handbook of the Arts in Qualitative Research: Perspectives, Methodologies, Examples, and Issues*, Thousand Oaks, CA: Sage, 511–25.

Lawrence, R.L. (2008), 'Powerful feelings: exploring the affective domain of informal and arts-based learning', in J.M. Dirkx (ed.), *Adult Learning and the Emotional Self*, San Francisco: Jossey-Bass, 65–78.

Leavy, P. (2009), *Method Meets Art: Arts-based Research Practice*, New York: The Guilford Press.

McNiff, S. (2008), 'Art-based research', in J.G. Knowles and A.L. Cole (eds), *Handbook of the Arts in Qualitative Research: Perspectives, Methodologies, Examples, and Issues*, Thousand Oaks, CA: Sage, 29–40.

Sullivan, A.M. (2004), 'Poetry as research: development of poetic craft & the relations of craft and utility', *Journal of Critical Inquiry into Curriculum and Instruction*, 5(2): 34–37.

Yorks, L., and Kasl, E. (2002), 'Toward a theory and practice for whole-person learning: reconceptualizing experience and the role of affect', *Adult Education Quarterly*, 52(3): 176–92.

EdD theses cited

Blockinger, C. (2007), 'On closer scrutiny: workplace educators examine the meaning of intercultural competence. A phenomenological exploration', unpublished thesis, National Louis University.

Blasingame-Buford, R. (2011), 'The blueprint: strategies for building a culture of excellence', unpublished thesis, National Louis University.

Donoho, B. (2003), 'Scrap mettle SOUL: community performance as a catalyst for adult learning through grassroots ensemble theater', unpublished thesis, National Louis University.

James, G. (2005), 'Crossing over, moving forward: personal narratives of Caribbean college women's struggles and strategies', unpublished thesis, National Louis University.

Mont, M. (2009), 'Perspectives of African American adult students and faculty on the use of arts-based learning in higher education classrooms', unpublished thesis, Penn State University.

Nieves, Y. (2009), 'The brown girls' chronicles: Puerto Rican women and resilience', unpublished thesis, National Louis University.

Patterson, F. (2011), 'Now I can dream: adult black males and the mentors that saved them', unpublished thesis, National Louis University.

Reed, S. (2008), 'Sentimental journey: the role of music in the meaning-making processes of older performing musicians', unpublished thesis, Penn State University.

Spaulding, J. (2010), 'The effects of experiential learning with playfulness in the adult education classroom', unpublished thesis, Penn State University.

Stuckey, H. (2007), 'Healing from dry bones: creative expression and adult learning in diabetes care', unpublished thesis, Penn State University.

Notes

1 An excerpt of the play can be found on YouTube www.youtube.com/watch?v=ML bj2R3GEmM (accessed 14 September 2012).

7

Collage-making for interdisciplinary research skills training in Northern Ireland

Shelley Tracey and Joe Allen

Setting the scene

This chapter shares our practice of collage-making for identifying and extending ideas for research in a course entitled Creative Thinking and Problem Solving (CTPS), part of a postgraduate research training programme. The programme provides a range of opportunities for doctoral students across the university to develop skills for designing, writing and presenting their dissertations and managing the demands of a PhD process. Research training ranges from half-day to three-day sessions, and is offered by academics with expertise in supervising and supporting research students. The CTPS course is unusual in its use of arts-based methods and in that it has two facilitators, the authors of this chapter. We are also unusual in that we come from the field of adult education and identify as adult educators. As with most universities in Europe, we have few colleagues from adult education in our department as the School of Education concentrates mainly on research, teaching and learning in the school sector.

This chapter explores the context, processes and outcomes of the CTPS course and the origins of our decision to introduce collage into this course. Collage is not only a method but also a metaphor for the differences and synergies between Shelley and Joe, the authors who collaborate on this programme. Moreover, Dietrich argues that a key principle of collage is 'bringing together of different realities' (1995: 70) and this is reflective of our experience with the students. They come from schools and areas across the university, including arts and humanities, languages and translation, engineering, biological and medical sciences, chemistry, politics and psychology, and they also speak a range of languages.

We begin this chapter with a discussion of our backgrounds and those of our students, and the principles of adult education on which we draw. From there, we move to the CTPS course and how we came to use collage as one of the core methods of this course. We focus on the first occasion on which we engaged students in collage-making, weaving together their reflections on the process with our own. We end the chapter with reflections on the applications of collage work to the higher education context, and on the ways in which collage enhances participation in learning and research. The notion of participation draws on frameworks and theories from adult education and from arts-based research.

Contextualising the authors and participants

Shelley's background is as a South African adult educator, poet and arts-based researcher. I was an adult literacy and numeracy practitioner and teacher educator in the apartheid years when adult literacy work was deeply political and involved with personal empowerment and social transformation. My work drew, and continues to draw, on Freirean pedagogy in terms of respect for existing knowledge, co-learning and active dialogue as a process of meaning making. At first glance the context for and members of the CTPS, namely higher education and PhD students, seems far removed from my previous community experiences as an adult educator working with people who often had little education, and were poor, frightened and lacking in confidence due to systemic cultural, social, political and institutional marginalisation. PhD students, one could argue, have clearly been successful within the traditional education system. However, when we asked our students on the CTPS course during a problem-solving activity to identify the strengths they brought to their PhD study, as well as the challenges faced, they identified a number of barriers to their full participation that were somewhat reflective of my past experience, such as a lack of self-confidence, sense of expertise, agency and or power in the institution and/or the research process itself. There were further institutional and social barriers for the international students, some of whom were experiencing difficulties in assimilating into the very complex Northern Ireland society.

Joe's realities contrast with Shelley's, and include the worlds of industry, electronic engineering and formal or school-based education. However, I also identify as an adult educator in the field of continuing professional development. But I work as a lecturer in teacher education, mainly involved with postgraduates who are working professionals and keen to enhance their academic qualifications with a Masters degree which offers a high level of research aimed towards strengthening their own professional context or workplace. I also research e-learning in higher education and the application of advanced technologies for the enhancement of teaching and learning. Not surprisingly in this fast-paced technological world, my learners often express a lack of confidence in using these technologies as well as in the research process itself.

While our learners face different barriers, our partnership as course tutors has allowed us to model interdisciplinary collaboration – the arts and non-formal education with formal education and science and technology – and different styles and ideas of research for our graduate students. Our backgrounds as adult educators have enabled us to draw on our own experiences and those of students, and to seek creative ways to help them overcome the challenges they face in learning and undertaking research. We turn now to how our contrasting yet complementary backgrounds and creative approaches brought an implicit acceptance of diversity and other advantages into the CTPS.

The Creative Thinking and Problem Solving course

The CTPS course has run on seven occasions since 2004, either once or twice in each academic year, with a total of 152 participants to date. In particular, the course acknowledges the importance of engaging with uncertainty and the liminal spaces between knowing that occur in the course of enquiry and learning (Barnett, 2004; Meyer and Land, 2006). Uncertainty about the processes and outcomes of learning and the concepts involved can inhibit self-confidence and hinder participation in learning. The CTPS course provides spaces for participants to explore these uncertainties, building on models from adult education which conceive of adults as active participants in knowledge creation, drawing on their experiences and previous knowledge as described in Knowles's theory of andragogy (1990) and Freire's (1970) notion of learning as participatory and rooted in culture and shared goals and experiences.

Participants in CTPS have opportunities to draw on their own knowledge and experience to explore and articulate ambiguities and uncertainties in research through problem-solving activities, particularly through arts-based methods, in this case collage and poetry in the form of haiku, although we focus more on the former in this chapter. Collage-making builds on the work of theorists such as Janesick (2004) who argues that creative methods allow researchers to access more intuitive processes that are often less consciously used in research. McNiff adds to this, suggesting that arts-based methods allow for 'immersion in the uncertainties of experience, finding a personally fulfilling path of inquiry, and the emergence of understanding through an often unpredictable process of exploration' (1998: 15).

At the beginning of the CTPS course, a series of ambiguous images portraying themes of searching and journeying stimulate discussion on the complexities of developing a PhD and the processes of discovery involved. This is the first of a series of activities that encourage metaphorical thinking and the capacity to explore research questions and themes from a range of perspectives, using different forms of meaning-making. One of these arts-based approaches we use, as noted above, is the Japanese poetic form of haiku. Haiku consists of three lines, with five syllables in the first and third lines and seven in the second one. What we have found is that this very conciseness of haiku is what enables students to capture or imagine their central research ideas. These three examples illustrate this:

Buildings tell
Stories of the city
Dividing its spaces
(architecture student)

Clean hydrocarbon
By using unique solvents
Improving process
(biochemistry student)

The function of peptides
Structure of proteins

Analysing the sequence of the peptides
(medical microbiology student)

While haiku allowed students to access aesthetic aspects of learning to create and convey their research themes more visually, the last two examples, rich in terminology, also provide an indication of the problems students involved in highly technical research in very diverse areas have in terms of actually explaining their research to each other. It should be remembered that this course brings together a diversity of students whose foci vary widely. But while the mastery of specialist knowledge is fundamental to a PhD, the final written product and the viva require the researcher to write up the research and to share it orally with subject specialists but also academics who may very well lack in-depth knowledge of the specific research topic. The haiku activity is what led us to the realisation that we needed to include more non-linguistic activities in the course, in the hope that this could take a step further towards addressing the research articulation difficulties students were having in explaining their research ideas, questions and even the terminology to peers from very diverse disciplines (although we also recognise some of these difficulties arise from the silo nature of the disciplines and their discourses themselves). Importantly, these articulation problems often parallel the challenges faced by the international students, who usually constitute approximately 60 per cent of the students we work with today. Participation in seminar discussions is stymied by a lack of vocabulary in their second language to explain what they mean, leading to a confidence issue. Of course the timeline of the CTPS was too brief to develop a model of sustained participation, but we did note how the use of images offered possibilities for communication across all language barriers. This developed what Wenger (1998) termed a community of practice in which the PhD students were visually and creatively able to share their diverse ideas. The process of collage-making specifically also offered students opportunities for making connections with their peers on the course, as well as between their own implicit ideas about their research and those already at the level of consciousness. This was important because it enabled them to recognise the significance of and build on their intuitive knowing and rational forms of meaning-making. Indeed, Butler-Kisber's notion (2008) that collage has the capacity for conceptualising research and memoing ideas about it, or recording ideas and questions for consideration, can lead to a more focused approach, particularly at the later stages of the research process.

Collaging creative thinking and problem solving

The course in which collage was first introduced took place in February 2009. There were 26 participants from 20 schools across the university. As on previous occasions on which the course had run, the majority of the students were in their first year of PhD study, with only one second-year and one third-year student. Most of the first-year students were still in the process of developing their research questions or designing their studies, so it was considered appropriate to use collage with this group to develop the initial stages of research and their confidence as researchers.

While the term 'collage' refers to any combination of found images, paint, text and three-dimensional objects, this chapter focuses on two specific forms of collage that we actually used. The first is an arrangement on a piece of card or paper of random words and images from magazines and newspapers. The second is an electronic document produced in PowerPoint that allows the creator to gather a number of images and words on a specific theme on one page. These images could then be moved, resized or rotated as desired by the individual collage maker to create the final composition.

The collage-making activity was introduced in the last session before lunch on the first morning of the course. Those who were working electronically went to a nearby computer laboratory with Joe, while the others remained in the class-room with Shelley. Newspapers and magazines, along with scissors and glue, were available on the tables, and there was background music to encourage working in silence to allow students to focus on their collages and to enter that space of 'flow' (Csikszentmihalyi, 1997) in which they were fully immersed in the process and able to develop their work without distraction. Students' responses to the process, which appear later in this chapter, suggest that their experience of collage-making did allow them to explore their research topic deeply in a supportive environment.

While each tutor had facilitated a different collage-making session (either paper-based or electronic), we were both present for the discussions that ensued when the students returned to class and presented their work to the rest of their group. Given the large number of students, and the time required to explain each collage, the presentations took place in groups of five or six students from a range of disciplines. The tutors circulated between these groups, recording key issues and reflections. Students took notes after they had presented their work to remind them of the implications of their collage for their future studies; some recorded their presentations on dictaphones, voice recorders or on their mobile phones. Photographs were taken of all the collages, and permission was obtained from the whole group to use the images for research purposes. At the end of the first day of the course, students completed questionnaires about their experiences of collage-making. The use of a questionnaire would allow students to identify issues that they might not have felt confident about raising in the group discussions; it also gave them an opportunity to develop their understanding through writing their reflections. Responses to the questionnaires are discussed in more detail shortly.

Typical points that the students considered in the small-group discussions were the aims and purpose of their research projects and how the collage-making process might have illuminated their understanding of their work. They also discussed the limitations or constraints on their research; typical barriers included their professional relationship with their academic supervisors and financial and other considerations in their personal and professional lives which were impacting on their research. Through these discussions, students built shared understandings of the research experience and the issues involved.

Reflection on collages: course tutors

Before we collated the responses to the questionnaires about collaging, we surveyed the photographs of the collages to identify common features and to establish whether there were significant differences between the paper-based and electronic ones. The first paper-based collage was an exploration of women's suffrage in Northern Ireland. It displayed a multitude of experiences and themes that would arise from, say, interviews. Looked at it more stylistically, however, there was a large amount of text, as with most of the other paper collages. This has to do with the high comfort level of students with words – reflecting the unmitigated emphasis on texts in the academy – rather than with images. It was also apparent, however, from the way in which the text was arranged that decisions were made about the positioning and the relative size of the text, as well as the relative importance of its content. This was both a thematic but also a visual 'analysis'.

This collage was typical of all of those made with paper in that they were not constrained by the page size and allowed individual pieces of text to extend beyond the edge of the page. By nature, this was not possible in the electronic collages. This collage was also typical of those of most of the PhD students from the arts, humanities and social and environmental sciences in its inclusion of the social and political factors that surround research. Collective discussions or analyses of collages allowed students to reflect on wider issues in Northern Ireland society and beyond and to create a shared understanding of the contexts of their research. We would argue that their collages demonstrated what Freire refers to as codes, or the use of images and shared cultural experiences and understanding to stimulate discussion and participation in the learning process.

This electronic collage created by another group of students, perhaps not surprisingly, was on the theme of wireless communication and the application of novel human–computer interfaces. Indeed, it too was typical of most of the electronic collages, with its use of regular shapes and gathering together of images on the theme. It was presented as a poster, illustrating thematic areas rather than using images as analogies and metaphors, as in the paper-based collages. The images may be perceived as examples of what Baxter Magolda (1992: 73) referred to 'absolute knowing' in that they are not interpreted, contextualised or mediated, other than in the decisions that were made about their relative size, or other picture properties such as rotation or positioning. Most of the electronic collages had no text added beyond what was already included in the images.

While this collage did not generate discussion about the political or social context in which the research was undertaken – although it could have if one thinks of discourses such as technical rationality – the group reflections offered opportunities for participants to share their knowledge and experience of wireless communications and to build a common understanding of that particular area. It was also much more image-based than the paper collages, and we will return to this.

In the process of making paper collages, students were able to use and find words that represented ideas from their research, while images were used in the main for the electronic collages. The predominance of words in the paper collages also suggests that the students were using the process of collage-making to draw on their own experience to theorise and to uncover their thoughts and feelings about the subject.

Those students who made electronic collages did so with a confident use of technology and skilful manipulation of images. This confidence and skill suggest that making the collages enabled them to develop and demonstrate their visual literacy, an important scholarly attribute not yet fully recognised and incorporated into mainstream higher education in Northern Ireland. Although we are surrounded with images this does not automatically make us able to analyse, manipulate and create them. Visual literacy involves a complex set of skills of interpreting, decoding, analysing, generating and synthesising images (Griffin, 2008; Langford, 2003). We will reflect on visual literacy and on the skills involved in making both kinds of collages at the end of this chapter but, for now, we turn to the responses to the questionnaire about the collage-making process and the insights they provide into participants' experiences of and views on using collage.

Students' responses to collage-making

While our observations of the collage-making process suggested that it was an effective research tool, we wanted to capture students' perceptions about it so that we could make decisions about using this method on subsequent CTPS courses. We wanted to explore our idea of collage as a tool for increasing participation in research, in particular the intrinsic aspect of participation: did collage offer students opportunities to engage closely with the processes of research and to develop their awareness of these processes? We surveyed students' views about collage-making with a questionnaire which asked about previous experiences of using collage, students' experience of creating collages on the course, their reflections on the processes involved in collage-making and possible applications of collages to other aspects of their research.

Eleven participants (42%) made paper-based collages, while 15 (58%) chose the electronic form of collage-making. We collated the responses about making each type of collage separately to identify distinctions between them. In most areas there was very little difference in the responses. A slightly higher proportion of those who made paper-based collage enjoyed it, and they were more likely to use collage in their vivas or at later stages in their research. The area in which there were sharper contrasts between those who had made electronic or paper-based collages was that of the cognitive and other types of processes involved in making collages. Details appear in the next part of this chapter.

The use of collage also allowed students to experience and reflect on the aesthetic aspects of research design and the range of cognitive processes involved in collage-making. In this part of the chapter, we include students' comments on these processes, framing these with the notion that collage is an effective tool in the early stages of research design because it gives students access to their intuitive notions about their research topics which they may never have articulated previously, thus developing their confidence in their understanding and capacity to undertake research. As Butler-Kisber (2010) suggests, collage allows close engagement with the subject of the research because it offers access to feelings and implicit beliefs as well as to cognition.

A participant described collage as 'a visual form of representation in the surrealist tradition that perhaps touches on unconscious motivations/interests/desires as regards the topic of research. It provides a complex range of signifiers that provide a potential stimulus for project development.' This suggests that collage was a useful tool for accessing hidden thoughts and assumptions about knowledge and researching and to develop confidence about engaging in research. The connection between collage-making and the unconscious suggests that it is a tool for meaning-making in the early stages of research. Moran, commenting on the nature of meaning-making in PhD research, suggests that meaning is 'an undiscovered continent, a terra incognita, until it is invited to come forward and reveal itself' (in Swanson et al., 2008: 90). Collage seemed to us to offer opportunities for students to make discoveries about their research topics. One noted that collage-making 'focused my thoughts on the subject of my research'. Another commented, 'It gives a chance to reflect on my own ideas to myself'; this highlights the intensely personal nature of meaning-making which collage facilitates, and its invitation to enter and participate in the research space. A further comment provides insight about the depth with which the research space is experienced during the collage-making process: 'I was focusing on the research idea, starting with a general image and then going deeply through the main idea.'

To facilitate students in their in-depth inquiry into their research topics, we ensured that the collage-making took place in a calm and quiet environment in which students had no concerns about interruption or being disturbed. Indeed, one comment was that the experience was 'Very relaxing and allowing my mind to build the bigger picture of my PhD', while another noted that the music that was playing in the background was 'Very supportive of the process. Amazed at how many ideas adhered to the central organising theme. Worked slowly, so did not construct an arrangement in class – only gathered elements.' These words suggest that this student did not feel pressurised, and that the space offered was sufficiently flexible to allow students to use it as they saw fit for their own purposes.

Other responses to collage-making indicate that it offered opportunities for engaging with and developing new ideas. One of these comments refers to the playfulness which collage stimulates: 'I thought it was a great way of playing with new ideas and concepts in my head and a great tool for generating new concepts/ideas.' Two responses indicate that collage helped with developing the conceptual basis for the research: 'It gives some ideas of thinking background about interesting subject like PhD study' and 'It is useful for developing background thinking.'

While some responses referred to the capacity of collage for idea generation, others suggested that collage helped to structure ideas and thinking processes. These include, 'Helps to organise ideas', 'I thought it was a very accurate way of getting my own thoughts and ideas into a coherent and concise fashion' and 'The process of collage-making gives an idea to represent the thinking in a structured way.' The following comments suggest that collage-making also enabled students to make connections between ideas in the research process: 'Helped me to see links to thesis topic in words and in images that I might not have thought of' and 'Links ideas especially from problem statement to the envisaged solution.'

One of our primary reasons for introducing collage on the courses was to enhance students' abilities to communicate their ideas about their research to their peers. The following comment on the usefulness of collage suggests that this aim was addressed: 'Collage helps to address it [research] to non-technical people – makes it simple. Aids to clarify the research in a simplistic manner.' When the students gave short presentations on their individual research topics at the end of the course, the impact of the collage-making was most evident: we observed a marked difference in students' abilities to express and to present their research ideas to their colleagues from those which they displayed when they were talking about their research at the start of the two-day course. In fact, one comment about the use of collage was that it 'may be more useful when presenting my ideas to others than generating new ideas for myself'. This suggests the power of collage to affirm the presenter's expertise in a particular field of knowledge, acting as a tool for communicating with others who are less knowledgeable.

Other comments about the use of collage for presenting ideas included 'I got a chance to present my idea with a completely different set of resources' and 'It increases my imagination and helped me to present my research idea in a simple visual way.' One of the final items on the questionnaire asked students whether they would use collage at other stages in their research; suggestions by the students for this included poster presentations and interim oral examinations for their PhD text and viva. Others thought that they might use their collages when presenting papers at conferences, in particular to interdisciplinary groups. All of these ideas point to the capacity of collage to enhance communication and connections with others. And even though one student said he would probably not use collage again, he would keep the collage and perhaps 'refer to it in the future to see if it still holds relevance to any research ideas or indicates to what extent my ideas and approach have evolved since then'.

Reflections on the processes involved in collage-making

To enhance participants' awareness of the cognitive processes involved in collage-making, we drew up for the questionnaire a list of these processes for participants to reflect on. They embraced the generation of ideas (divergent thinking and playing with ideas), organising ideas (making connections, clustering, structuring ideas) and analytical processes (convergent thinking, critical analysis and reflection). We asked students to identify those which they believed to be intrinsic to collage-making. This was the item on the questionnaire that generated the greatest divergence between those who had made the paper collages and those who had produced the electronic versions. The former each identified between five and six processes, while the average for the latter was 4.9. It is not possible to extrapolate from such a small sample, but this finding confirmed our sense that the process of making a paper collage generated more ideas than did the electronic format. In addition, comments about the paper-based process, including those from students who had made electronic collages, suggest that there might be more complex processes at work in the making of paper collages than electronic ones.

Those who made paper collages chose the processes of idea generation (divergent thinking and playing with ideas) most frequently, along with clustering ideas. The next most frequent choices were reflection, making connections and structuring. Convergent thinking was selected less frequently, with critical analysis as the lowest choice. These results indicate that collage was seen as a tool for generating and organising ideas more than for analysing them; it therefore seemed to be useful in the earlier stages of research, for identifying and playing with ideas, rather than for analysing them in the later stages of research.

There was a more uneven distribution of processes for the electronic collages, with structuring and playing with ideas as the two highest categories. This may have to do with the format of electronic collages, which involves manipulating and arranging largely regular shapes and therefore foregrounds the processes of organising the images rather than generating ideas. The students who made electronic collages also selected critical analysis the least frequently; this does not imply, however, that collage is not a useful analytical tool in the research process, but suggests that students might need to be supported to recognise the analysis that was going on and that the process of discussing their work with their peers would enhance their awareness.

Participants were also asked to identify other processes they had used for collage-making. One pointed out that in making paper collages, 'the manual process of construction based on a limited range of visual resources seems to force a certain creativity and greater abstraction [than perhaps the electronic collage], providing a rich and allusive document that can serve to enlighten and refresh the research process'. For one student, the limited range of materials was an issue: 'More magazines would be better! From other fields, e.g. pharmaceutical newsletters, cars, video games, film magazines, even a child's colouring book!' This comment was a prompt to inform students before subsequent courses about the collage-making activity and to offer them the opportunity to bring relevant images along with them, if they so desired. It should be noted to that few chose to do so, however.

Another student, commenting more positively on the impact of limited resources, suggested that collage-making involved 'Using metaphor to represent message (because very limited pictures and words related to my research topic from the magazines available!)' A student who made a paper collage proposed that one of the processes involved in collage-making was 'Being inventive: use of metaphors – free association, translation of concepts/ideas into images.' These references to metaphor suggest that collage-making supports abstraction and conceptualisation, as well as the representation of research ideas. This provokes the notion that the act of collage-making needs to be followed by a reflection on the process to build on the ideas that emerged.

Implications for higher education and research

This chapter began with the proposition that the use of collage in a creative thinking and problem-solving course for PhD students might offer opportunities to enhance participation and confidence in their studies. Participation was understood in terms of the individual with regard to their metacognitive engagement with the research process and also in terms of the learning group and the integration of the knowledge and experiences of all participants. Students' responses to the questionnaires suggest that the use of collage enhanced their awareness of the research process and their sense of ownership of this process. Therefore, although the collage work was based partly on ideas about participation in adult education, these often seem to have limited application in that the PhD process has traditionally been perceived as a largely solitary pursuit. And yet students appeared to benefit from sharing the outcomes of the collage-making with their peers on the CTPS course; their discussions on their experiences built on socio-cultural aspects of learning more common in participatory adult education than in higher education, and make a case for a collaborative culture of research training, drawing on experience and the use of arts-based approaches to provide stimuli for sharing ideas.

The comments from other students to those presenting their collages were invariably supportive and constructive, and participants reported gaining many valuable insights and suggestions for ways forward with their research. In their final evaluations of the CTPS course, participants on all of the courses commented that they had learned a great deal from discussions with their peers about their research and processes of exploration, especially those from different disciplines. It appears that giving research students access to accounts of their peers' research processes has the potential to enhance their own insights about research.

The outcomes of this small-scale enquiry suggest that collage is useful for supporting engagement in and developing ideas about new research projects in all disciplines, including the arts and humanities as well as the sciences. We are not suggesting that collage should be used on its own in research training; collage-making was one activity in a series on the course which involved divergent thinking exercises and individual and group problem-solving activities and reflections, all of which students identified as useful for developing their research. What we did learn from using collage was that aesthetic aspects of learning have the capacity to enhance participation and address some of the barriers which face PhD students the initial stages of their studies.

Another interesting aspect to this work is the question of technology. We live in a 'wired' world and the push to use technology in every aspect of our lives is sometimes overwhelming. There is no doubt that the paper-based collage generated more text ideas and provoked more social responses than the electronic collage. And yet the paper collage remained text-based while the people using technology went for images to metaphorically depict ideas that would emerge from a research question. So while some students argued that there was too much information on the Internet – as opposed to the magazines and other limited numbers of resources we had supplied for the collage-making – and that this was confusing and overwhelming, others gravitated to the vast, visual feast the Internet affords. We think of the selection of images from the Internet in the making of the electronic collages as a sophisticated process of accessing, evaluating and filtering suitable images, drawing on expert knowledge of the relevant subject area. As Natharius's (2004) well-known aphorism about visual literacy reminds us, the more we know, the more we see. Images are resonant constructs which bring together layers of cultural, historical, artistic and conceptual meanings. We argue that the use of electronic collage draws effectively on and supports the development of knowledge and understanding about the research area.

With their richer array of images than that available for the paper collages, and the potential which technology offers for changing the size and colour values of the images, the electronic collages provided the space to allow more imaginative or creative ways of displaying and analysing 'data' than did the paper versions. Students on the CPTS course with limited ICT skills chose to make paper collages, while their colleagues who were more confident with ICT than with paper-based forms of art-making chose the alternative format. To offer students access to different ways of using images to make meaning about their research, we would suggest that opportunities should be given for all students to try both versions in order to experience the benefits of each process. We also think the idea of text versus images as it emerged from the collages should be more fully explored, perhaps through the lens of visual literacy, but also within the context of what is valued in higher education.

Participants on the CTPS courses described in this chapter appeared to benefit from the opportunity to use arts-based approaches to explore their research questions and to share their insights with their peers. In this case, collage appears to be useful as a heuristic for the initial stages of the research process, and for enhancing collaboration and communication. Equally as important are opportunities for both verbal and non-verbal reflection since not everyone, as adult educators argue, learns in the same way. Moreover, Mason argues that a non-verbal reflective environment develops a stronger capacity for 'noticing a possibility in the present moment and reflecting back on what has been noticed before in order to prepare for the future' (2002: 15). And what is a research course if not preparing for the future? Engagement with images also supports participation and learning across language barriers and academic disciplines, the environment of our course. Indeed, collage-making represents a multimodal pedagogy and tool, operating across semiotic modes, to transcend and extend linguistic and pragmatic/objective forms of knowing (Kress and van Leeuwen, 2002). Going further, Hoggan (2009) explores the role of images in transformative learning, suggesting that image-based research affords greater access to unacknowledged assumptions and stimulates changes in perspective. Elkins (2002) and Metros and Woolsey (2006) go so far as to suggest that all higher education programmes should be cognisant of the potential of the visual, aesthetic and affective in learning. We would concur, although we fear that with the vested interest in written text and cognitive engagement that defines the university we may be a long way from this goal. But let us go even further. We would argue that the different backgrounds of the tutors enhanced the interdisciplinary collaborative nature of the course – cutting itself across the disciplines while remaining firmly grounded in the theory and practice of adult education. While again this is not something that higher education promotes, given its emphasis on the individual 'expert', we strongly advocate the practice of co-teaching through and with the arts to bring together and bridge difference in the classroom. We believe we must demarcate spaces in which to avoid the constraints of our increasingly neoliberal educational institutions, by combining collaborative teaching and artistic engagement as an aesthetic that challenges recurring distinctions.

Perhaps nothing can speak to the potential of the arts in general and collage-making in particular in the graduate research classroom than the students themselves, so we give the final word in this chapter to one of them: 'It is a good intuitive approach, and could be applied to any difficult situation which positively needs out of box thinking.'

References

Barnett, R. (2004), 'Learning for an unknown future', *Higher Education Research and Development*, 23(3): 247–60.

Baxter Magolda, M. (1992), *Knowing and Reasoning in College*, San Francisco: Jossey-Bass.

Butler-Kisber, L. (2008), 'Collage as inquiry', in J.G. Knowles and A.L. Cole (eds), *Handbook of the Arts in Qualitative Research: Perspectives, Methodologies, Examples, and Issues*, Thousand Oaks, CA: Sage, 265–76.

Butler-Kisber, L. (2010), *Qualitative Inquiry: Thematic, Narrative and Arts-informed Perspectives*, Thousand Oaks, CA: Sage.

Csikszentmihalyi, M. (1991), *Flow: The Psychology of Optimal Experience*, New York: HarperPerennial.

Csikszentmihalyi, M. (1997), *Creativity. Flow and the Psychology of Discovery and Invention*, New York: HarperPerennial.

Dietrich, D. (1995), *The Collages of Kurt Schwitters: Tradition and Innovation*, Cambridge: Cambridge University Press.

Elkins, J. (2002), *Visual Studies: A Sceptical Introduction*, New York and London: Routledge.

Freire, P. (1970), *Pedagogy of the Oppressed*, Harmondsworth: Penguin Education.

Griffin, M. (2008), 'Visual competence and media literacy: can one exist without the other?', *Visual Studies*, 3(2): 113–29.

Hoggan, C. (2009), 'The power of story: metaphors, literature, and creative writing', in C. Hoggan, S. Simpson and H. Stuckey (eds), *Creative Expression in Transformative Learning: Tools and Techniques for Educators of Adults*, Malabar: Krieger Publishing Company, 51–74.

Janesick, V.J. (2001), 'Intuition and creativity: a pas de deux for qualitative researchers', *Qualitative Inquiry*, 7(5): 531–40.

Janesick, V.J. (2004), *"Stretching" Exercises for Qualitative Researchers*, Thousand Oaks, CA, and London: Sage, 2nd edn.

Knowles, M.S. (1990), *The Adult Learner: A Neglected Species*, Houston: Gulf Publishing, 4th edn.

Kress, G.R., and Van Leeuwen, T. (2002), *Multimodal Discourse: The Modes and Media of Contemporary Communication*, London: Edward Arnold.

Langford, L. (2003), 'Are you visually literate? Word as image, image as word', *Access*, 17(4): 12–13.

McNiff, S. (1998), *Art-based Research*, London: Jessica Kingsley.

Mason, J. (2002), *The Discipline of Noticing*, London: Routledge.

Metros, S.E., and Woolsey, K. (2006) 'Visual literacy: an institutional imperative', *EDUCAUSE Review*, 41(3): 80–81.

Meyer, J.H.F., and Land R. (eds) (2006), *Overcoming Barriers to Student Understanding: Threshold Concepts and Troublesome Knowledge*, London: Routledge.

Natharius, D. (2004), 'The more we know, the more we see: the role of visuality in media literacy', *American Behavioural Scientist*, 48: 238–47.

Swanson, D., Moran, J., and Honan, E. (2008), 'Voices in the silence: Dalene Swanson's story', in Four Arrows (aka Don Trent Jacobs), *The Authentic Dissertation: Alternative Ways of Knowing, Research, and Representation*, London: Routledge, 83–94.

Wenger, E. (1998), *Communities of Practice: Learning, Meaning and Identity*, Cambridge: Cambridge University Press.

8

Theatre-based action research in Denmark

Mia Husted and Ditte Tofteng

Background

This chapter discusses our use of theatre and drama as tools of action research within an adult education programme at Roskilde University, Denmark. Our use of art in research is in essence embedded in the Scandinavian tradition of what we call worklife studies and adult learning. In Scandinavia, researchers within the field of worklife studies and adult learning share a history of working towards empowerment and enhanced participation in the collective development of an organisation. This worklife studies focus is based on the theoretical inspiration of Lewin (1948) who worked with groups of employees in the early days of organisational studies and found that more democratic organisations tend to enable new learning and enhance both discovery and development of solutions. Building on this, Scandinavia in particular has evolved its own history of action research that focuses on how democratic processes of participation can contribute to social development and learning (Toulmin and Gustavsen, 1996; Nielsen and Svensson, 2006). Bringing these ideas together, the state currently funds many programmes designed to improve and democratise work and organisations, and funds are available to encourage researchers to participate more fully in diverse action-oriented studies to develop local and practical knowledge.

Our research takes place outside the university in cooperation with local communities and with people engaged within the labour market or living on the edge of the labour market. Most often, our role is to design methods that allow workers to participate more actively and equally in studies that aim to better their working conditions. Our methods actually go beyond the more normative approaches to workplace research and learning generally found in Scandinavia by drawing on the principles of adult education, including the arts. By this we mean that the research fully respects and draws upon people's knowledge and their ability to understand and address the issues confronting them and their communities (Brydon-Miller et al., 2003). To us, adult education-oriented action research means bringing parties and interests together, allowing all voices, critiques and needs to be heard through both the collective investigation aspects of the project as well as the final analyses and decision-making processes. Continuing to develop new and more creative methods is a part of our challenge as researchers, and of course this is where the arts have come in. But our challenge is also to bring these new practices back to our students at university. By this we mean we must work to legitimise these new, creative or arts-based practices within the discourse of qualitative research, but also to engage students in discussions about the real-life difficulties of developing and using these new methods in workplaces. What we share in this chapter is an arts-based research programme that we developed called 'Stop Stress'. This theatre-based action research programme was designed for people working in the healthcare sector in Denmark. In this chapter, we illustrate how the creative potential of bringing together the arts, adult learning and collective enquiry helped the participants explore and alleviate the stressful aspects of their lives.

Adult education embodied in action research

Before we turn to the programme, it is important to look at where the inspiration for our work has come from. The construction in 1972 of Roskilde University in Denmark, the location from which we work, ushered in a new era for adult learning and research. Emerging alongside the bricks and mortar were new forms of project-based, real problem-oriented learning and research that later became progressive models for other types of educational institutions (Jensen and Salling Olesen, 1999). The works of John Dewey were one of the important foundations for this engaged, problem-based learning and study method. Dewey (1916) argued that 'learning by doing' could be an effective educational practice if students were encouraged to focus on problems related to their own experiences. Moreover, if students were given sufficient time and resources to explore the problems they believed to be important, they would engage more actively in new learning activities and create new knowledge, understandings or even answers or solutions to the problem. Another important cognitive and social shift that steered the work at Roskilde University was the educational concept of Oskar Negt, *exemplarisches Lernen* or exemplary learning (Negt, 1969). Negt argued that the challenges and dilemmas of society, and in the workplace, needed to be critically analysed but this analysis had to culminate in some form of collective action for change. At Roskilde University these ideas were distilled into what we call today the 'Problem-Based Work Project'. These ideas also had an impact on action research in that creating critical learning environments within the research process itself became valued, since it enabled participants to explore everyday experiences and stimulate democratic discussion around organisational development and make decisions for change regardless of the person's position within the work environment.

However, although Scandinavian action research within the academy has adopted many of the principles of workplace adult education, the same cannot be said in regard to the use of arts and aesthetics as part of the educational methods in Scandinavian academia. The coming together of art and adult education can first be found in the folk high-school tradition developed by Grundtvig (1991) in the late nineteenth century. Grundtvig, a priest who wrote many of the Christian hymns used today in Denmark, was concerned with how to educate people to take a more active part in culture and society. He proposed that the state should take on the responsibility of running a 'school for life' to educate people and that these schools should encourage curiosity, wonder and a desire to learn. Folk high schools were originally founded to educate farmers and unskilled workers, providing them with a general education in relation to worklife and the trades. Grundtvig stressed the need for interplay between enlightened teaching, skills acquisition and enlivened artistic experience, and these are still the foundations of Danish folk high schools today. Indeed, one simply cannot imagine a Danish folk high school without singing, dance, theatre, painting, musicals or literary activities. These artistic methods do not turn everyone into artists, but they do provide people with joy, insight and with new ways to express and learn about themselves. This tradition of using art forms has in fact paved the way for the work we do. The action research projects we conduct all use theatre and music. It is this socially oriented drama – what popular educators call popular theatre – and its ability to produce or strengthen visibility, recognition and social imagination that interests us (Tofteng and Husted, 2011). We are theoretically inspired by a dialectic materialistic view on the world and the potentials for social change therein; our use of arts in our action research processes is in line with a pedagogy that fosters inquiry in students' critical consciousness and empowers them to pose problems and to deliberate new answers. We use theatre as a link between education and social change, as we consider theatre to be able to mirror senses, experiences and emotions that resonate with the audience, causing new thoughts, feelings and insight (Brecht, 1964). Drama/theatre can be extremely effective in highlighting certain aspects of life, certain experiences and feelings that would otherwise be difficult to voice in public.

This approach also brings us into line with more political educational thinkers who point out the potential of critical pedagogy to help students to learn to take control over their lives and to live together in more human and democratic ways (Freire, 1970; Horton and Freire, 1991; Boal, 1995). Taking a critical stance means that the use of arts, including drama, must make pedagogical, political or social contributions that can pave the way to more humane, just or democratic ways of living (Eisner, 2008). We believe that theatre can often show us new paths into working life development and working life research that elevates feelings, emotions and aesthetics in relation to the often-assumed superiority of language. Moreover, visibility and the performing of emotions and experiences can help raise and explore difficult, systemic issues, making a contribution to the democratisation of the workplace and even society.

'Stop Stress': a programme to counteract work-related stress

'Stop Stress' is a state-funded action research programme conducted by us and inspired by an educational concept of theatre as a method in the Problem-Based Work Project. 'Stop Stress' is designed to highlight and counteract work-related stress among health- and homecare employees. The programme began in January 2010 and will run until 2013. It takes place in Næstved, a community situated approximately 100 kilometres outside Copenhagen, and involves the homecare service within District West. District West provides homecare for elderly or disabled citizens living at home or at one of three elderly care centres in the district. The district covers a circle of 80 kilometres in diameter and employs 250 caretakers, healthcare assistants, nurses, kitchen crew and cleaning operatives. The employees in District West are divided into 12 teams managed by seven team leaders, one sous-chef and one head of the district.

'Stop Stress' is funded by the Prevention Fund, a large national programme designed to reduce health deterioration or disabilities related to work and the improvement of occupational health and safety in the workplace. We designed the 'Stop Stress' programme as our contribution to assisting with this concern over work-related stress. We proposed the programme to the health and safety committee of District West and they were immediately in favour. Through collective discussions, we settled on the following activities: an opening conference, workshops, follow-up meetings and the use of theatre to uncover problems and create new knowledge and strategies.

The 'Stop Stress' programme has three main steps. The first step was to identify the issues the employees feel to be critical in terms of creating stress, and by extension ill health, in the workplace. This phase takes place over the period of a year and leads to the creation of problem-based projects. Everyone in District West attended workshops, formed small working groups, identified issues and organised meetings to explore the meanings, implications and interpretations of the problems. The second step was to develop ideas for how the problems could be addressed if they themselves were to decide how to organise their 'corner', so to speak, of their workplace. The final step was to take the ideas and develop plans of action complete with timelines, agreements, distribution of tasks, deadlines, monitoring and evaluation of the changes.

Methodological challenges in 'Stop Stress'

'Stop Stress' contains some methodological challenges in terms of trying to promote deeper learning and practical answers to work-related stress as well as accommodate the use of theatre. The overall challenge of the project was how to manage action research and learning processes for 250 people at the same time and at the same workplace. Dealing with so many people at once makes it important to develop a conceptual framework that features reflexive educational procedures, techniques and processes. Such a framework enables us to respect the educational and political objectives of our work while at the same time allowing us to be open to accommodate, critique or respond to resistance and/or the need to develop a completely different methodological approach. In other words, the educational processes of 'Stop Stress' demanded, as do all community-based adult education and research processes, that we were open to democratic change yet at the same time kept things manageable. The methods, therefore, needed to be able to encourage all employees and managers to participate and reflect upon their own diverse experiences from their everyday experiences on the job. Yet the practical challenge was that there was little time or resources for individual suggestions and local needs to be met. We wondered, therefore, how to design something concrete enough to be a large-scale developmental process but also sufficiently open to ideas or suggestions for new emergent directions as suggested by the participants.

A second related challenge was the very limited number of days allocated for participation in workshops. The employees participated in courses twice: a three-day event followed by a two-day event. The courses provided the employees with the opportunity of discussing and reflecting on how and why some everyday work processes caused stress. However, the courses also provided them with information that might be of use for further investigation of their working environment. For example, several job-satisfaction occupational health and safety surveys had been conducted in their district (Tufte et al., 2011). Primarily, this data presented 'professional' interpretations of stress as these have implications for health-related and governmental regulations.

The third problem or challenge was that we wanted to introduce the concept of what we call project-based learning into the overall process of 'Stop Stress'. But many of the participants had little education and were not accustomed to attending educational courses of any kind. We therefore developed a relatively 'non-academic' approach, using adult education. This meant developing ideas and actions, as alluded to above, related to our own problems in relation to work-related stress. The projects conducted by participants in 'Stop Stress' were also different from traditional academic education, as it was long project period of almost two years, wherein they were able to explore problems and test ideas for solutions in their everyday work environment. Group meetings and follow-up meetings in various workplaces supported this process. The educational choice of project-based learning was effective as a response to the little time available at the workshops, because the programme gave time and resources at the workplace during regular work hours.

Theatre-research as a learning process

The use of theatre in 'Stop Stress' was designed to help the participants overcome some of the challenges outlined above and to engage in a learning process based on critique, active participation and a will to do something that would bring about change. We, the researchers, did not act in or produce the plays ourselves. We worked together with a theatre group called the Travelling Stage. The Travelling Stage is a Danish adult education association that produces plays professionally using scriptwriters, directors, actors and musicians. This theatre group cooperates with employees and workplaces or organisations to design and stage plays around issues that the groups themselves identify. We have a history of cooperation with the Traveling Stage, having used them in the past to translate, visualise and share some of the data or knowledge that has emerged from past action research projects (Tofteng and Husted, 2011). In 'Stop Stress' we used the Travelling Stage to produce short vignettes that could serve to express the significance, emotions and extent of specific experiences.

The participants form project groups on the first day of the workshops based on practical matters related to development of teams, their schedules and location. The first session focuses on sharing work-related problems causing stress or difficulties and finding examples from their daily work where they faced the problem in question. The professional actors join the groups and lead the discussions, bringing out the stories and examples of the various or multiple problems each person experiences in their workplace. Using this material, the actors create vignettes based on what they see as some of the key or recurrent themes raised. These are then performed for the audience.

This performance method is often referred to as 'mirroring the problem' and it is a technique inspired by both Brecht (1964) and Boal (1995), although they differ in their approaches. Brecht believed that the emancipatory potential of theatre lay in its ability to 'show' social inconsistencies and contradictions on stage directly to the audience. His point was that the provocative recognition of everyday challenges, and therefore the ability to be able to confront and deal with them, arises from watching issues and problems in society illuminated or performed. In other words, by watching familiar conflicts and challenges unfold on stage from a reflective or critical distance, we are better able to study and explore them in new ways. Boal (1995) was also concerned with social change and learning through theatre, but his approach was much more participatory. He used role-playing called 'forum theatre', in which audience members were invited to take part in re-forming the narratives that had been played out before them as a means of investigating these narratives for opportunities to change, develop or overcome the difficulties within the story. Both forms of theatre, we would argue, are involved in the struggle for consciousness change and the envisioning of new possibilities. While Brecht always worked with paid professional actors, in Boal's Theatre of the Oppressed actual community members were taught the techniques of theatre, created the images based on their own experiences, performed the play then re-enacted the vignettes along with the audience to transform the images.

Our work, we would argue, is a combination of Brecht and Boal in terms of forming and altering a small piece of reality theatre, using professional actors, but based in and on the experiences and stories of the different workers from District West. Saldaña (2011) refers to this as an 'original approach'. Research data, gathered by professional actor-researchers, is represented through a fictional story inspired by study findings and composed by extrapolating key themes. This gives voice to and is representative of the 'collective realities of its original sources' (Saldaña, 2011: 17). Professional actors transpose participants' lived experiences into an aesthetically effective piece of research-based theatre.

As we mentioned earlier, the professional actors from the theatre troupe gathered the data and then presented a 'mirror' of the key themes they felt and observed from the group discussions about workplace stress. Following this, the audience was asked to comment on what they had just seen and to write their responses on large pieces of paper visible to all. We then turned to the group who 'owned' the mirror and asked if they recognised what the actors had just played. Their answers were also recorded and these formed pathways for further research and development. The mirroring is a critical starting point for discovery and questioning, as the vignettes present a poignant visualisation of the problem. But actors who have a professional distance and an eye for emotions, conflicts and incoherence actually perform the mirror. This process makes it possible for the audience members to somewhat dislocate themselves from the problem and to watch and reflect from the sidelines. They can decide whether or not the mirror reflects the problem as they see it, sharpens the problem, illuminates something noticed before or allows them to explore their own feelings about what they have seen and the role they might play in creating the stressful environment.

Making the mirrors is mostly about creating a scene for shared and individual recognition and reflection. It is possible to have various reflections in the mirror. Quite often the audience see something more or different in the mirror than what the group discussed. Creating a visualisation of the problem seems to offer the potential to embrace differences in the perception of reality. Visualisation is a powerful technique for gaining new understandings but also for recognition, as is the process of the actors collecting the stories of problems and reinterpreting this material. By recognition we mean that this process tells the participants that the 'Stop Stress' programme takes their experiences of worklife seriously. Presenting the mirrors offers another kind of recognition: the mirrors presented to all the participants in the course create a voice that makes the problem distinct and visible for the whole group, and in turn encourage the audience to recognise that this problem exists and needs to be addressed. Most of the participants in 'Stop Stress' have little time together in the course of a day and limited resources in their worklife for insisting that difficulties be investigated and dealt with. It takes confidence, resources and time to raise one's difficulties in the everyday workplace alone in as visible and defined a way as the mirror. The mirrors are in essence a shortcut that makes it possible to present a voice and to insist that this piece of reality be recognised, but they also enable us to define the research foci within a short timeframe.

In the following section we show how the mirrors help to facilitate the processes intended in 'Stop Stress'. We present this through two stories. The first story is called 'Lack of presence'. It was a mirror created from the stories of the team leaders when they attended the first course. The second story is a vignette called 'Lark Meadow'. It is in fact a synthesis of common problems or themes illuminated through 50 mirrors that had been produced during the first step of 'Stop Stress'.

Lack of presence

The upper managers and team leaders in the district attended their own separate 'Stop Stress' workshops. Our experience was that regular employees sometimes needed to attend courses with no management present. But the managers and team leaders needed an extended course as they had a dual role in 'Stop Stress': they were to reflect on the processes in 'Stop Stress' in terms of management and they were to make a 'Stop Stress' project confronting their own worklife as well.

The managers who attended the same workshops were seven team leaders, one vice-chief of district and one chief of district. The project groups were divided into three; two groups of team leaders and a small group comprised of the vice-chief and chief of the district or what we refer to as senior management. The two groups of team leaders separately discussed difficulties of 'presence' (being there, being fully present in each moment) in their workplace and the actors then combined their stories into one mirror that reflected the problems for both groups. This is the performance mirror:

Joan, a team leader, shows up at her office and starts to work with a new document. There is a knock on the door. It is Marie, who is working as carer. She looks sad and nervous.

MARIE: Do you have a little time?

JOAN: Sure, come in … sit down.

Marie sits down on the edge of a chair.

MARIE: It's just because … things are not going so well … and I can't seem to …

A caretaker knocks at the door and enters the room. He starts to fiddle with the window.

CARETAKER: It's today we are repairing windows in this wing, remember? You'll have it back before evening.

Caretaker leaves the room with the window. The phone starts to ring. Joan ignores the phone and buttons her cardigan. She is cold. She faces Marie again.

JOAN: Yes… you were saying?

MARIE: Well it's just because I keep getting this …

The phone keeps on ringing and ringing. Joan answers the phone.

JOAN: Yes? … Oh, I'm sorry to hear that … Yes, I'll list you as sick. Take care and call in again tomorrow … Bye.

Joan faces Marie again. A planner knocks on the door and enters the room, holding some papers.

PLANNER: You have to approve of the new plan for team 8. I had to rearrange seven routes and we need two more substitutes.

The planner leaves the papers on Joan's desk and leaves the room. She meets Kirsten, a carer, in the doorway.

KIRSTEN: We still haven't received facilities for Mr Jensen and for Mrs Hansen and Mrs Hansen is about to have a serious bedsore. Could you please remind facility service division?!

Joan nods and turns to her computer. Kirsten leaves the room as another team leader enters.

TEAM LEADER: Joan … the management meeting started 5 minutes ago. Are you coming?

Joan looks from the computer to the phone to Marie and to her colleague in the door.

JOAN: Sure … just give me five minutes … Marie … I'm so sorry, but I have to go … maybe you could come back after lunch?

Marie avoids her eyes, nods and leaves the room. Joan picks up papers and her phone and tries to leave the room, but a man is now standing in the doorway.

MAN: Good morning. This is a health inspection …

When the vignette concluded, we asked the participants what they saw in the mirror. The responses of the team leaders ranged from it being a very good representation of their daily lives on the job to suggesting they did not feel that they looked that stressed but, in fact, they did 'feel' that stressed. Almost all talked about the inability to be 'present', hence the name of the project, in any one particular situation, given the push and pull of needs. The responses from senior management, however, were quite different. They focused on the inability of the team leader, saying things such as: 'She needed to prioritise and book a meeting later and don't answer the phone'; 'I see a team leader who doesn't use her opportunities to get help.' So while the team leaders recognised themselves and their problematic everyday worklife in the mirror, the reaction and comments from senior management were about how they could avoid or counteract what was represented in the mirror. These diverse responses created an atmosphere of conflict, of bad feeling and a lack of ability to address the problem of 'presence' that the team leaders were feeling. Therefore, following this event, several meetings with team leaders were organised by the senior management to address these conflicts.

In this case, the mirror served as a means of illuminating what the stressful work conditions looked like from the perspective of the team leaders. The team leaders preferred to talk about the feelings, difficulties and conditions of their employees. The workshop encouraged them to address their own difficulties and they were able to articulate the lack of presence and continuity as a stressful side-effect of the many tasks and shifts in focus they experienced during a workday. The actors created a mirror that showed the stressful situation and the growing feelings of frustration. The team leaders felt recognised and relieved as the mirror 'called a spade a spade'. The reaction from senior management, as noted above, was to suggest that the lack of presence could be solved by better organisation and prioritisation. They expressed frustration, as they believed the mirror showed a rift in their conception of 'management'. The senior managers believed that they and the team leaders were a 'unit' that shared the same managerial responsibilities in trying to make working conditions better for all. The frustrations revealed in the mirror addressed conditions that were shared by all in management positions, but the team leaders experienced the performance as if the senior managers were not doing what they should to deal with the problem, and they felt vindicated.

The mirror made us all aware of how difficult it is to address stressful working conditions. It also brought into question the integration of senior management and team leaders in the same workshops. As a result of bringing them together, all parties experienced major problems in pursuing their projects; their units were disrupted and they were not able to bridge the gaps. We therefore recommended that senior management should pursue and explore their own projects and recognise their own conflicts. Engaging a psychologist to undertake supervision and coaching with senior management and team leaders in separate groups was how we carried out this recommendation. By the time 'Stop Stress' moved to the second step and senior management were to participate in the next workshop to develop new ideas to counteract stress, they had progressed in several ways. For example, no one perceived 'management' any longer as a cohesive unit. Team leaders were now meeting by themselves, discussing their own experiences, but many spoke of new dialogues among senior management and the teams related to differences in how the function of manager or leader should be fulfilled and how to support each other in their clearly different roles.

The value of the mirror was to visualise, present and insist that the team leaders' experiences which were causing them stress be recognised. However, the mirroring activities also have their challenges. There have to be resources, a willingness to communicate across hierarchies and a readiness to meet the challenges reflected in the mirror. If the organisation is unable to fully comprehend and accept the conflicts presented and the need for further assistance, the mirror might have visualised too much for the organisation to handle. In other words, the difficulties in fulfilling their roles as team leaders, both professionally and humanly, were over-exposed in the mirror. If various frustrations about how to fulfil one's role in an organisation are neglected by the leaders who claim to be on each other's side, it can leave employees vulnerable with nowhere to go.

'Lark Meadow'

We had arranged follow-up meetings with all the groups six months after the first workshops to inform us on how the projects were coming along and to offer some feedback on the process. Most of the projects had survived and were about to be investigated or discussed. Some had collapsed and some had difficulties in sustaining what the project was all about and how they could move on. As 'Stop Stress' was moving into the second step – a year of interventions and the devising of new initiatives and activities to counteract work-related stress – we had to consider how all the work done so far could be sustained and communicated. We turned to the mirrors produced in the first-year workshops. How could we use the mirrors to review the critical reasons for new initiatives to counteract stress?

Fifty-seven groups were formed as a result of the first series of workshops, and critiques and difficulties in relation to projects were reflected in almost 50 mirrors. We reviewed all the mirrors and discussed their significance, their conflicts and emotions with the actors of the Travelling Stage. We found that it was possible to outline some common features of the problems reflected in the mirrors. These features can be best understood through three themes.

The first theme was *relationships*. Difficult or conflict-ridden relations existed between colleagues, between carers and planners or team leaders, or between teams. The second theme was *technology*. Technology and facilities played an important role in how care was organised and carried out in District West. A lot of the mirrors told us about daily situations where technology broke down and occupied enormous amounts of attention that was supposed to be given to, for example, elderly citizens. The third theme concerned *planning and influence*. The planning of daily routines and assignments is undertaken in District West by a team of planners; critique of irrational, confusing or impractical planning formed a consistent theme.

These three themes formed a background for a scriptwriter who transformed the material into 'Lark Meadow'. 'Lark Meadow' is not exactly a mirror. It is a vignette drawing on the three persistent themes in the form of a narrative about a nursing home called Lark Meadow where affiliated teams provide home care. 'Lark Meadow' contains three scenes addressing each of the three themes. We used 'Lark Meadow' to welcome the groups back to the second series of workshops. The actors performed the theatre piece and then we asked the participants in the workshop whether they recognised their critiques and realities in Lark Meadow. This was not always the case, and during three or four of the first workshops we had to correct and modify both minor and major details of the play. One of the scenes had to be rewritten altogether as it did not make any impression on the participants.

'Lark Meadow' served as a reminder of the critiques and problems that were highlighted the previous year. We knew that the brief time available to attend workshops or meetings during 'Stop Stress' would create challenges of continuity, so this was a way to bring everyone back to the same starting point. 'Lark Meadow' was a narrative that created a shortcut, so to speak, back to the experiences and emotions of the members of the groups, but also the challenges they wanted to address or solve. The play shares, as we noted above, themes common to all groups but without singling anyone out who might be able to be identified by their specific mirror. In other words, it offers anonymity to those individuals who might feel exposed. This created what we call a 'free space' that was both safe and able to reflect the 'power reality' that critical pedagogues and researchers argue is necessary to investigate social issues, problems and sufferings (Marcuse, 1941; Jung and Müllert, 1987). Free spaces create an atmosphere in which those involved can systematically reflect upon structures of power to strengthen democratic processes (Nielsen et al., 1996). Free spaces also encourage learning based in and on the social imagination, everyday life experiences and subjectivity (Skjervheim, 1996). The goal of art-based free spaces is to allow participants to perform – or in our case see performed – the creative ways that allow them to become more conscious of ambiguities, but also possibilities.

Conclusion

We have found that the use of theatre to combine adult learning and research encourages sharing and the recognition of different experiences and views visually and poignantly. Although it is not always perfect, this Brecht/Boal combination of theatre has worked well to critique and illuminate the workplace struggles that cause stress. Theatre-based research and learning, drawing from Brecht (1964), illuminates contradictions, challenges false harmonies and idealisations, and provokes emotions and analysis, not just empathy, ensuring that people feel, think and respond. Indeed, our approach is a 'creative shortcut' towards getting at key common themes that it might otherwise be difficult to find the resources and space to name and address. Our approach constitutes a praxis that is rooted in a more creative struggle for change in the workplace, health and lives of the committed workers of District West.

References

Boal, A. (1995), *The Rainbow of Desire*, London: Routledge.

Brecht, B. (1964), *Brecht on Theatre*, London: Methuen.

Brydon-Miller, M., Greenwood, D., and Maguire, P. (2003), 'Why action research?', *Action Research*, 1(1): 9–28.

Dewey, J. (1916), *Democracy and Education: An Introduction to the Philosophy of Education*, New York: Macmillan.

Eisner, E. (2008), 'Persistent tensions in arts-based research', in M. Cahnmann-Taylor and R. Siegesmund (eds), *Arts-Based Research in Education*, New York and London: Routledge, 16–27.

Freire, P. (1970), *Pedagogy of the Oppressed*, New York: Continuum.

Grundtvig, N.F.S. (1991 [1834]), *Selected Educational Writings*, Copenhagen: The International People's College.

Horton, M., and Freire, P. (1991), *We Make the Road by Walking: Conversations on Education and Social Change*, Philadelphia: Temple University Press.

Jensen, J., and Salling Olesen, H. (1999), *Project Studies: A Late Modern University Reform?* Copenhagen: Roskilde Universitetsforlag.

Jungk, R., and Müllert, N.R. (1987), *Future Workshops: How to Create Desirable Futures*, London: Institute for Social Inventions.

Lewin, K. (1948), *Resolving Social Conflicts*, New York: Harper and Row.

Marcuse, H. (1941), 'Some social implications of modern technology', in A. Arato and E. Gebhardt (eds), *The Essential Frankfurt School Reader*, New York: Urizen Books, 138–62.

Negt, O. (1969), *Soziologische Phantasie und examplarrisches Lernen*, Frankfurt am Main: Eur. Verlagsanstalt.

Nielsen, K.Aa., Olsén, P., and Nielsen, B.S. (1996), 'From silent to talkative participants: a discussion of techniques as social construction', *Economic and Industrial Democracy*, 17: 359–86.

Nielsen, K., and Svensson, L. (eds) (2006), *Action and Interactive Research: Beyond Practice and Theory*, Maastricht: Shaker Publishing.

Saldaña, J. (2011), *Ethnotheatre: Research from Page to Stage*, Walnut Creek: Left Coast Press.

Skjervheim, H. (1996), 'Participant and spectator', *Skriftserien*, 12.

Tofteng, D., and Husted, M. (2011), 'Theatre and action research: how drama can empower action research processes in the field of unemployment', *Action Research*, 9(1): 27–41.

Toulmin, S., and Gustavsen, B. (1996), *Beyond Theory: Changing Organizations through Participation*, Amsterdam: John Benjamin.

Tufte, P., Nabe-Nielsen, K., and Clausen, T. (2011), 'Client-related work tasks and meaning of work: results from a longitudinal study among elder care workers in Denmark', *International Archives of Occupational and Environmental Health*, 85(5): 467–72.

PART III

Community cultural engagement

9

Weaving tales of hope and challenge: exploring diversity through narrative *métissage*

Catherine Etmanski, Will Weigler and Grace Wong-Sneddon

It all came to a head when one of my male classmates asked how I felt about what Oprah had done for 'my kind of people'. That is when I truly felt that all some of the people in that room were seeing was my colour. (Administrative support staff member)

I wanted to raise my voice and draw attention to their exclusive practices, but had seen other female colleagues who had tried to assert themselves, with the result being eye-rolling and hallway conversations about strident frustrated females – I wasn't yet brave enough for that. (Former sessional instructor)

That commitment to, and relationship with Canada's First Peoples[1] doesn't end when students graduate. Make it concrete – put something in the [University] Strategic Plan that is a specific commitment regarding hiring, retention, and promotion of Canada's First Peoples as professional employees. (Technical support staff member)

They never did come back to see if the building was being cleaned to their standards, which in fact, are probably not as good as mine! (Custodial support staff member)

There is an ongoing dialogue on diversity taking place at the University of Victoria (UVic), Canada. Although this dialogue has occurred in many locations across the university over time, it is rendered more public at an annual, campus-wide, interdisciplinary Diversity Research Forum hosted by the university's Office of the Provost.[2] In the months leading up to the 2011 forum, the planning committee decided to experiment with an arts-based method called *métissage*: an approach to storytelling that weaves different people's narratives together (we describe this in more detail shortly). The four quotations above are the closing lines from the four participants' narratives that were brought together in this *métissage* project.

In this chapter, we document the process leading up to the *métissage* performance, describe the effect it had on the audience, and reflect on lessons we learned along the way. While this chapter incorporates the views of the three key organisers of this project and authors of this chapter, sections written in the first-person singular voice represent Catherine's perspective.

We have two key reasons for writing this chapter. First, in sharing our experience, we are in fact advocating for more widespread use of arts-based methods in university settings. Conferences, classrooms, meetings and research projects continue to be dominated by more traditional methods such as PowerPoint lectures, panel presentations or debates. While these time-honoured methods certainly have their place, they are but a few among endless possibilities for teaching, learning and scholarly communication. We suggest that the unexamined ubiquity and dominance of these traditional methods limits our ability to learn more holistically in academic settings. As many have argued before us, arts-based methods tend to have a different effect on the audience than these more traditional methods, and can create more possibilities for engaging our hands, hearts, spirits *and* minds. In documenting how an arts-based method was successfully employed as part of a Provost's research conference, our desire is to join our voices with the many arts-based practitioners and scholars who inspire new ideas for what is possible – not only for conference organisers, but for administrators, educators and researchers alike.

For readers who are already convinced of the power of the arts, our second purpose in writing this chapter is to provide a behind-the-scenes look at the process leading up to the *métissage* performance. We offer this as a description, not a prescription, and invite you to take what is useful from our experience and adapt it to the nuances of your own context. We hope that the key decision points we have highlighted here and the particular way in which we have employed *métissage* will inspire new ideas for your practice.

We open the chapter with an introduction to diversity and multiculturalism in Canada. This section provides background information on UVic's Diversity Research Forum and, by demonstrating the intersecting elements of the diversity debate, sets the stage for why *métissage* – a method that showcases intersecting narratives – was an appropriate method to choose for this context. We then describe *métissage* in more depth, revealing the link to arts-based research in general, and the theoretical nuances of this method. Next we move to an overview of how we employed *métissage* in the context of the Diversity Research Forum: our creation process and a discussion of the quality of conversation that resulted from the performance. Here we emphasise the importance of conversation following the performance, and discuss the measures we took to create a welcoming space for the deeply personal dialogue that ensued. We close with a hope that other scholars and practitioners will continue to encourage the use of arts-based methods and working to create holistic ways of engaging within academic settings.

Note that this chapter is intended to accompany and complement – not replace – the performance. We therefore encourage interested readers to view a recording of the *métissage* online (see Etmanski et al., 2011).

The diversity dialogue in Canada: why is this forum important?

The Provost's Diversity Research Forum has been an annual occurrence at UVic since 2008. The purpose of this forum is to provide a space for faculty, staff and students to showcase their work on issues related to diversity in its various manifestations. Members of the university community come together to build strategic alliances, hold critical conversations and address discrimination and oppression of all kinds. The forum is fully funded by the university, and organisers make every attempt to put values of diversity into practice. The existence of controversies and human oversights mean that the conference cannot satisfy everyone, but it is a sincere effort to tackle difficult and seemingly intractable topics related to diversity. The forum has been growing with every year, and attendees report through anonymous feedback forms that this is a unique space for holistic academic engagement with ideas and actions on diversity in our home university context.

Such diversity conversations are shaped by Canada's complex colonial history, which includes waves of settlement by peoples from around the world. The Canadian Multicultural Act 1985 is an attempt to promote equity and equality among people of all cultural backgrounds. However, the dominance of European colonisation remains enshrined in the two official languages (English and French) and there is a growing body of literature exposing the inconsistency of achieving equality in practice (e.g. Abu-Laban and Gabriel, 2002; Bannerji, 2000; Lee and Lutz, 2005; Razack, 2002). Such scholars suggest that a contradiction exists between the welcoming discourses of multiculturalism and the myriad real challenges endured by people outside of the 'Euro-white', English-speaking Canadian norm. Goldberg describes this contradiction as a key paradox of modernity: 'the more open to difference liberal modernity declares itself, the more dismissive of difference it becomes' (1993: 6). This dismissal of difference has implications for how people interact in a university setting, as standardised evaluative and pedagogical practices are often employed to assess and teach a diverse range of people.

In addition, the disproportionate level of poverty among Canada's indigenous peoples creates a significant challenge to the rhetoric of multiculturalism. The University of Victoria is located on the traditional territories of the Coast Salish and Straits Salish First Peoples of Canada, and many indigenous people assert that their traditional territories are occupied or have been stolen (a view supported by some of their non-indigenous allies). This fundamental struggle over waterways and land, as well as blatant social and economic inequity, adds complexity to conversations around diversity in Canada. Various efforts are currently underway at UVic to support indigenous-centred education (e.g. Williams and Tanaka, 2007), bridge indigenous–non-indigenous relations, and build and sustain meaningful relationships between settlers and the surrounding indigenous communities. Unlike most academic conferences, organisers of the Diversity Research Forum make significant efforts to follow protocols for acknowledging the traditional territory, welcoming newcomers and visitors to the territory, and inviting Elders from local indigenous communities to hold a place of honour during the conference, especially during meals and opening/closing ceremonies. These efforts, as well as the content of some of the conference sessions, encourage non-indigenous people not only to become more aware of the struggle for land and basic human dignity, but also to work as allies in this struggle.

This forum, however, is not simply about cultural diversity. Forum organisers endeavour to recognise a breadth of human possibility. Presenters highlight their work around intersecting elements of power and privilege, including how class, for example, intersects with sex, gender, sexuality, religion (dis)ability, country of origin, language, culture and more. In recent years forum organisers have sought to weave an ecological analysis into the conversations as well, thereby drawing clearer links between diversity and biodiversity, social and environmental justice.[2]

During the summer of 2010, organising committee members started to plan for the 2011 forum. Feedback from previous years indicated that while the conferences had been successful in generating inclusivity among faculty and students, there was one group of people whose voices had been absent from the conversations to date: members of university staff. While Grace, in her position as lead organiser and diversity advisor to the Provost, goes out of her way to ensure that staff members can take time away from work to attend this forum if they so wish, the reality of institutional constraints means that many do not or cannot participate in a meaningful way. As a result, committee members began pondering how they could create an opportunity for staff voices to be heard. Adding another panel presentation to the conference schedule was a possibility, of course, but, as the resident artist on the committee, Will had a different idea. He had previously seen Catherine and her students facilitate a *métissage*-based dialogue related to graduate student experiences on campus and suggested to the committee that this method might be a good fit for this purpose. He then got in touch with Catherine to help facilitate the development of *métissage*-based presentation.

What is *métissage*?

Métissage is an arts-based method of enquiry and education, which, by its nature, defies categorisation and concrete definition. It draws from the traditions of life writing, storytelling, theatre and – symbolically – from the art of weaving or braiding. When presented in written form, the genres can vary, as multiple personal narratives are woven together with theory, poetry, photographs and more. When performed orally, *métissage* is similar to Reader's Theatre, in which people read openly from their scripts, with minimal attention to staging or costumes – though these are also welcome. Projected still images, video and other creative possibilities may complement the reading as well. Part auto-ethnography, part performance, *métissage* resists '19th century scholarly conventions of discrete disciplines with corresponding rhetorics for conducting and representing research' (Chambers et al., 2008: 142). It is a process of uncovering and co-constructing knowledge about self, others and the world around us, and a means of making that knowledge public.

The simple practice of narrative *métissage* (i.e. without images, poetry and so on) results in the interweaving of short personal stories. To enable this process, a small group of three to five participants can self-organise, or a researcher-teacher-artist can facilitate the writing of participants' narratives. These narratives are often, but not necessarily, on the same theme. Participants write independently then come together to share their narratives with others. The individual texts are then divided into vignettes or shorter segments so that people can take turns reading segments of their narrative aloud. Person A shares one vignette or a few sentences, then person B speaks, then person C, back to person A, and so on. The weaving or order of segments can be negotiated as a group, or prepared by one person. The ordering of segments creates a further layer of meaning, as the juxtaposition of different scenes can demonstrate how individual stories diverge and converge, complement and contradict. Through this braided storytelling, one person's story is interrupted by another's – just as our lives and identities are often overlapped and interwoven with the people with whom we come into contact. *Métissage* can highlight both the threads of individuality *and* the common experiences of our collective human tapestry.

As with other arts-based methods, audience members frequently report at least two (of many potential) categories of experience upon witnessing *métissage*. First, as storytellers speak, members of the audience are often able to see themselves reflected in the stories. This can allow for greater self-knowledge, as people's experiences are either validated through the understanding that they are not alone, or, conversely, spectators gain some awareness about the hurtful effect their behaviour could have on others. Secondly, stereotypes and assumptions become dismantled as we learn more about people's life experiences (e.g. contesting preconceptions that social privilege precludes pain). People can feel greater compassion and empathy as the complexity of another person's life unfolds before them. In this way, the *métissage* moves from expressing individual stories to becoming 'a means of conveying truths about the human condition' (Furman, 2006: 138). These personal narratives are not didactic or necessarily intended to convey a particular message. Rather, as points of connection are made between the tellers and the audience, people can extract their own meaning and apply these 'truths' in their own contexts.

Though not a uniquely Canadian art form, the practice of *métissage* has gained momentum in western Canada over the past decade through the work of University of British Columbia and University of Lethbridge authors and educators (see Hasebe-Ludt et al., 2009), and at the University of Victoria through scholars Wanda Hurren, Antoinette Oberg and Kathy Sanford, among others. I was first introduced to *métissage* in 2009 by Sheila Simpkins, who, through her doctoral work, was employing *métissage* to promote peace through dialogue between Kurdish and Arab students in Kurdistan, northern Iraq (Simpkins, 2012). Sheila and fellow classmates introduced narrative *métissage* to me as a simple but surprisingly powerful arts-based method. I have since come to better appreciate the complex, decolonising world-view that this method represents.

Why *métissage*?

Barndt cautions that 'there is always a danger of art-making processes being reduced to tools or techniques when using them as integral to qualitative research, making them devoid of meaning in relationship to the deeper purposes of the research' (2008: 359). Though it could pass as a simple reading and writing exercise, the practice of *métissage* is deeply rooted in an ontology of liminal, transformational spaces and creative, constructivist epistemologies. Chambers, Donald and

Hasebe-Ludt suggest that *métissage* 'is a site for writing and surviving the interval between different cultures and languages; a way of merging and blurring genres, texts and identities; an active literary stance, political strategy and pedagogical praxis' (2002: para. 1). Hasebe-Ludt and Jordan have further attested, 'in our life writing, we are committed to promoting emancipatory projects of learning and teaching by attending to the ways that life writing constantly explores, contests, and negotiates the imaginative possibilities of knowing and being in the world' (2010: 2). The ontological and epistemological stances that these authors express support our choice to employ *métissage* for this project.

The concept of *métissage* is particularly meaningful in Canada in relation to the colonial history and ongoing multicultural agenda described earlier. Derived from the Latin word *mixtus*, meaning mixed, the word *métis* originally refers to cloth woven from two different fibres (Chambers et al., 2008). In the Canadian context, the term *Métis* specifically refers to people of a mixed indigenous and European settler cultural heritage. While *Métis* peoples across Canada maintain a unique cultural identity and nation, the act of claiming *Métis* status cannot be separated from ongoing colonial interventions in family, identity and historical records (Barman and Evans, 2009). The racial prejudice that historically accompanied the concept of *Métis* must also be understood as context for this work, including both fear of the 'Other' and fear of the 'familiar-strange' (Nishad Khanna, pers. comm., 5 February 2010/14 December 2011). People of so-called mixed heritage have historically defied categorisation, never fully belonging to one cultural group or another. In recent years the postmodern era has helped to reconceptualise in-between spaces as important and productive epistemological sites. As a result, diasporic, post-colonial, hyphenated, hybrid and transnational identities are increasingly celebrated (Anthias, 2002; Grewal and Kaplan, 1994; Ifekwunigwe, 1999).

This reclaiming of mixed identity harkens back to Greek mythology, in which a Titaness named *Metis* was revered as a wise 'figure of skill and craft, and of cunning, a trickster with powers of transformation who resisted notions of purity by weaving and blurring textiles' (Hasebe-Ludt and Jordan, 2010: 2). As both a methodology and pedagogy, then, *métissage* disrupts modernist ideals of linearity and rationality by weaving in 'strands of place and space, memory and history, ancestry and (mixed) race, language and literacy, familiar and strange with strands of tradition, ambiguity, becoming (re)creation, and renewal' (Chambers et al., 2008: 152). Viewed as a response to colonial encounters, the practice of *métissage* becomes a way of working with and through the experience of dislocation, and the 'messiness' of a reality that defies fixed categories.

In addition to cultural heritage, the juxtaposition of multiple narratives through *métissage* promotes an intersectional analysis of identity, power and privilege. Intersectionality is a concept that attempts to address the multiplicity of complex dynamics embedded in human relationships, organisations and global social structures, as well as the oppressive or enabling circumstances to which these dynamics give rise. It is defined as 'the interweaving of oppressions on the basis of multiple social identities as well as marginalisation that [is] both relational and structural' (Moosa-Mitha, 2005: 62). Proponents of intersectionality claim that no one element of identity or oppression can stand alone (e.g. sex or sexism; 'race' or racism); rather, these dimensions of difference are deeply interconnected and are expressed differently through individual people's identities. The idea of intersectionality acknowledges that the human experience is complex and constantly in motion. While some attributes are seemingly fixed, others are more fluid. Our unique positions in axes of difference at any given time influence, though they do not predetermine, both our experience of the world and our life chances.

With the theoretical and political underpinnings of *métissage* outlined, the remainder of this chapter focuses specifically on employing this method as a strategy for promoting dialogue around diversity within and for a university community.

Our process

*M*étissage, like many arts-based media, is better understood when it is experienced, not simply described – indeed, this is why we urge readers to view the online video that accompanies this chapter. After discussing the possibility of facilitating this process with Grace and Will, I requested the assistance of three volunteers to help demonstrate what a *métissage* performance could look like in practice. The four of us (two faculty colleagues, Will and I) agreed to pilot a simple performance that would serve as an experiential demonstration to others on the committee.

To begin, we sought a central organising theme for our story-writing and performance. The invitation that my students had previously extended to me, and which had proven to be powerful in our context, was the phrase 'standing outside'. In the interest of keeping this part of the process as simple as possible, we used this invitation again and each of us wrote a narrative of less than 300 words to describe experiences of being an outsider. For the purpose of this simple demonstration, this was an open invitation to write as personally or as superficially as we wished, and our stories of 'standing outside' could directly relate to academic experiences or not. I explained that the piece could be written as one continuous story, or as a few shorter vignettes and asked the other storytellers to remember that our narratives would be separated into segments and woven with three others. Therefore we endeavoured to incorporate natural pauses or spaces for interruption. The four of us met once to read our stories aloud and determine the order in which we would share this initial *métissage* with the rest of the committee at an upcoming meeting.

After hearing this pilot *métissage* performance, committee members instantly agreed to move forward with the idea. Our narratives stimulated a range of responses, and through the conversation many individuals commented that they could see themselves in the stories we had presented; as suggested above and as is often the case, it was an empathy-building process. Encouraged to proceed, we began to consider how we could integrate *métissage* into the larger structure of the Diversity Research Forum.

The planning committee, which consisted of staff, faculty and a few students, raised a number of concerns about employing *métissage* with staff members.

High among them was whether or not it was in fact appropriate or ethical to ask staff members to put themselves in a potentially vulnerable position by publicly sharing personal stories about challenges they may have encountered. We were fully aware that most community-driven arts-based practices encourage people to tell their own stories, in their own voices, and there are many examples of people feeling empowered through this process. Our reality, however, was that this was not a bottom-up process with staff members self-organising, or with a group coming forward and requesting to be heard. As organisers, we wanted to ensure that staff voices were part of the discussion around diversity on campus; yet we also knew that universities tend to have long memories. We found ourselves in a place of not wanting to reinscribe dominant norms that silence uncomfortable truths and experiences of oppression, while simultaneously recognising that it is not always safe or strategically wise to disclose too much personal information about the workplace within those same institutional walls.

Will was a doctoral candidate in the Department of Theatre at that time and was well connected to a network of local actors. He suggested that we consider breaking with the traditional *métissage* format by finding actors to read the narratives, rather than asking staff members to read their own words in the public forum. We found this to be a useful innovation, and a good compromise for our particular circumstance, especially as Grace was able to allocate some funds to pay the actors. We brainstormed a few options for how we might incorporate *métissage* into the forum, including whether we should send out a general call to see how many interested participants would come forward, or whether we should use a more intentional approach of eliciting stories from a known, purposive sample. We also debated whether we ought to set this up as a performance with audience reflection and discussion afterwards, or make the workshop more interactive, with audience members writing their own narratives and weaving them together with others.

We ultimately chose to invite specific individuals to participate and called upon actors to read the narratives as a performance. Grace was intentional in inviting participants who represented four campus unions and she sought a diversity of job position, ethnicity and class within those groups. The four excerpts that open this chapter are part of the 300-word narratives written by a former sessional instructor and three participants from administrative, technical and custodial support services. Except for one narrative that was forwarded directly to me, we maintained a level of anonymity for the writers. To facilitate this, Grace initiated contact with the participants during the writing process and then sent the narratives to me without identifying the authors by name. I subsequently worked with these narratives, looking for vignettes or natural breaks in the story, and collaborated with Will to weave them together. We sent the compiled (or woven) version to Grace, who forwarded the document to the participants for feedback and their final approval.

In the meantime, Will began recruiting actors who would read each of the four scripts. To maintain the integrity of the authors' voices, he felt that it was important to involve actors who were willing, more or less, *just to read* the texts rather than feel the need to create characters. Certainly we asked that they ground the passages in authenticity and sincerity, and it was evident that they were committed to the vision of the work. However, as he explained to the actors during rehearsal, they would be standing in for real people, not fictional characters – people who might in fact be in attendance at the performance. The process required that the voice of the writer come through unimpeded by the extra layer of an actor's interpretation. Will had previously seen verbatim theatre in which the performers had felt it necessary to make their characters dramatic, funny or otherwise interesting as they tried to fill out the text. In our case, he believed that these layers would interfere with the purpose of the exercise. Drawing from his experience as a theatre director, he believed that this particular process required a simple reading by actors who were willing to serve as neutrally as possible as conduits for the writers' words.

The actors met with Will and me for one rehearsal before the performance. We also extended an invitation to the writers to attend this rehearsal. By sending the woven version of the text to the writers for their input, and later inviting them to see the rehearsal (and to feel entitled during that preview to weigh in on what they felt ought to be adjusted before the actual performance), we were attempting to communicate that this was an open process – that we were not just collecting data from *them* to use for *our* project. It turned out that none of the writers took us up on the offer. Still, we felt it was important that the offer be made, and that it be made in good faith with a clearly communicated understanding that the writers were entitled to play a role as co-authors in the staging and reading of their words. The use of actors as stand-ins became an important part of our deliberate approach to maintain anonymity. Nevertheless, we attempted to honour the intent of the work, which was for individuals to share and control their own stories.

The final performance was offered as a plenary address on the second afternoon of the forum. We used minimal staging (four different chairs), and the actors did not wear costumes per se, though they did dress in clothes appropriate to their roles. After an introduction by Will and me, the actors read from the scripts, while a sign language interpreter simultaneously translated.

The performance was followed by a long period of conversation. Although the audience members had provided their consent to be video-recorded upon registration for the forum, due to the personal nature of the comments inspired by this performance, we decided not to place their conversation online. To ensure that people could hear each other in a large room, and also since the sessions were being recorded, we used microphones during this conversation period. Knowing that some people feel uncomfortable approaching a standing microphone, we chose instead to bring the microphones to people who indicated that they wanted to speak.

To add another layer to this conversation, we adapted an educational activity that uses yarn to literally weave connections between people. Will custom-built spools to fit around the microphone handles, and when people spoke we asked that they hold on to the yarn before the microphone was carried on to the next speaker. By the end of the discussion, the yarn that connected one voice to the next created a colourfully woven web, tangibly displaying the interconnections among those in the room.

Effects of arts-based communication in an academic setting

The legacy of Cartesian dualism, positivism and Enlightenment thinking encourages not just a split between mind and body within the academy, but an emphasis on developing the mind *above* the body, heart and spirit. As a result, in our experience it is still rare to find academic spaces – particularly conferences – that intentionally seek to engage learners as whole beings. Barndt suggests that 'the arts, when applied appropriately and facilitated sensitively, can involve participants as full human beings, touching minds AND hearts, healing the body/mind split inherent in Western scientific research methods' (2008: 359, emphasis in original). Based on our observation of the in-depth conversation that followed this *métissage* performance, we believe that this plenary address had the hoped-for effect of touching hearts and minds. This was confirmed by anonymous feedback comments such as this: 'I was particularly fascinated by the storytelling plenary and how it was able to voice individual stories while illustrating common themes experienced by the people who had come forward. It was very powerful and something I would like to be able to do in my work.' People also commented directly to us that the storytelling genre fitted well with indigenous oral histories, which opened a space to discuss the ongoing effects of colonisation.

We left plenty of time for conversation following the performance and many of the audience members were moved to share very personal, detailed accounts of their own experiences. Though spoken by actors, the staff members' stories shared during the *métissage* served as powerful catalysts that enabled people to speak from the heart. While we intentionally problematised the idea of a 'safe' space through both our choice of utilising actors and our introductory comments, one participant told us we had created a 'brave space', where the tone of discussion was accessible and supportive for those who wished to share their own hopes, challenges and experiences. These individuals' stories became symbolically interwoven with the staff members' original stories and the conversation following the performance became part of the *métissage* itself. To move beyond performance into deeper levels of analysis, empathy and trust, this space for discussion is essential to the practice of narrative *métissage*.

A critical question raised during the performance was the common concern about whether we were reaching the right audience at this kind of self-selected gathering. This discussion led to Grace securing a spot for a follow-up performance at a subsequent all-staff conference hosted by the university's Office of Human Resources. Although I could not attend this performance, Grace and Will reported that it was also very well received, and that it created another place in the academy for equally rich, heart-centred conversation. Several participants chatted with Grace about how watching *métissage* affected them and disclosed some of the experiences they have had on campus. For example, one staff member talked about her recent (and still raw) experience when someone in authority made a stereotypical assumption of who she is based on her cultural background.

While many speakers, panel presentations or facilitated discussions can have the effect of generating dialogue, as practitioners of other community arts will attest, 'the process of "thinking with our hands" can short-circuit the censorship of the brain' (Jackson, 2002: xxiii). Similarly, a performance such as this one has the ability to touch people – not all people of course, but many – at an emotional level, thereby lowering defences and enabling a different kind of conversation to the seemingly rational, intellectual engagement normally called for in academic settings. As one feedback respondent stated, of the sessions at the Diversity Forum, the *métissage* staff members touched her the most.

Tying a knot

In this chapter we have provided one example of narrative *métissage* in practice. Through our experience we have learned that *métissage* is a powerful method for fostering greater understanding and empathy between people of diverse backgrounds. When employed mindfully, methods such as this can provide unconventional opportunities to encourage heart-centred dialogue in academic settings such as meetings, workshops, conferences, classrooms or other environments that aim to move beyond the simple transfer of information. In our contemporary global context in which we might interact with people from a range of backgrounds on any given day, it behoves us to deconstruct stereotypes and learn more about the range of possible human experiences. In our context, we were fortunate that, under Grace's leadership, members of the conference organising committee were supportive of arts-based methods. In sharing our story, we hope that others in your community will be equally supportive, and that you may be inspired to try *métissage* yourself. In so doing, perhaps you will weave elements of our story into your own.

References

Abu-Laban, Y., and Gabriel, C. (2002), *Selling Diversity: Immigration, Multiculturalism, Employment Equity, and Globalization*, Peterborough, ON: Broadview Press.

Anthias, F. (2002), 'Diasporic hybridity and transcending racisms: problems and potential', in F. Anthias and C. Lloyd (eds), *Rethinking Anti-racisms: From Theory to Practice*, London: Routledge, 22–43.

Bannerji, H. (2000), *The Dark Side of Nation: Essays on Multiculturalism, Nationalism and Gender*, Toronto: Canadian Scholars' Press.

Barman, J., and Evans, M. (2009), 'Reflections on being and becoming Métis in British Columbia', *BC Studies*, 16(1): 59–91.

Barndt, D. (2008), 'Touching minds and hearts: community arts as collaborative research', in J.G. Knowles and A.L. Cole (eds), *Handbook of the Arts in Qualitative Research: Perspectives, Methodologies, Examples, and Issues*, London: Sage, 351–62.

Chambers, C., Donald, D., and Hasebe-Ludt, E. (2002), 'Creating a curriculum of métissage', *Educational Insights*, 7(2), http://ccfi.educ.ubc.ca/publication/insights/v07n02/metissage/metiscript.html (accessed 15 September 2012).

Chambers, C., and Hasebe-Ludt, E., with D. Donald, W. Hurren, C. Leggo and A. Oberg (2008), 'Métissage: a research praxis', in J.G. Knowles and A.L. Cole (eds), *Handbook of the Arts in Qualitative Research: Perspectives, Methodologies, Examples, and Issues*, London: Sage, 141–53.

Etmanski, C., Weigler, W., and Wong-Sneddon, G. (2011), *Weaving Tales of Hope and Challenge: Exploring Diversity through Métissage* [video recording], edited by J. Dalderis-Moore and M. Groves, Victoria, BC: University of Victoria, https://dspace.library.uvic.ca:8443//handle/1828/3391 (accessed 15 September 2012).

Freeman, V. (2005), 'Attitudes toward "miscegenation" in Canada, the United States, New Zealand, and Australia, 1860–1914', *Native Studies Review*, 16(1): 41–69.

Furman, R. (2006), 'Poetry as research: advancing scholarship and the development of poetry therapy as a profession', *Journal of Poetry Therapy: The Interdisciplinary Journal of Practice, Theory, Research and Education*, 19(3): 133–45.

Goldberg, D.T. (1993), *Racist Culture: Philosophy and the Politics of Meaning*, Cambridge: Blackwell.

Grewal, I., and Kaplan, C. (eds) (1994), *Scattered Hegemonies: Postmodernity and Transnational Feminist Practices*, Minneapolis: University of Minnesota Press.

Hasebe-Ludt, E., Chambers, C.M., and Leggo, C. (2009), *Life Writing and Literary Métissage as an Ethos for our Times*, Oxford: Peter Lang.

Hasebe-Ludt, E., and Jordan, N. (eds) (2010), '"May we get us a heart of wisdom": life writing across knowledge traditions', *Transnational Curriculum Inquiry*, 7(2), http://nitinat.library.ubc.ca/ojs/index.php/tci (accessed 15 September 2012).

Ifekwunigwe, J.O. (1999), 'Old whine, new vassals: are diaspora and hybridity postmodern inventions?', in P. Cohen (ed.), *New Ethnicities, Old Racisms*, London: Zed Books, 180–204.

Jackson, A. (2002), 'Translator's introduction to the first edition', in A. Boal, *Games for Actors and Non-actors*, 2nd edn, New York: Routledge, xxii–xxix.

Lee, J., and Lutz, J. (2005), *Situating "Race" and Racisms in Space, Time, and Theory: Critical Essays for Activists and Scholars*, Montreal: McGill-Queen's University Press.

Moosa-Mitha, M. (2005), 'Situating anti-oppressive theories within critical and difference-centred perspectives', in L. Brown and S. Strega (eds), *Research as Resistance: Critical, Indigenous, and Anti-oppressive Research Approaches*, Toronto: Canadian Scholars' Press, 37–70.

Razack, S. (ed.) (2002), *Race, Space and the Law: Unmapping a White Settler Society*, Toronto: Between the Lines.

Simons, H., and McCormack, B. (2007), 'Integrating arts-based inquiry in evaluation methodology: opportunities and challenges', *Qualitative Inquiry*, 13(2): 292–311.

Simpkins, S. (2012), 'Narrative métissage: crafting empathy and understanding of self/other', unpublished doctoral thesis, University of Victoria.

Williams, L., and Tanaka, M. (2007), 'Schalay'nung Sxwey'ga: emerging cross-cultural pedagogy in the academy', *Educational Insights*, 11(3), http://ccfi.educ.ubc.ca/publication/insights/v11n03/articles/williams/williams.html (accessed 15 September 2012).

Notes

1 The term 'First Peoples' is the original author's choice. Some readers may prefer terms such as indigenous, First Nations, Aboriginal or Indian. All of these terms are somewhat inadequate, however, as they generalise and homogenise vastly different nations, with people who speak various languages and hold diverse cultural traditions. Elsewhere in the narrative, this author problematises use of the term Aboriginal. This author self-identifies as Tlingit, a nation located in the Pacific Northwest Coast of what is now the border of Canada and Alaska.

2 More information on the content of the Provost's Diversity Research Forum, including a list of UVic sponsors, can be found online at http://web.uvic.ca/vpac/diversity/forum2011/index.php (accessed 15 September 2012).

10

In a new 'Age of Enlightenment': challenges and opportunities for museums, cultural engagement and lifelong learning at the University of Glasgow[1]

Maureen Park

Inspiration and enjoyment are powerful motivators to learning, and the unique importance and extraordinary diversity of the collections held in university museums are undoubtedly a potent resource to this end. (UMG, 2004: ii)

During the last forty years a revolution has taken place in the role of many of our museums. Once defined as centres of culture and learning, they are now adopting an extra dimension as agents of social change. Museums have always been perceived as *loci* of learning and research. From its foundation in 1753, the British Museum offered free entry to 'the learned and the curious' members of the public (Crook, 1972: 39); in 1816 Viscount Fitzwilliam gave his collection to the University of Cambridge for 'the Increase of Learning and other Great Objects of that Noble Foundation' (Fitzwilliam Museum, 2011). But in our current political climate museums must also respond to the agendas of their funders, in particular the policy priorities for social inclusion, widening participation and lifelong learning. Now, more than ever, education is not simply an adjunct to a museum's provision but plays a central role in defining its policy, displays, exhibitions and activities. As Anderson reports, 'education is the golden key, which opens doors to resources of skills, money and facilities in their communities' (1999: 1). This means that museums are becoming increasingly visitor-centred institutions, places of lifelong learning for everyone. New theories on how visitors learn in museums have contributed to our understanding of active engagement as a key process of learning and the significance of the individual participant's prior knowledge and personal experience in shaping the learning process (Roberts, 1997; Hein, 1998; Hooper-Greenhill, 1999). Museums are increasingly aware of their role as a learning resource, their need to provide formal, informal and self-directed learning opportunities for visitors of all ages (as well as 'virtual' visitors) and the importance of reaching out to new target audiences in the community. This is all very well for municipal or national museums for whom widening of cultural engagement is top of their funders' agendas, but it can a particular challenge for university museums whose primary function is to serve as a resource for a much more focused audience – students and researchers. Nevertheless many do contribute to widening participation, offering a 'welcoming and comparatively undaunting gateway to the university' and playing a role 'in local and regional life of which their governing universities are all too often only dimly aware' (UMG, 2004: ii). Located within an environment of ambitious strategies, global aspirations and ever-decreasing budgets, university museums face daunting challenges.

In 2010 the University of Glasgow launched its new strategic plan, *Glasgow 2020: A Global Vision*, in which it set out its mission 'to undertake world leading research and to provide an intellectually stimulating learning environment that benefits culture, society and the economy' (University of Glasgow, 2010: 7). At the heart of its new agenda lies the ambition to raise its standing within the world university rankings. To achieve this it is laying greater emphasis than ever before on promoting excellence in innovative research, enhancing its undergraduate and postgraduate student experience, attracting increasing numbers of international students and extending its global impact. Promoted against a backdrop of internal structural changes, economic cuts and redundancies, the strategic plan sets challenges for its staff to review their contribution to this vision. The document showcases a number of priority research centres identified as models of global excellence but no reference is made either to the university's museum, The Hunterian, or to its adult and continuing education provider, the Centre for Open Studies, or to their role in the university's commitment to widening participation. Indeed both have undergone recent review and their relevance to the university's vision has been carefully scrutinised.

Somewhat depressingly, this lack of recognition for a cultural asset on its very doorstep does not appear to be unusual. In its 2004 report, *University Museums in the United Kingdom: A National Resource in the 21st Century*, the University Museums Group UK (UMG) examined the relationship between these museums and their parent universities, their contribution to the mission of research and teaching in higher education and their role in lifelong learning and cultural engagement (UMG, 2004: ii). The report included remarkable statistics: university museums hold 30 per cent of all collections designated to be of national or international importance and yet comprise only 4 per cent of the total UK museum sector. It concluded that, while for many museums their 'research, teaching, international collaboration and engagement with the general public all enhance the profile and status of their universities', their contribution can, and often does, go unacknowledged by their parent institutions (UMG, 2004: ii). More than half of the report's recommendations place the onus on universities to support their museum services but how realistic is it to expect universities to respond to this call when they have so many other demands upon their time and resources? Would one such report landing on the desk of a principal really be enough to change perceptions or should university museums adopt a more proactive approach to the problem? That is exactly what is happening at The Hunterian. It is rising to the challenges set by the university's *Global Vision* by embedding its activities within the heart of the university and realigning itself as a core service for the institution and for the wider community. The Hunterian's strategy and ambitious plans for collaborations in cultural engagement and lifelong learning within the city are the focus of this chapter.

The University of Glasgow and The Hunterian

> University museums make an important contribution both to the research and teaching goals of higher education and to the wider engagement of universities in the cultural life of the nation. (UMG, 2004: ii)

For such a small country Scotland has an extensive range of museums, galleries and historic buildings – more than 350 – run by national and local authorities, universities, the National Trust, Historic Scotland or independent organisations. It is estimated that they welcome 25 million visitors every year and boost Scotland's economy by around £800 million (MGS, 2011). Few cities in the UK are more engaged in the provision of cultural and lifelong learning opportunities than Glasgow. Designated 'European City of Culture' in 1990 and 'UK City of Architecture and Design' in 1999, it is home to the largest municipal museum service outside London and the most significant university museum in Scotland, The Hunterian. Almost three million visitors are welcomed into the city's museums every year, many of whom are unaware that Glasgow has another side to it: almost 30 per cent of its population experiences some of the worst levels of poverty, health and educational attainment in the UK (O'Neill, 2007: 381). The local authority, under the auspices of Glasgow Life, is addressing these problems in part through its support for museums and lifelong learning initiatives as agents for social change. Adult education provision is also offered through local colleges, the University of Glasgow and Strathclyde University.

The University of Glasgow is the fourth oldest in the UK, having been founded in 1451 to make 'the minds of men illuminated, and their understandings enlightened'.[2] 'Men' here is important, as no women attended, nor quite possibly were they expected to. A member of the Russell Group of leading UK research universities and a founder member of Universitas 21, the university was listed 102 in the world university rankings in 2012, up 26 places from 2010–11. The university receives its main financial support from the Scottish Funding Council as well as income generated from its tuition fees and research grants. At a time of economic recession and squeezed budgets, added pressures are coming from the Research Excellence Framework, the system for assessing the quality of research produced in UK higher education institutions, which is due to be completed in 2014. The assessment outcomes will be used to inform the allocation of research funding from 2015–16. Like so many of the top-ranked world universities, including Harvard, Oxford and Cambridge, it is served by a museum, The Hunterian, and by an adult education unit, the Centre for Open Studies.

Scotland's university museum network is small in comparison to its metropolitan museums but its collections are substantial, totalling more than 1.8 million items and including '32% of Scotland's science history, 31% of its coins and medals, 24% of its fine art, 20% of its natural science and 18% of its world culture' (UMIS, 2011). The Hunterian is by far the largest of these museums. It was founded during the Age of the Scottish Enlightenment through the bequest of the celebrated anatomist and 'man-midwife' Dr William Hunter (1718–83). His extensive collection of 'precious and rare objects' – works of art, medical and scientific material, numismatics and medieval manuscripts – was an extraordinary 'cabinet of curiosities' that was 'a centre of instruction and enlightenment' (Vicq d'Azyr, 1805, quoted in Black, 2007: 168). In 1783 Hunter bequeathed his private collection to his *alma mater*, the University of Glasgow, to be used in a way 'most fit and most conducive to the Improvement of the Students'.[3] When it opened in 1807, The Hunterian was Scotland's first public museum and the third oldest in the UK, after the Ashmolean in Oxford and the British Museum.

The Hunterian's holdings have continued to expand and its 1.3 million objects are currently scattered over four separate sites on campus: the museum with its medical, scientific, historical and numismatic collections; the art gallery, in a venue purpose-built in 1980, with works by J.A.M. Whistler (1834–1903) and a partial reconstruction of the home of Charles Rennie Mackintosh (1868–1928); the zoology museum; and a small anatomy museum. Core funding comes from the Scottish Funding Council (50%) and from the university (50%), supplemented by successful grant applications. In 2007 the entire collection was recognised as a Collection of National Significance by the Scottish government (Scottish Government, 2007). Part of University Services, The Hunterian has around 50 curatorial, education, support, technical and front-of-house staff. Closure of the main hall due to major roof repairs in 2009 led to reduced attendance figures: in 2009–10 The Hunterian attracted 162,000 visitors including 6,200 schoolchildren for educational classes and had 182,000 visits to its website (Hunterian, 2010: 14).

The Hunterian has found itself walking on a tightrope above a chasm of economic downturn, funding cuts and shifting university strategies. Balancing on one hand the need to address the university's new key objectives, it is also required to meet the Scottish Funding Council's performance targets for high-quality collections care and management, teaching and learning provision for the research and wider higher education community, as well as widening participation activities. So how is The Hunterian responding to such challenges? In 2008, as a result of an internal review, the museum had already begun to reflect upon its future development. The arrival of a new director, Professor David Gaimster, in September 2010 offered an opportunity to re-evaluate The Hunterian's purpose and direction. Spurred on by the university's *Global Vision*, since 2011 The Hunterian's strategy has become more clearly defined and targets have been set for the next few years. Rather than attempting to be a museum service providing 'all things to all men', it is instead focusing upon enhancing its reputation as an internationally leading university museum, addressing the needs of its academic community and committed to the university's research agenda. What once may have been perceived by some as marginal or adjunct to the university's activities is rapidly becoming a central and essential part of its new strategic vision. This is indeed a remarkable turnaround for The Hunterian in only one year.

The Hunterian: realignment from the margins

It is clear that a close alignment of the university museum with the mission of the university offers the greatest likelihood of museums realising their true potential. Fully integrated within the university's strategic planning, the university museum can earn recognition and support as an academic and public institution of unique value, as an irreplaceable repository of knowledge and skills, and as the custodian of material culture of national and international significance. (UMG, 2004: vi)

In 2004 the influential University Museums Group UK published its report, *University Museums in the United Kingdom: A National Resource in the 21st Century*. This advocacy document summarises the diverse activities of university museums, showcases examples of best practice (The Hunterian is mentioned several times in this respect) and calls for greater recognition from their parent institutions. The Hunterian's new plan addresses many of the report's recommendations. Its mission is 'to care for and develop' its collections (a primary task for museums) and 'to share and communicate' its knowledge of them (Hunterian, 2011a: 5). Like so many museums it has to balance curatorial responsibilities with duties as a service provider. Its stated 'vision' is to become 'a facilitator and contributor to the research and learning objectives of the University of Glasgow' and 'a cultural asset with national and international reach' (Hunterian, 2011a: 5). Curatorial staff are not just 'facilitators' for research but rather 'equals' to other academics through their own research contribution. The diversity of The Hunterian's art and science collections is one of its greatest strengths, permitting focused research for the traditional disciplines such as history of art, archaeology, medicine, Egyptology and natural history; but its diversity also lends itself to cross-disciplinary study, a field of enquiry promoted as a key component of the university's strategy. By building closer links with staff in subject-related areas, The Hunterian is making its collections more relevant to the academic disciplines, and stimulating collections-based research.

In line with the university's strategy for providing an excellent student experience, The Hunterian is working with the internal colleges to develop its offer for the undergraduate and postgraduate student community. It is facilitating collections-based experiential learning, taking a lead role in the Museums Studies MSc through the expertise of its staff and the provision of innovative work-related and volunteering opportunities. The College of Arts and The Hunterian are piloting a postgraduate research programme for public engagement in which students become museum 'associates' and contribute to its public programme. Projects with the School of Education will allow postgraduate trainee teachers to engage in voluntary subject-specific sessions in schools. Another development is the involvement of student volunteers in the MUSE (Museum University Student Educators) programme offering free daily guided tours to highlights of the collection. A Student Engagement Officer is coordinating student participation in the museum's activities. The Hunterian's status as a Collection of National Significance already serves the university's ambition to extend its global reach and reputation. Its displays and activities are being designed to create a culturally diverse learning experience and it provides learning placements for the international student community. Curators are developing international partnerships by collaborating on major exhibitions and projects. Further, by hosting the University Museums in Scotland conference in October 2011 The Hunterian has taken a leading role in shaping future museum policy and practice in the UK.

The Hunterian: engaging with the wider community

[University museums] are superb vehicles for widening participation in higher education, for engaging the public in the importance of research, and more generally for opening up the universities to the community. (Higher Education Funding Council for England, 2011: 2)

Many of the developments identified in The Hunterian's plan are designed for the benefit not only of its academic community but also of the wider public. Improving visitor experience and understanding of the collections through the development of its permanent galleries, temporary exhibitions and engagement in learning is an important objective. Publicity information and accessibility to the various collections is being improved by the extension of weekend opening times; until recently the museum was closed on Sundays, one of the busiest days for its close neighbour, Kelvingrove Art Gallery. Virtual access to the collections for research and learning has also been developed through enhanced digital resources. The Hunterian has collaborated on *Revealing the Hidden Collections*, a University Museums in Scotland partnership project that offers an online portal to their entire collections (UMIS, 2011).

The Hunterian has sought external funding for major projects, extending and upgrading its display areas such as the Kelvin Gallery, now a modern exhibition and conference space within the museum. In 2011 the zoology museum storage facilities were installed to allow better access for students and researchers; the art gallery reopened in September 2012 following major refurbishment. Displays focus on the strengths of the collections and use different interpretative approaches. *Lord Kelvin: Revolutionary Scientist* incorporates hands-on activities to engage a non-specialist audience, appropriate for an exhibition focused upon a man whose achievements were the result of practical experimentation. By contrast, a new permanent gallery, *The Antonine Wall: Rome's Final Frontier*, highlights The Hunterian's spectacular collection of Roman monumental distance slabs and artefacts without the use of any interactive technology – 'no gimmicks, just the living stone' (Higgins, 2011: 5). The Hunterian adopts two approaches to museum displays: the 'aesthetic' – the lighting of objects and use of imagery is visually stunning – and the 'educational' – its informative (but not intrusive) text panels and labelling provide the historical and social narrative for the objects (Duncan, 1995). Hooper-Greenhill (1999: x) notes that education in museums 'is rarely about conveying factual information [which] can be done elsewhere in a more competent way'; instead it has 'moved more firmly from the transmission of information to the enabling of the construction of personal relevance'. It has been argued that a model of learning and cultural engagement 'based on dissemination of the knowledge of experts ... goes against fostering participation in cultural activities' (Barr, 2005: 105) and 'leaves little room for critical or social reflection as it cements notions of expertise' (Clover et al., 2010: 9). But in today's world, need they be mutually exclusive? A prime function of university museums is to facilitate access to the expertise of scholars and staff; exhibitions are powerful vehicles for this. The sensitive use of displays as educational 'tools' can be directed towards facilitating self-learning, challenging perceptions and stimulating critical engagement for a wide range of visitors.

The Hunterian's research-led special exhibition programme is now timed to map on to the university's teaching calendar (Hunterian, 2011b: 19). Exhibitions capture themes that can be exploited for academic teaching but at the same time are designed to have wider public appeal. A cultural engagement programme involving contributions from other sections of the university is planned around each exhibition. For *Colour, Rhythm and Form: J.D. Fergusson and France*, the offer included public lunchtime talks, children's art activities, a research forum for College of Arts postgraduate students, an art history public lecture, and a public symposium involving cross-disciplinary themes delivered through the Centre for Open Studies.

The development of new audiences is key to The Hunterian's strategy. Autumn 2011 saw the launch of The Hunterian Friends scheme directed at alumni and the general public and offering enhanced opportunities for engagement directly with staff and collections. In the past it has run very successful, innovative outreach initiatives with young people – with a grant from BBC Children in Need in 2009, staff developed the *Touching Lives* project which involved children with vision impairment and their sighted peers visiting and engaging with the collections (Hunterian, 2010: 12). It is also a key coordinator of Glasgow's annual Science Festival, more than two weeks of science-inspired events, demonstrations and exhibitions held throughout the city. In one respect, however, its community reach is being lessened by the withdrawal of its schools provision; UCL has also recently adopted this strategy. School groups will continue to be made welcome in the museum but their visits will be led by the teacher rather than by museum staff. The Hunterian defends the decision by pointing out that its provision was directly overlapping that offered by Glasgow Museums; with such limited resources, all its expertise and energies are being channelled into serving its university community. In real terms, however, such a decision means that fewer schoolchildren will be introduced to its collections and its 'elitist' status will only be reinforced.

The Centre for Open Studies and lifelong learning opportunities

> For adult learners, university museums are well placed to stimulate new areas of interest through liaison with their university's Extra-Mural or Continuing Education Department. (UMG, 2004: iv)

The Hunterian is also forming partnerships with other education providers, the university's Centre for Open Studies for lifelong learners and Glasgow Museums' for visitors of all ages, tapping into their expertise and market. University museums and adult education units are natural allies in lifelong learning and cultural engagement but they have not always taken full advantage of each other's resources. This is now changing in Glasgow. In the eighteenth century University of Glasgow professors such as Francis Hutcheson and John Anderson provided free lectures for the general public (Hamilton and Slowey, 2005: 12–13). The concept of public engagement within the university became linked to a wider 'democratic ideal of education' in Scotland that stimulated 'a thirst and demand for education in adulthood' (Hamilton and Slowey, 2005: 12). From the early nineteenth century organisations such as the Association for Procuring Instruction in Useful and Entertaining Sciences and the Mechanics' Institutes flourished throughout Britain, often attracting audiences of hundreds (Cooter, 1984: 149–50). The university's commitment to adult education was formalised in 1951 through its Department of Extra-Mural Education (now known as the Centre for Open Studies), the largest such unit in Scotland. Most of the UK's Russell Group universities are also committed to adult education initiatives (Open Programme, 2011: 7).

A core activity for the Centre for Open Studies is the Open Programme of courses for adults. Led by academic subject specialists, administrative and support staff as well as 200 part-time academic tutors, it provides lifelong learning opportunities in Glasgow and the west of Scotland. Its annual programme of over 400 courses and special events covers diverse interests from Egyptology and history of art to languages, music, literature, astronomy and biology. Closely linked to this is the Access Programme. It provides an introduction to university study for mature students who have no previous qualifications or whose qualifications are now out of date. During session 2010–11, the Open Programme attracted more than 4,200 students and 6,000 enrolments – some students enrol on more than one course (Open Programme, 2011: 2). One-third of students receive the Scottish government's Independent Learning Account award which contributes £200 to the cost of learning of any individual on a low income. Outreach courses off campus support specific widening participation initiatives organised in partnership with local councils and community organisations, and are targeted at socially excluded groups.

Like The Hunterian, the Centre for Open Studies is having to consider its contribution to the university's *Global Vision*. Since 2012 the Centre has been reviewing its strategies. It would do well to reflect on the plan adopted by The Hunterian to increase its 'visibility', realign its activities and strengthen its ties within the institution. The Centre's subject specialists contribute to research excellence through their publications and through participation in national and international projects on lifelong learning and in their own subject-specific areas. Its Open Programme achieves the highest levels of student satisfaction every year for content and delivery of courses, thereby meeting the university's drive for excellent student experience. The subject of a consultation exercise in 2010, the Centre's Open Programme emerged with an acknowledgement of its contribution to the 'personal and professional development of the community', its role as 'a key mechanism' for the university's wider engagement, and its 'positive impact on the intellectual, social and cultural life' of Glasgow (Open Programme, 2011: 7).

The Centre's new strategy involves strengthening links with the university's colleges and schools, running a Summer School in 2012 and taking the lead on high-profile public lectures and events. It is also making a more significant contribution to The Hunterian's educational provision. The Centre has delivered history of art, practical art, Egyptology and biology courses, teaching directly in front of the collections and handling museum objects to enhance the student experience. By extending that offer, the Centre for Open Studies can provide a continually fresh and vibrant programme that reaches target audiences and brings benefits to all concerned. It can contribute to cross-disciplinary events by pulling together expertise from its own tutors and other academic experts, and through its many contacts with community groups it can help to disseminate knowledge of, and stimulate wider public engagement in, The Hunterian's collections.

Glasgow Museums: agents of social change

As the loci for two-way exchange between a university and its locality, museums bring tremendous potential for partnership with regional agencies and local businesses. A strong and long-term relationship between a university and its region on the one hand, and on the other a positive attitude to experimentation and personal development can also stimulate exceptional urban regeneration initiatives. (UMG, 2004: 20)

The Hunterian is developing much stronger ties with Glasgow Museums. Their strategic objectives and provision for cultural engagement and lifelong learning – one university-led, the other driven by local authority agendas – make for interesting comparisons. Glasgow's municipal museum began in 1854 when town councillor Archibald McLellan bequeathed his magnificent art collection and a suite of galleries to the citizens of Glasgow. Kelvingrove, Glasgow's most popular museum, was opened in 1901 in the city's west end. Run by Glasgow Life, it is one of a network of museums (Glasgow Museums), including the Burrell Collection, Gallery of Modern Art, St Mungo Museum of Religious Life and Art, People's Palace, the Open Museum, Glasgow Museums Resource Centre and the Riverside Museum. There are 420 members of staff employed to look after its collection of 1.4 million objects; in 2010 the museums welcomed 2.5 million visitors (Kelvin Hall, 2011: 4). All the municipal museums are free to visit and most are open seven days a week. Glasgow Life's objective to create a culture of creativity and learning for everyone is met in part by its museum service, designed to act as 'an agent for social change' and 'a force for learning in the city' (Riverside Museum, 2004: 35). Glasgow Museums aim to 'provide a socially inclusive and stimulating museums and galleries service that addresses the barriers to access, connects with the lives of everyone and reflects the cultural and social diversity of the city' (Riverside Museum, 2005: 43).

Kelvingrove's £30 million refurbishment plans, begun in 1990, took sixteen years to complete; during that time extensive consultation with visitors, education, community and disability groups was undertaken. The project's strategic objective was to create a narrative-based museum with as wide a visitor appeal as possible (O'Neill, 2007: 385). Reflecting upon the 'deep sense of ownership by

Glaswegians of their museums in general and in Kelvingrove in particular', Mark O'Neill, Kelvingrove's director at that time, adopted a radical strategy for creating the new displays (O'Neill, 2007: 380). This involved discussions with a range of stakeholders to 'break down the barriers to museum visiting', the inclusion of 'hidden and neglected histories, especially of excluded groups', the introduction of 'difficult' themes to challenge 'prejudices and negative heritage', and ways to engage with 'the most deprived and excluded even in the most prestigious sites of civic pride' (O'Neill, 2007: 395). Using prime objects from the collection, 100 'stories' are located throughout the building, but with minimal information so as to allow individual visitors to construct 'their own particular interpretation of their educational experiences, according to their existing knowledge, skills, background and personal motivation' (Hooper-Greenhill, 1999: xi). Closed in 2003 for refurbishment, Kelvingrove reopened in 2006 and welcomed more than three million visitors in its first year.

A key policy objective for Glasgow Museums is to meet the needs of diverse audiences and provide activities and learning opportunities, both formal and informal, for its visitors. The needs of those lifelong learners with specialist interest in the collections are acknowledged through a variety of channels: the well-established support organisation, Friends of Glasgow Museums, has more than 1,800 adult members who benefit from special programmes of tours, talks and events; opportunities for volunteer guiding (and training) and working along-side curatorial staff to develop collections research; and access to resource facili-ties for individual researchers. In 2009–10, a total of 381 volunteers contributed 42,269 hours of service in Glasgow Museums (Kelvin Hall, 2011: 4).

Glasgow Museums' outreach service, based at the Open Museum, has been parti-cularly creative in extending its 'arena for learning' to 'care homes, community centres, children's centres, hospitals, libraries and prisons' and using its collections 'through collaborative projects, loans kits, travelling exhibitions, community museums' (Lane, 2011). *The Gardener's Ark*, a 2010–11 collaborative project with Community Learning, Occupational Therapy and Acorn Project, involved adult learners from the city's Leverndale Hospital who created a plant-filled boat inspired by Glasgow's art collections. Combining art, writing and gardening skills, the *Ark* has been displayed in various city venues. Another partnership involving the Scottish Prison Service, Carnegie College and Scottish Book Trust resulted in the publica-tion of a leaflet, *The Alternative Guide to Glasgow* – 'a tourist-style map with a twist' – produced by long-term male prisoners at HMP Glenochil (Glasgow Life, 2011a).

The philosophy behind the Riverside Museum showcasing Glasgow's rich industrial and transport heritage, which has proved so popular since its opening in June 2011 (800,000 visitors in its first 14 weeks), is to 'create displays which connect with people's lives and that allow visitors to make links and perceive inter-relationships between diverse groups of objects' (Riverside Museum, 2004: 5). The museum uses key items, including giant locomotives, to tell around 150 'stories', each with an interpretation focused on one of five target groups: under 5s, schools, teenagers, families with children and the sensory impaired. Adult educa-tion provision within the museum is offered through different modes of presentation: labelling, multimedia, interactive and live interpretation, guided tours and a lifelong learning library facility. The Riverside's Learning and Access team is involved in several local Clydeside initiatives, one supporting apprenticeships at Rolls Royce and another developing shipbuilding industry projects with BAE Systems (Glasgow Life, 2011b: 16). Such collaborations are not simply 'bolting on education as an optional extra' to museum objectives; rather, they offer a 'slow, sustained approach to social inclusion which is committed to finding new ways to work with people and the objects which they as citizens own' (Barr, 2005: 107).

Glasgow Museums and The Hunterian are also collaborating on a major initiative involving the regeneration of the Kelvin Hall in Glasgow to provide shared state-of-the-art museum storage facilities and resources. The main objectives are to promote knowledge and use of their shared collections, widen access, provide a shared physical centre for collections research and learning and create a shared online portal for accessing both collections (McAdam, 2011; Gaimster, 2011). The university's Centre for Open Studies would facilitate community engagement by developing collections-based courses and maximising lifelong learning opportunities for the public. The project has the potential to enhance research activity, cultural engagement and lifelong learning in a way that will impact on the lives of so many both in Glasgow and beyond. In January 2012 the funding application for £4.83 million to the Heritage Lottery Fund received first-stage approval. If the project succeeds in its second-round application, due to be submitted in early 2013, and full funding is awarded, the results could be truly breathtaking.

Conclusion

> The full cultural value of a museum or collection resides not only in its intrinsic significance, but also in the benefits of the activities developed around it. Consequently, what university museums do is as important as what they have. (UMG, 2004: 8)

Even so prestigious a university museum as The Hunterian, with its wealth of collections and reputation for excellence, is not immune to the changing strategies of its parent institution. Having to justify its relevance to the university's core mission and examine its strategic fit has been a challenging exercise but one that has led to a better understanding of the strengths and weaknesses of its educational provision. Its strategy to strengthen ties with internal colleges, develop research and learning initiatives, and promote itself as a gateway for cultural engagement with the wider community may help to secure its future. For many university museums their collections can be promoted as invaluable resources for collaborative and interdisciplinary research initiatives. It is their potential to be flexible, creative and experimental in their approach that makes their contribution to a university's 'vision' unique and allows them to adapt to constantly changing strategies. With its links to other learning providers such as the Centre for Open Studies and Glasgow Museums, The Hunterian can provide a much more effective service to the university and the wider community. The museum has learned much from the exercise, not least that collaboration may be the key to success and a more secure future.

References

Anderson, D. (1999), *A Common Wealth: Museums in the Learning Age*, Norwich: Department for Culture, Media and Sport.

Barr, J. (2005), "'Dumbing down intellectual culture": Frank Furedi, lifelong learning and museums', *Museum and Society*, 3(2): 98–114.

Black, P. (ed.) (2007), *"My Highest Pleasures"*, London: The Hunterian and Paul Holberton Publishing.

Clover, D.E., Sanford, K., and Jayme, B.D.O. (2010), 'Adult education and lifelong learning in arts and cultural institutions: a context analysis', *Journal of Adult and Continuing Education*, 16(2): 5–20.

Cooter, R. (1984), *The Cultural Meaning of Popular Science*, Cambridge: Cambridge University Press.

Crook, J.M. (1972), *The British Museum*, London: Allen Lane, The Penguin Press.

Duncan, C. (1995), *Civilizing Rituals: Inside Public Art Museums*, London and New York: Routledge.

Fitzwilliam Museum (2011), 'History of the Fitzwilliam Museum', www.fitzmuseum.cam.ac.uk/about/museumhistory.html (accessed 28 September 2011).

Gaimster, D. (2011), 'Development of Kelvin Hall Project Notes', unpublished, The Hunterian, University of Glasgow.

University of Glasgow (2010), *Glasgow 2020 – A Global Vision*, Glasgow: University of Glasgow.

Glasgow Life (2011a), *The Open Museum*, www.glasgowlife.org.uk/museums/our-museums/open-museum/about-the-Open Museum/Pages/home.aspx (accessed 15 October 2011).

Glasgow Life (2011b), 'Glasgow Life Annual Review 2010/11', unpublished, Glasgow Life, Glasgow.

Hamilton, R., and Slowey, M. (2005), *The Story of DACE*, Glasgow: University of Glasgow.

Hein, G. (1998), *Learning in the Museum*, London: Routledge.

Higgins, C. (2011), 'The Antonine Wall sculptures at the Hunterian Museum', *The Guardian*, www.guardian.co.uk/culture/charlottehigginsblog/2011/sep/21/museums-roman-britain (accessed 21 September 2011).

Higher Education Funding Council for England (2011), *Briefing on University Museums and Galleries*, www.umg.org.uk/wp-content/uploads/2011/05/Briefing-on-University-Museums-and-Galleries-May-2011.pdf (accessed 2 October 2011).

Hooper-Greenhill, E. (1999), *The Educational Role of the Museum*, London: Routledge.

The Hunterian (2010), *The Hunterian Impact Report 2009/10*, University of Glasgow, www.gla.ac.uk/media/media_207206_en.pdf (accessed 2 October 2011).

The Hunterian (2011a), 'The Hunterian Draft Forward Plan 2011–12 and onwards', University of Glasgow, unpublished.

The Hunterian (2011b), 'The Hunterian Outline Strategic Development Plan', unpublished, The Hunterian, University of Glasgow.

Kelvin Hall (2011), 'Application Draft', unpublished, Glasgow Life, Glasgow.

Lane, J. (2011), 'Glasgow Museums/Glasgow Life: a learning institution and an agent of social change?', Glasgow Stimulus Paper, Pascal International Exchanges, pie.pascalobservatory.org/pascalnow/blogentry/pie/glasgow-stimulus-paper (accessed 14 October 2011).

McAdam, E. (2011), 'Finding new friends: collaboration between Glasgow Museums and the University of Glasgow', UMIS conference paper, unpublished, Glasgow Life, Glasgow.

MGS (Museums Galleries Scotland) (2011), www.museumsgalleriesscotland.org.uk (accessed 4 October 2011).

O'Neill, M. (2007), 'Kelvingrove: telling stories in a treasured old/new museum', *Curator*, 50(4): 379–99.

Open Programme (2011), 'Academic Shape Consultation, 2011', unpublished, Centre for Open Studies, University of Glasgow.

Riverside Museum (2004), 'Audience Development Plan', unpublished, Riverside Museum, Glasgow.

Riverside Museum (2005), 'Business Plan', unpublished, Riverside Museum, Glasgow.

Roberts, L.C. (1997), *From Knowledge to Narrative: Educators and the Changing Museum*, Washington, DC, and London: Smithsonian Institution Press.

Scottish Government (2007), 'Recognising collections of national significance', www. scotland.gov.uk/News/Releases/2007/06/25102143 (accessed 7 October 2011).

UMG (University Museums Group UK) (2004), *University Museums in the United Kingdom: A National Resource in the 21st Century*, umg.web.its.manchester.ac.uk/wp-content/uploads/2010/03/UMG_Advocacy.pdf (accessed 2 October 2011).

UMIS (University Museums in Scotland) (2011), *Revealing the Hidden Collections*, Aberdeen: UMIS.

Notes

1 This research has been made possible by the generosity of Professor David Gaimster, director of The Hunterian and Ellen McAdam, director of Glasgow Museums, who gave of their time and expertise and allowed me access to their strategic plans. I would also like to thank Lawrence Fitzgerald, Rachel Lees, Mark O'Neill and Peter Black.

2 Papal Bull, 7 January 1451, GU Special Collections, University of Glasgow.

3 'Will of William Hunter, Doctor in Physick of Windmill Street, Westminster, Middlesex, 4 April 1783', PROB. 11/1102, The National Archives, Kew.

11

Empowering literary educators and learners in Northern Ireland: university–community engagement for peace

Rob Mark

Not all issues are amenable to resolution through rational discourse. (Welton, 1995: 35)

This chapter illustrates how a university–community partnership incorporated creative, non-text-based approaches into adult literacy work to contribute to the efforts towards creating greater equality and peacebuilding in Northern Ireland. The university–community partnership, known as the Literacy and Equality in Irish Society project (LEIS), was based on the fundamental belief that low levels of literacy among adults was one factor contributing to inequalities and violence in Irish society and, therefore, that literacy practice had to be re-contextualised within an equality and peacebuilding agenda. The project aimed to explore how more creative approaches to literacy practice could assist literacy educators and learners to explore more deeply and provocatively the inequalities and mistrust perpetuated in Northern Irish society that negatively affect people's lives. As arts-based adult educators around the world have argued, the arts – and I will refer to these as creative methodologies or practices – are powerful means to deal with embedded, problematic cultural, political, social and/or religious beliefs. They can also provide imaginative and creative alternatives to normative literacy approaches that often simply revolve around reading print texts. I would argue that, in the case of Northern Ireland, to be even more effective literacy educators should understand and learn to use these new methods.

I begin this chapter with a brief background of the context of Northern Ireland. This discussion is by no means exhaustive, nor does it capture all the complexity of Northern Ireland's recent conflict or 'the Troubles', as they are most often referred to. What it does do, however, is to provide a snapshot of the fragile context in which literacy practitioners and their academic partners are engaging with a post-conflict situation. Following this, I provide a description of the LEIS project, locating myself in this work and discussing in more detail the nature of the community–university partnership. From there, I provide an example of how a particular arts-based methodology was used and, by examining the comments of the various people involved, show how these new approaches to literacy learning helped them locate themselves in the conflict. Although not without their challenges, I argue that these methodologies provided new ways for expressing inner feelings and, in many ways, a much more creative, engaged and informed understanding of conflict and peacebuilding.

Peacebuilding in the Irish context

Northern Ireland's conflict is a tangled web of interrelated questions around how social and economic inequalities – especially in the field of employment – can be tackled, religious and cultural differences accommodated/accepted, and diverse political aspirations understood and worked through in a deeply divided society. Darby (2003) noted four issues – politics, violence, community relations and inequality – as having become particularly intractable. As a result Northern Ireland, and indeed other parts of the islands of Ireland and Great Britain, have over the last three decades experienced rioting, street fighting and bombing between 'hostile' groups in various religious, cultural and political camps. These violent and deep-rooted confrontations became known as 'the Troubles'. The result of this protracted conflict is that many people have known little save violence and distrust, high levels of economic and social deprivation, restricted access to education and exclusion from any type of political system that they felt valued and respected who they were or their democratic freedom. But in the 1990s a peace process was ushered in, offering a new kind of environment in which these issues underlying the Troubles could be at least talked about if not yet fully addressed or acknowledged. Today, Irish society is involved in a process that is seeking to help people from all sides of the divide to live together through developing a shared understanding of each other's political, cultural, social and religious beliefs and building stronger cross-community cohesiveness. It concerns not only post-conflict reconstruction, but also prevention of the recurrence of violence and assistance with the transition from conflict to a self-sustaining and durable peace.

This process is popularly known as 'peacebuilding', although there is in fact little agreement about what that term truly means. Common definitions associate it with strengthening the relations and positive patterns of engagement between individuals and groups (Hamber and Kelly, 2004). Given the grand scope of peacebuilding, it cannot be viewed as a mechanistic or short process but rather must be seen as a long and complex process that draws on a wide range of human capabilities and, in our case at the university, focuses on creating opportunities for education and learning. Lederach (2005) views peacebuilding as a way of envisioning new and dynamic patterns of relationships and developing new forms of engagement, as well as the courage to pursue the concretisation of a peaceful, caring vision of the world. It also speaks to what is possible in terms of the creation and recreation of human societies, and imagines new actions and ways of working together. Thus, while peacebuilding may emerge in reaction to a situation of (post-)conflict, as in the case of Northern Ireland, it seeks to be proactive in laying the foundations to prevent conflict in the future and in this sense, I would argue, it can be seen as an essential life skill. In workplaces, homes and communities, and in education and learning environments, the process of peacebuilding can play a role in transforming the present and moving people towards a future with greatly reduced incidences of conflict.

Peacebuilding scholars and practitioners recognise that a movement away from conflict, violence and inequality towards sustainable peace requires more than simply cognitive, rational engagement with ideas (Hamber and Kelly, 2004; Lederach, 1997). The understanding that peacebuilding transforms the cognitive domain of learning and affective modes of expression provide a reason for focusing on adult literacy education using alternative, creative, cultural methods.

In addition to the lack of understanding about the value of creative practice, there has also been little recognition of the relationship between peacebuilding and adult literacy vis-à-vis conflicts such as Northern Ireland. Indeed peacebuilding has not before been identified as part of the adult learning curriculum. In other words, the opportunity to connect adult literacy and peacebuilding to challenge the problems of a society so deeply divided by religion and politics, as well as class and gender, had not been previously realised.

The Literacy and Equality in Irish Society project

The LEIS project brought together a number of partners with an interest in literacy to experiment with some new creative/non-text methodologies. The two academic partners were University College, Dublin, a centre for research and teaching on equality, and the School of Education at Queen's University, Belfast, a provider of tutor training in adult literacy, which came together with literacy groups across the various communities. Together the partners pooled their skills and knowledge to improve educators' and learners' understandings about how better to learn about and from experiences of inequality in society and its negative effects on their own lives as well as lives of others as a contribution to the larger peacebuilding process in Northern Ireland. In addition to introducing and training educators to use various creative, non-text methods to engage the learners in a very different type of cross-cultural learning experience, the LEIS project included an action research component and in this chapter I draw on some of the findings of that collective process.

Each of the partners had a particular contribution to make. Queen's University possessed a well-developed understanding of the theoretical bases of adult literacy, equality and peace, as well as using creative and engaged arts-based adult education practices. Moreover, the university had a background of working with literacy educators through ongoing professional development programmes. Other community partners had a particular expertise in the more formal management and delivery of adult literacy programmes, placing them in a position to identify groups where teachers and learners were already working together across the 'troubled' divides within communities of Northern Ireland.

My own involvement in the project began with preparing and submitting the application for funding, and I was later a project coordinator. The project extended over a two-year period and employed three full-time staff (two development workers and a secretary). The work was supported through a management committee that included representatives from various providers including the Waterford Institute of Technology, a higher education institution involved with training teachers and the National Adult Literacy Agency for Ireland (NALA), an independent charity committed to making sure that people with literacy and numeracy difficulties can take part fully in society and have access to learning opportunities that meet their needs. The provision of financing from the European Union as well as the British and Irish governments' peace funding for Northern Ireland was also important in allowing ideas to be translated into practice. The partners worked together using their particular expertise to develop an ongoing dialogue about literacy and equality linked specifically to the peacebuilding process in Northern Ireland.

One way in which this was achieved was by bringing groups of students together, using a variety of creative practices, to discuss their feelings of disempowerment as a result of living and growing up in a conflict-ridden society where individuals had experienced inequalities as a result of their religion, class and/or gender. In our literacy work, we believed that creative arts could provide modes of expression that could go beyond words and give voice to deeply ingrained thoughts and feelings. But like various other scholars such as Clover and Stalker (2007) we too believe that arts-based practices are 'cognitive' practices, so we developed our creative methodologies to stimulate dialogue and critical discussion as well as to encourage the imagination and, in our case, the right to imagine a conflict-free world. This coming together of the rational, cognitive, spiritual, imaginative and affective arguably mirrors our real-life experiences.

The creative, non-text approaches used in the project included image theatre, visual arts, storytelling and music. The students shared their stories, visually creating, singing or performing lived, painful experiences of inequality in a creative journey of literacy development. These imaginative, non-text-based activities can be valuable processes in themselves that not only prepare individuals for reading and writing, but also make a real contribution to peacebuilding, as have others in other places. For example, Barefoot Artists is a non-profit organisation that works with poor, violence-ridden communities around the globe using the arts to bring healing, self-empowerment and social change in poor and marginalised communities. It aims to bring the transformative power of art to impoverished communities through participatory and multifaceted projects that foster community empowerment, improve the physical environment, promote economic development and preserve and promote indigenous art and culture. Their creative methodologies have been used not only to overcome violence but also to make the foundations stronger for a more lasting peace. Of course, not all art forms are benign, neutral or positive. Various walls across Dublin continue to carry large, full-colour murals that visually represent 'the Troubles' such as the face of a sniper whose ferocious gaze transfixes the children who play on the pavement below.

Literacy programmes in Ireland have a strong basis in text-based curricula that often focus on individual assessment of learners. It can be argued that this text-based approach with its narrow range of literacy skills does not promote equality. In contrast, Gardner's (1999) work on multiple intelligences acknowledges not only the importance of verbal/linguistic and logical/mathematical skills, but also the value of visual, musical and interpersonal skills in making sense of the lived world. Gardner's theories of multiple intelligences provide a more pluralistic picture of intelligences as well as a holistic approach to how humans learn. In addition,

Tisdell's (2003) work outlines the value and power of various symbol-making activities and the importance of these experiences through ongoing creative activities in the arts. Problematically, adult literacy education programmes – like much formal adult education – have most often been perceived as 'serious' spaces of learning and, as a consequence, many adults are unsure about their capacity to engage in creative practices and fear that enjoyment and play may not be effective means towards becoming literate. Indeed, during the development of the LEIS project, it became clear that in order to help adults learn from creative methods there would need to be an explicit emphasis on the value of creativity and imagination for their learning and their lives.

A further challenge in the LEIS project was to connect literacy discourse with an equality and peacebuilding discourse. Similar to the concept of peacebuilding, considerable controversy surrounds the meaning of literacy and how skills and competences can be developed (Crowther et al., 2001). How one defines literacy has implications for the development of literacy programmes including the content and approaches used for learning. Popular usage of the term literacy extends from the simple notion of the ability to read and write to a host of other ideas including the possession of complex multi-literacy skills which may include computer, technical, information, media, visual, cultural, financial, economic, emotional and environmental skills. Moreover, a review of the literature shows that there is no single universally effective or culturally appropriate way of teaching or defining literacy. Rather, definitions of literacy are viewed as a function of social, cultural and economic conditions with different discourses becoming dominant at different times and in different places. Writing about the meaning of literacy Crowther, Hamilton and Tett note:

> Definitions of what it means to be literate are always shifting. It is socially constructed and cannot be seen outside of the interests and powerful forces that seek to fix it in a particular way. The common way to think about literacy at the moment is by seeing it as a ladder that people have to climb up. (2001: 1–2)

Our project took the view that literacy is about acquiring a set of complex capabilities rather than a simple set of basic skills or a ladder to climb, and that literacy is a key dimension of learning for community regeneration. Fundamental to the project was the idea that adult literacy is an equality issue often linked to traditional issues such as religion, class and gender in Northern Ireland and that these divisions in society are a manifestation of inequalities that can contribute to the cause of illiteracy. There has been a radical rethink of the need to confront issues of illiteracy in national policies, which now recognise the importance of improving literacy for citizens who wish to actively participate in modern, industrial, democratic societies. However, while there is almost complete acceptance that literacy has a profound impact on life chances around the world, there is somewhat less agreement on how adult literacy learning should be developed. Freire and Macedo (1987: 6) argue that ideology, culture and power can limit, disorganise and marginalise more critical and everyday life experiences. They emphasise the need to move towards an understanding of literacy that encourages individuals' critical thinking about the conditions of their lives. So, as an integral part of the equality agenda, the development of literacy becomes an important tool in the construction of a more just and equal society.

Paulo Freire placed an emphasis on the arts in his teaching and work. He believed that adults could learn to read rapidly if reading were not part of a cultural imposition. Moreover, adults speak an extraordinarily rich and complex language that they can set down graphically with the proper tools to do so. In one particular example, Freire realised that many Brazilian non-literates were so submerged in their daily struggles that they had little or no awareness of whether or how they could change their lives. During literacy classes, they resisted being told they had problems, choosing to believe instead that these were conditions of fate. In order to transform this debilitating notion of powerlessness to change their circumstances, Freire introduced the concept of culture. He used a series of images of their lives drawn by a local artist to stimulate very different ways of seeing culture and talking about culture. He believed that 'images or theatre or songs or any cultural expression could serve as codes representing a common social reality and could be engaged or decoded by learners to deepen their critical consciousness of [their] situation' (Barndt, 2011: 11). Boal (1979), also from Brazil, developed a process that he called Theatre of the Oppressed. Using image theatre, he helped students to articulate their experiences of specific inequalities and oppressions including situations of conflict in everyday life and in the community. In particular, this form of interactive theatre aims to illuminate and challenge racial and class inequality.

LEIS set out to develop clearer links between an understanding of equality and practical approaches to reconciliation using creative methodologies. To do this, it applied an equality framework developed by Baker, Lynch and Cantillon (2004). The project focused on four interrelated dimensions of their equality framework: respect and recognition; love, care and solidarity; access to resources; and power relations. These dimensions provided an opportunity to look at the economic, political and cultural dimensions of inequality as well as how the affective or emotional realm affects learning.

Universities and tutor training

The first step of the project was to focus on and train the tutors. Considerable responsibility is placed in the hands of tutors in Northern Ireland who are charged with the development of literacy skills and competences across communities. Moreover, while literacy tutors may work with some of the most marginalised groups in society, educational training programmes for them have not tended to focus on promoting and understanding these inequalities and how the curriculum might assist learners to learn from their inequitable experiences. Neither have they focused on the development of an understanding of peacebuilding and how this connects with literacy learning. For these reasons, the two universities proved to be excellent partners for the LEIS project. Queen's University, Belfast, is a major provider of training programmes for teachers of adults that included a series of initial and continuing professional development courses in literacy and numeracy. In addition, it had already developed a number of programmes for teachers of literacy that included various arts-based approaches. The Equality Studies Centre at University College, Dublin, had an interdisciplinary understanding of equality supported by ongoing research into connections between literacy, equality and peacebuilding. Their work is based on Freire's principles of emancipatory literacy, grounded in the everyday life situations of learners and woven into this fabric of creative practices. It was imperative to instil into the LEIS tutors a full understanding of how inequalities adversely affect individual lives and for them to learn how to apply the equality model with a variety of new and creative teaching tools.

Over a period of three years, 125 people attended short training courses organised in seven different locations in Northern Ireland through the university and college. The programme included seven continuing professional development courses each lasting ten hours and a further five courses in which training was part of an initial and ongoing professional development course for adult literacy tutors and managers. Some of the courses included community activists and literacy volunteer tutors lacking formal education and training. Most of the courses were offered as accredited courses and 107 individuals were awarded accreditation. The focus groups and seminars emphasised the need for support materials and resources for tutors and learners.

Specialist creative learning methodologists were engaged to develop training in the use of creative/non-text methodology using drama, image theatre, storytelling and music. The expectation was that, after experiencing and learning from the methodologies and equality framework, tutors could then use the innovative methods to engage with and empower marginalised literacy learners from across the divide in Northern Ireland. From these experiences, a resource guide was developed. This guide sets out a rationale and includes project aims as well as discussion of the equality framework and methodologies employed with practical examples of how to use the methodologies (Lambe et al., 2006). Many of the tutors who attended the workshops were already teaching in a variety of community contexts and following the training were able to try out some of the new methodologies.

Using creative methodologies

The LEIS project used creative/non-text-based methodologies to create spaces for the exploration of equality issues in learners' lives. The methodologies were also intended to empower tutors and learners to discuss issues arising from their experiences of conflict in Ireland.

Storytelling is one example of a creative method that can empower learners to understand experiences of inequality in their lives and the lives of others. Individuals are asked to share stories from the past that highlight experiences of exclusion, particularly those referring to inequalities experienced as a result of the conflict situation. Very often these experiences had never before been spoken about and the need for unconditional acceptance and confidentiality within the group was discussed and agreed on in advance in our work. Group members are encouraged to think about real-life stories, both recent and in the distant past. Some examples of stories were also given to assist individuals when selecting and preparing their stories. The range of examples is endless and can include both large events in people's lives, such as attending court, dealing with the impact of a shooting incident or the effect of a bomb explosion, and everyday issues such as not being able to travel to school or to visit a family member on the other side of the divide.

Individuals are placed in small groups of four to six and provided with instructions on how to prepare and present their stories. Before the stories are told the group members are given guidance on how to select their story, what bits of the story to tell, what to leave for discussion later, how to present their story and to link it to their experience of exclusion, and how to listen and respond to stories. After the stories are told the group is given the opportunity to respond and to share similar experiences. Time is always given for consideration of what could be learned from the stories and what might be done differently in the future.

Impact of methodologies on individuals

A variety of responses to the positive but also the sometimes negative impacts of the work were recorded and I share just a few here. One tutor commented on how attending the storytelling sessions had helped her develop skills and knowledge about new approaches to learning and how these could be used to facilitate understanding about the causes and consequences of conflict. Through the use of stories her students had talked to her and in the group about real-life experiences of unemployment, alienation and isolation. This led to a group discussion on issues such as the effect of unemployment on people of all religions, class and gender that united as well as divided individuals; many said it had enabled them to develop an understanding and empathy for other points of view. The creative/non-text approaches enabled them to discuss issues in more interesting ways. Storytelling, for example, enabled the issues to be linked more closely to real-life situations; the use of art, sculpture and drama allowed for different ways of representing experiences that often engendered feelings of hurt and shame because the individual lacked confidence to put feelings into words. These strategies were also seen as a more appealing way of engaging others and as a way of provoking discussion. A range of other skills that included bonding, inclusivity, working in groups and ability to empathise with others' experiences of different situations were mentioned as spinoffs from being involved.

Another tutor who taught on a literacy programme for young men took along a sculpture of a man whose head was bowed. She had made it especially to discuss with the group. She believed that it was a good stimulus to discussion about guilt and wrongdoing as she was sharing her own feelings and thoughts with the group in a very open way. She felt that having a concrete object made it easier to raise more complex issues about equality that were generally hard to introduce in other types of discussion. It was a good stimulus to get the group thinking, rather than asking the group to write down their thoughts, a strategy she felt would not have worked as it would have limited their thinking simply to something they could write. Commenting on the use of sculpture to explore inequalities, the tutor noted:

> In the course I met with people from lots of different areas. I felt worried about making a sculpture about peace because I'm not artistic and I didn't want to expose myself in front of strangers. Anyway we worked in groups and it was great because doing it together led to lots of discussion. We found that what we made together was much more interesting than what we could have made on our own. When everybody talked about what their sculpture represented, you got right to the heart of things because it was a safe space and we were all able to speak honestly.

To my mind, this comment demonstrates how creative arts act as a stimulant and encourage individuals to open up and express their feelings on a range of topics which otherwise might be difficult to express. It indeed demonstrates how art can be used to share views, ideas and feelings and to build a sense of cohesiveness or community. This may be particularly relevant for men of all ages who are very often unwilling, as a result of habits of socialisation and 'manliness', to express their feelings at all, particularly within group situations.

Another tutor working in a rural setting used a collage to encourage students to represent their views about inequalities in their lives. What she found was that collage worked to enable students to think more deeply about issues, such as equality, but without inhibiting them in a way that writing down their thoughts often did. By using collage she discovered a new and powerful way of fully engaging learners that was both meaningful and evocative, thus enabling learners to participate more fully in the learning experience. This tutor reported that students worked well together and talked about their individual experiences using the collages as a medium for the discussion. Issues discussed included their previous lack of educational opportunities and their feelings of powerlessness in creating change. The tutor reported that the discussion also revealed a lack of understanding arising from the religious and political divisions in society, and the discussions about the collage provided a way of addressing these misunderstandings. For these students, putting pen to paper could be particularly problematic, never mind writing about their feelings about equality. The discussions enabled them to approach things in an open and honest way and at the same time developed their confidence in speaking about issues usually not discussed.

For many tutors, the new creative methods enhanced their understanding about the causes of conflict and enabled them to confront equality issues about living in a society in conflict and how it had affected their opinions, attitudes and ability to participate in education and schooling. They also felt that it had made them more confident about using the methodologies with their own students to help them resolve conflicts arising as a result of living in a community that was religiously segregated. One participant felt the training had provided her with some simple yet powerful exercises for conflict resolution. When she used them, she noted how even those with learning difficulties were able to easily understand the idea that you need to learn how to cooperate if you are going to solve conflict.

Other tutors spoke of the potential value of creative methods to create safe spaces for groups from both communities to explore equality issues impacting their lives, leading to an improved understanding of how a lack of literacy skills can create inequalities. For example, in the Irish context, Catholics very often did not perceive Protestants as people who had been disempowered through a lack of literacy skills and Protestants very often didn't perceive Catholics as people who could understand their feeling and opinions.

This cultural, religious divide exists not just within the literacy learners but also within the tutors. They too come from diverse communities and have been raised within the same context of fear, mistrust and disrespect. Therefore a powerful aspect of the creative methodologies training was that it enabled literacy tutors from the different sides of the community to develop new levels of cooperation and understanding. Moreover, as this tutor stated so emphatically, 'I found working with tutors from other sides of the religious divide made me look at my own practices more openly. It was a bit uncomfortable to have the things I see as "common sense" challenged, but it did improve my practice.' This is important in helping tutors to understand learners who come from different backgrounds and who share different experiences, enabling them, if not to value, at least to be exposed to something they might find difficult to understand or accept.

Finally, some tutors saw creative approaches as a way of democratising learning as well as working across national and global networks. Understanding difference at the local level might enable learners to also understand wider international issues about equality and peacebuilding and in so doing introduce a range of skills and competences going far beyond improvement of literacy skills. In the case of Northern Ireland, creative approaches enabled tutors and adult learners to face up to difficult issues in their lives and in so doing facilitated cognitive and affective learning which empowered them to make real changes.

However, as I noted above, the new methodologies also presented some key challenges for tutors. First, some felt that the activities required a high level of preparation and might be perceived as 'childish' by learners, while others questioned the value of activities that were too much enjoyed by learners. This is of course not uncommon, and scholars have drawn attention to the derision and scorn that accompany a view of the arts as mere forms of 'entertainment' that negate the seriousness of learning (Clover and Stalker, 2007; Greene, 1995). Secondly, while tutors were very enthusiastic about incorporating these creative methods into their literacy practice of exploring equality issues more visually and imaginatively, they also indicated that ongoing advice and support was necessary to build confidence in their abilities to use the new methodologies. They also spoke of the need for a clear rationale to validate this learning in the eyes of managers and funding bodies. These comments showed that, while tutors were enthusiastic about the new methodologies, they were also aware of the limitations and offered a critique highlighting a number of practical problems that might curtail the power of the new creative methodologies if not taken into account.

Working in partnership to develop and improve learning

This project showed how working with partners across different sectors can facilitate the integration of new knowledge and ideas, which in turn can improve professional practice. The use of creative approaches was ultimately able to change the ways teachers and learners thought about inequalities and peacebuilding. It also provided tutors and learners with opportunities to work together as researchers on ideas about equality and peacebuilding and the development of new learning practices. In this respect, one of the most significant achievements of the project was that of building greater insight and understanding of the causes and consequences of inequalities and the possibilities that exist for peacebuilding. The project's approach to literacy work challenged the widely held view of deficit among learners and instead focused on people's ability to do what they wanted in their lives. A tutor commented, 'It opened my eyes and mind to what is possible through using other creative, non- text methods.'

The project was based on the premise that literacy is far more than a set of basic skills, but rather is a set of social practices. Adult literacy education is in itself an issue of inequality since adults with low literacy skills are more likely to be unemployed, living on low incomes, and experiencing poor health and early morbidity (Bynner and Parsons 2001; Hammond 2004; Raudenbush and Kasim 2002). Through the use of a 'social practices' account of adult literacy, rather than viewing literacy as a de-contextualised, mechanical manipulation of letters, words and figures, it can be located in social, emotional and linguistic contexts. Literacy practices become more than just routines and skills and are better understood by teachers and learners as linked to specific contexts which take account of people's feelings and values.

By focusing on equality and creativity, the project demonstrated how creative arts and non-text methods of learning can be integrated into literacy learning for peacebuilding. The project also demonstrated how universities can work in partnership to enhance creativity, promote the arts and develop new ways of working with partners across different sectors. In this project the focus was on connecting research on equality with new pedagogical approaches that would contribute to an evolving peace process. It also provided a transferable model that can be used to support further cross-departmental or inter-university cooperation for the promotion of the arts in universities. It thus created a new opportunity for the universities in Ireland to get involved in peacebuilding through the promotion of arts-based approaches to learning. This particular approach to training teachers for a particular situation is perhaps just a starting point and might well provide opportunities to consider how creative approaches might be developed in other professional programmes such as social worker and community work training. In support of this approach to learning, Shor argued that 'this kind of literacy ... connects the political and the personal, the public and the private, the global and the local, the economic and the pedagogical' (1999: 1). The challenge for the future will be to develop lifelong learning and literacy policies and practices that promote dialogue between different stakeholder groups, and for universities to promote and engage in teaching and research that encourages dialogue that recognises the importance of the principles of equality and social justice as a core tool for promoting peacebuilding in Northern Ireland.

References

Baker, J., Lynch, K., and Cantillon, S. (2004), *Equality from Theory to Action*, Dublin: Palgrave Macmillan.

Barndt, D. (ed.) (2011), *Community Arts and Popular Education in the Americas*, Albany: State University of New York Press.

Boal, A. (1979), *Theatre of the Oppressed*, New York: Urizen Books.

Border Action Ireland (2006), Consortium with responsibility for the implementation of the Peace & Reconciliation Projects in Ireland, https://www.pobal.ie/Pages/Home.aspx (accessed 16 September 2012).

Bynner, J., and Parsons, S. (2001), 'Qualifications, basic skills and accelerating social exclusion', *Journal of Education and Work*, 14: 279–91.

Bruner, J. (1986), *Actual Minds, Possible World*, Cambridge, MA, and London: Harvard University Press.

Clover, D., and Stalker, J. (2007), *The Arts and Social Justice: Re-crafting Adult Education and Community Cultural Leadership*, Leicester: NIACE.

Crowther, J., Hamilton M., and Tett, L. (eds) (2001), *Powerful Literacies*, Leicester: NIACE.

Darby, J. (2003), *Northern Ireland: The Background to the Peace Process*, http://cain.ulst.ac.uk/events/peace/darby03.htm (accessed 16 Septermber 2012).

Fegan, T. (2003), *Learning and Community Arts*, Leicester: NIACE.

Freire, P. (1970), *Pedagogy of the Oppressed*, New York: Continuum.

Freire, P., and Macedo, D.P. (1987), *Literacy: Reading the Word and the World*, South Hadley, MA: Bergin and Garvey.

Gardner, H. (1999), *Frames of Mind: The Theory of Multiple Intelligences*, New York: Basic Books.

Greene, M. (1988), *The Dialectic of Freedom*, New York: New York Teachers College Press.

Greene, M. (1995), *Releasing the Imagination. Essays on Education, the Arts and Social Change*, San Francisco: Jossey-Bass.

Hamber, B., and Kelly, G. (2004), *A Working Definition of Reconciliation*, Belfast: Democratic Dialogue.

Hammond, C. (2004), 'Impacts on well-being, mental health and coping', in T. Schuller, J. Preston, C. Hammond and A. Brassett (eds), *Wider Benefits of Learning*, London: Routledge, 37–56.

Hardy, B. (1974), 'Narrative as a primary act of mind', in M. Meek, A. Warlow and G. Barton (eds), *The Cool Web, the Pattern of Children's Reading*, London: Bodley Head, 12–23.

Lambe, T., Mark, R., Murphy, P., and Soroke, B. (eds) (2006), *Literacy, Equality and Creativity: A Resource Guide for Adult Educators*, Belfast: Queen's University, Belfast.

Lederach, J. (1997), *Building Peace: Sustainable Reconciliation in Divided Societies*, Washington, DC: USIP Press.

Lederach, J. (2005), *The Moral Imagination: The Art and Soul of Building Peace*, Oxford: Oxford University Press.

Morris, C. (n/d), 'What is peacebuilding? One definition', http://www.peacemakers.ca/publications/peacebuildingdefinition.html (accessed 16 September 2012).

Norton, M. (2005), 'Welcoming spirit in adult literacy work', *Research and Practice in Adult Literacy*, 58(6): 3–7.

Raudenbush, S., and Kasim, R. (2002), *Adult Literacy, Social Inequality and the Information Economy, Findings from the National Adult Literacy Survey*, Ottawa: Statistics Canada and Human Resource Development Canada.

Schutzman, M., and Cohen-Cruz, J. (eds) (2002), *Playing Boal: Theatre, Therapy, Activism*, London: Routledge.

Shor, I. (1999), 'What is critical literacy?', *Journal for Pedagogy, Pluralism and Practice*, 4(1): 2–10.

Tisdell, E. (2003), *Exploring Spirituality and Culture in Adult and Higher Education*, San Francisco: Jossey-Bass.

Welton, M.R. (ed.) (1995), *In Defence of the Lifeworld: Critical Perspectives on Adult Learning*, New York: State University of New York Press.

12

Creative pathways: developing lifelong learning for community dance practitioners

Victoria Hunter

This chapter discusses a collaborative pilot project led by staff from the University of Leeds BA dance programme and Yorkshire Dance, the West Yorkshire region's national dance agency. The one-year pilot aimed to engage key industry stakeholders in the development of continuing professional development opportunities for dance professionals within the area of what is known as community dance practice. Funded by the West Yorkshire Lifelong Learning Network, the project was a response to current concerns regarding dance training and lifelong learning within the United Kingdom community dance sector. Research had suggested that dance graduates, while retaining a specialism in their art form, often lacked the broader range of leadership and facilitation skills necessary to support and develop careers as freelance practitioners in a range of dance contexts (e.g. Burns, 2006; Hall, 2007). Furthermore, a discernible lack of distinct career progression routes for currently practising community dance artists had already been identified as a cause for concern at the University of Leeds.

The West Yorkshire Dance Leadership project explored these issues through the creation of a pilot project that engaged two 'apprentices' in a year-long programme of work-based learning placements, career development and individual mentoring opportunities. These opportunities were provided in a collaborative manner through consultation with regionally based dance companies, established community dance practitioners and local community arts employers.

Context

The BA dance programme is housed within the School of Performance and Cultural Industries at the University of Leeds, a research-led university in the north of England. As suggested by its title, the school prioritises the study of the arts in relation to their application within the wider fields of the cultural industries. As opposed to studying the performing arts disciplines in isolation, the school's remit is to combine discipline-specific study with entrepreneurialism, innovative arts practice, applied practice and industry/community-related study.

The University of Leeds is committed to a wide range of what it calls 'knowledge transfer' initiatives. This type of initiative is defined as the application of scholarly expertise across a range of community and industry contexts for the general benefit of society. The ability to demonstrate relevance and connectivity at both a local and national level has become of key importance to many UK higher education institutions in recent years in the face of an ever more competitive marketplace in which institutions and degree programmes compete for market share. This ethos is reflected through the School of Performance and Cultural Industries' development of partnership relationships with regionally and nationally based arts organisations including Opera North, Bradford Media Museum, the National Coal Mining Museum, Dance United and Phoenix Dance Theatre. These partnerships operate in a number of ways from providing work-based learning opportunities for undergraduates to informing academic research projects and developing widening participation work with local schools and colleges. Partnerships also help to inform the school's curriculum development and planning and, for industry partners, provide access and insight into valuable arts research processes that in turn serve to develop and disseminate their work through public performances, seminars, industry workshops and conference presentations. These relationships are important for the school's ongoing development and its commitment to developing graduates with skills and experience for future employment. These partnerships help to foster relationships in which the exchange of particular skills, expertise and sets of knowledge serve to refresh, inform and engage both partners in a myriad of creative ways and to benefit their communities.

This chapter shares the project outcomes and the experiences of those individuals (mentors, employers and apprentices) engaging with the West Yorkshire Dance Leadership project and reflects upon these experiences and outcomes in relation to broader issues pertaining to lifelong learning, social inclusion and continuing professional development within the field of community dance practice. Furthermore, the chapter demonstrates how collaborative projects involving higher education and the dance industry can develop mutually beneficial relationships that serve to strengthen the locally based community dance 'ecology', its organisational infrastructure and the individuals participating in this type of dance activity.

Community dance practice and professional development

Dance and its inherent transformational properties has received an upsurge in interest and increased popularity in the UK in recent years. Fuelled by the rising popularity of televised dance talent shows and creative approaches to addressing national health and fitness issues, dance and its transformational, life-enhancing qualities appears to be back in favour and developing visibility in a range of government and educational agendas.

Community dance, the focus of this chapter, describes an area of dance activity occurring within a range of community and educational contexts. Involving a wide range of activity from youth dance to older peoples' dance, work with the disabled and socially excluded groups, it is an area of activity that places emphasis on participation and process as opposed to vocational dance training. Community dance serves many educational, therapeutic and recreational functions and is best defined as 'primarily a social activity, uniting creativity and physicality in a way that offers the experience of *communitas*, of solidarity and significance in an immediate and grounded way;' (Thompson, in Amans, 2008: xi). It can be further defined as a field of practice with the potential to effect personal and social change. Sara Houston observes, 'at the heart of the community dance movement lies a set of principles founded on the idea that dance is for everyone' (2005: 169). Alongside this set of principles lies also the belief that participatory dance, with its emphasis on group activity and collective responsibility, can be a force for good. Houston comments,

> Because the community dance movement emphasises the idea that anyone can dance, it has been linked to groups that have been termed 'socially excluded' and the movement has been instrumental in delivering dance to disenfranchised communities and individuals for several decades. (2005: 169)

The facilitation of community dance experiences requires careful development reliant upon the lead practitioner's skill, commitment, awareness (of self and others) and enthusiasm for engaging with this particular form of dance work.

Despite the increasing interest in dance and its application in a range of educational and community contexts in the UK (such as healthcare, youth work, rehabilitation and social integration work), industry definition and regulation guidelines are elusive and the career path for those individuals wishing to engage with this type of work remains unclear. Moreover;

> In community dance, there are no formal or universally agreed criteria that determine an individual's 'readiness' to practice as a professional. Expectations around standards, competence and 'professionalism' have evolved organically, over time and in tandem with the nature and demands of the work, so there is no prescribed route into the profession and few 'must haves' or 'must dos' on the way to becoming a professional practitioner. (Ackroyd, in Amans, 2008: 121)

The 'organic' nature of the practitioner's world of work is understandably a key component of a practice that relies upon a degree of malleability in order to respond to the needs and demands of a wide range of client groups. However, this lack of regularity inevitably gives rise to a range of issues pertaining to the training and development needs of dance professionals and undergraduate dance students in preparation for entering this field of rapidly developing work. The need for ongoing professional development is crucial; however, the *Making a Move* report (Burns, 2008) revealed (through the results of a questionnaire with over 200 respondents) that only 50 per cent of community dance practitioners had either undertaken or were undertaking development in the form of apprenticeships, mentoring, volunteering and shadowing.

In a survey of dance training and employment contexts, dance consultant Susanne Burns comments that, for many years, higher education establishments such as universities have produced dance graduates with a bias towards performing and choreography, with few graduates actually gaining employment in these areas due to high levels of competition and limited employment opportunities:

It is evident that, despite the primacy often designated to the performer and chore-ographer, they make up a very small proportion of the dance labour market. The market demand appears to be for dance practitioners who can teach, facilitate dance work in community contexts and manage and produce the work. (2008: 5)

As a result, Burns observes that the industry itself has followed its own, home-grown approach to professional development, as evidenced by the UK's Founda-tion for Community Dance's framework for continuing professional development which identifies key competencies such as session planning, personal presenta-tion skills and health and safety awareness. In addition, Burns suggests that both higher education and the community dance sector could work together more closely to address issues pertaining to training, skills development and graduate employability.

The pilot project analysed in this chapter arose from my own desire to explore and address these issues and to consider ways in which higher education dance programmes and the community dance industry could work together to facilitate the dance graduate's transition into the world of work and identify further profes-sional development opportunities for current practitioners.

Lifelong learning and the West Yorkshire Dance Leadership project

In April 2009 the School of Performance and Cultural Industries at the Univer-sity of Leeds and Yorkshire Dance received funding from the West Yorkshire Lifelong Learning Network to support a curriculum development project. The network is a government-funded partnership of higher education institutions, further education colleges and other organisations throughout West Yorkshire aimed at promoting quality vocational experiences for learners to progress into and through higher education. In the UK lifelong learning refers to a process of 'lifelong, voluntary and self-motivated' learning (Department of Education and Science, 2000) in which an adult might seek to pursue work-based vocational learning experiences or more holistically based personal self-development.

The partnership project led by me as project leader and Yorkshire Dance's professional development coordinator aimed to identify a range of graduate and continuing professional development work-based learning opportunities avail-able in the region and, by doing so, provide opportunities for career progres-sion into and within the community dance sector of the industry. Throughout the project a number of tensions were encountered between definitions of and approaches to the concept of 'lifelong learning'. It became apparent to both me and the project partners that the term itself can be nuanced and interpreted in a number of ways often producing a certain tension between the rather pragmatic, quantifiable skills development and acquisition approach promoted by universi-ties and other academic institutions and the less quantifiable, subjective approach promoted by dance artists and community dance practitioners themselves. This more holistic and organic approach to lifelong learning facilitated by a 'knowing-through-doing' approach became foregrounded as a defining feature of the project described here and was influential in the development of the project design.

The aims of those involved in the project were, first, to support and maintain dance networks and relationships between artists, dance companies and dance education providers in the region in order to develop a greater sense of collegiality and encourage dialogue. Secondly, we aimed to trial continuing professional development work placements provided by the local dance industry, which included a range of medium-scale dance companies (Phoenix Dance Theatre, Northern Ballet Theatre, RJC Dance Company), small-scale, project-based companies (such as Ascendance Rep, Motion Manual and Instant Dissidence dance theatre), independent choreographers (Gary Clarke, Douglas Thorpe, Jenni Wren), government-funded community dance initiatives (Dance Action Zone Leeds, Youth Dance England) and vocational training/higher education institutions providing dance education (University of Leeds, Northern School of Contemporary Dance, Leeds Metropolitan University).

The project was driven by a desire to harness and develop local dance network relationships in the West Yorkshire region in preparation for the implementation in 2010 of a new vocationally based community dance leadership qualification. Commissioned by Youth Dance England, the level six qualification (equivalent to level three of an undergraduate degree programme) resulted from the nationwide Dance Training and Accreditation project (Burns, 2008) and the *Making a Move* initiative led by the Foundation for Community Dance, and aimed to provide the first nationally recognised qualification in this field. In light of this development, the West Yorkshire Dance Leadership project sought to prepare the ground for the local provision and collaborative 'hosting' of this qualification within the region through the development of a collaborative and supportive dance infrastructure network.

An initial networking meeting was held to launch the project formally, held at Yorkshire Dance and involving representatives from Leeds City Council, Youth Dance England, Yorkshire Dance, the University of Leeds, York St John University, Dance Action Zone Leeds, Phoenix Dance Theatre, Ascendance Rep Dance Company, Northern Ballet Theatre and Dance United. Following a joint presentation by me with Yorkshire Dance's professional development coordinator concerning dance graduate employability and community dance leadership, the participants were asked to provide feedback. In particular, the representatives were asked if they could identify (from an employer's perspective) the key skills required by a community dance leader and suggest ways in which these skills could be best evidenced to employers. Finally, the representatives suggested potential ways forward for the development of community dance leadership training in the Yorkshire region and stated whether they would be willing to provide work placements, mentoring opportunities and support.

In their feedback, the representatives identified that, alongside a good level of practical dance skills, community dance practitioners need to possess a high level of business and marketing skill to manage a freelance career. Time management and professional presentation skills were also identified and the ability to market and promote a range of differing dance facilitation skills was deemed important. The industry representatives also discussed the importance of the practitioner's own personal development (in terms of developing confidence, professional behaviour, and so forth) and work experience vital to developing their knowledge and understanding of the field of community dance practice.

The representatives also stressed the importance of self-evaluation in terms of dancers needing to know their own skills and strengths and weaknesses as a practitioner and then seeking out professional development opportunities to develop their craft. They identified that many of the skills required could not be taught 'off the shelf' and that, within the industry itself, there is an expectation that in order to gain work experience individuals will often have to volunteer or take unpaid work to develop their portfolio; they observed that employers respect this type of work experience and the commitment shown by the individual. They also felt that, on paper, an undergraduate dance degree provided few insights into the actual skills and experience gained by individual graduates and expressed a consensus view that evidence of extra-curricular work experience gained while studying was a key indicator of the individual's commitment to the profession. For more established practitioners, the representatives felt that letters of recommendation from previous employers, work experience placements or commissioning bodies were of key importance as they acted as 'quality assurance markers' from within the industry itself. However, it was also acknowledged that quality assurance is often a 'judgement call', only made possible by evidencing an individual's work. This discussion raised a series of questions regarding quality assurance within the industry per se; in particular the participants questioned how employers (who might not always be dance specialists) identified good practice and how they identified quality or discrepancies. Equally, the representatives' acknowledgement of an over-reliance on anecdotal recommendations as an indicator of 'quality' echoed Susanne Burns' observation that 'the lack of benchmarks and accredited provision inhibits the ongoing development of this work and means that employers are contracting the same practitioners on a regular basis as a means of ensuring that standards are maintained' (2008: 10).

In order to address some of the issues identified in the meeting, representatives suggested that further liaison between the region's dance industry and locally based higher education institutions was required to produce graduates with employable skills. Participants observed that, while core dance skills are a 'given', additional 'soft skills' (defined as time management, personal presentation, interpersonal skills etc.) gained from work experience alongside their degree programme makes graduates employable. Following the consultation, a number of placements, mentoring and peer observation opportunities were suggested by the group, which led to a range of experiences for the project's two apprentices

The apprenticeship programme

Two dance 'apprentices' were selected from a range of applicants to take part in the year-long project. Both had studied on a regionally based BA dance degree course that included aspects of community dance practice. Both had been graduates for two years and in that period had demonstrated a commitment to community dance practice through their developing work in the industry. However, both individuals expressed frustration at the lack of discernible career progression routes within the field and identified significant skills and experience gaps in their professional portfolios. Skills gaps common to both apprentices included teaching experience, project management, funding application preparation, working across other dance genres (i.e. site-specific work and large-scale participatory project work), time management and confidence/network building.

In order to introduce the apprentices to the programme and as a means of introducing them to new experiences and working methods, both participated in a three-day training course held at the University of Leeds prior to embarking upon their work placements. Dance United, a national dance company working in the field of dance and social inclusion, facilitated the course. The aim of the course was to introduce participants to the company's proactive training approach focused on resolving challenging behaviour, resistance and non-engagement within participant groups. Dance United is the UK's leading company working in this field; the company's *mission is to demonstrate that interventions modelled on professional contemporary dance training can transform behaviour in a sustainable manner.* They have developed an international reputation for creating quality contemporary dance training and performance projects with disadvantaged and marginalised individuals and communities from street children in Ethiopa to young offenders in Bradford and 'reluctant' young gangsters in East London.

Burns' (2006) observations regarding skills shortages within particular areas of the UK's dance industry are exemplified through Dance United's own experience of recruiting dance artists with appropriate background training The company identified an acute shortage of suitably trained dance artists confident enough to work with challenging groups. They have developed their own training course in order to address this particular skills gap. The training course focusing on how to deal with confrontation, conflict and challenging behaviour was one of the programmes provided to the apprentices. The apprentices engaged with a range of role-playing and practical dance exercises that gradually introduced them to Dance United's philosophy and practical methodology. The training course functioned as a precursor to the apprentice's work placements and introduced them to an unfamiliar area of community dance practice that challenged them to step outside their comfort zones and discover new skills.

Following these initial experiences, the apprentices were asked to further consider their own particular needs and skills gaps in order to identify and allocate a specific work placement and mentor. The skills gaps identified by the apprentices included a lack of experience in teaching groups of adults, specifically approaches to class management, teaching methods and the structuring of workshops for this type of client group. The apprentices also felt that they lacked sufficient knowledge of choreographic methods appropriate to a range of community dance performance-making contexts, such as choreographing for youth dance groups versus choreographing for intergenerational groups. They also felt that they lacked experience and knowledge of the wider field of community dance practice, specifically in dance and disability and dance and mental health contexts.

Additionally, both apprentices identified a lack of confidence and experience of sole-trader business practices such as 'pitching' for work, assessing pricing structures for commissions and compiling funding applications.

From this task, the apprentices identified the type of placement and mentoring that would benefit them. Placements were arranged through local partners and partnership agreements and targets were put in place. Clear expectations from both placement providers and the apprentices were established regarding the type of training and mentoring that would be delivered and the company's expectations. The apprentice's travel and subsistence was funded and industry partners were funded for their placement provision, ensuring that their time and expertise was acknowledged.

Apprentice A's first work placement was helping to deliver adult contemporary creative dance classes as part of the Northern School of Contemporary Dance's community outreach programme. The placement involved the apprentice shadowing the dance artist as she prepared and delivered contemporary dance workshops to adult learners. Participation in the class was voluntary and the cohort comprised of adult learners from a range of socio-economic backgrounds and locations across the city. As the placement progressed, the apprentice began to lead parts of the workshop herself and received feedback from the dance artist in a mentoring capacity on her planning, teaching and facilitation skills. As the placement developed further, the adult dance group worked towards a performance of their work which the apprentice helped to choreograph. This aspect of the placement provided a new challenge for the apprentice as she developed choreographic strategies for the development and management of dance material and learned how to motivate the dancers and develop their performance skills.

Apprentice A's second placement was with a locally based dance artist who has over thirty years' experience of working as a freelance community arts practitioner, choreographer and teacher. The practitioner's specialisms included working with disability groups and adults with mental health issues. The apprentice attended an initial dance/art workshop with the mentor at the start of the programme which provided her with first-hand workshop planning and delivery experience. From there the apprentice worked with the mentor in both a shadowing/work placement and mentoring capacity that focused on the apprentice's professional development, time management and forward planning, assessing potential opportunities for future skills development.

Following the completion of the placement a report was written by both the apprentice and the placement provider including details of the individual's expectations, progress and future development plans. This feedback identified key areas of achievement for the individual apprentice and outlined areas for improvement and suggestions for future development.

Apprentice B's first placement was with Ascendance Rep Dance Company, a project-based small dance company based in Leeds, and involved working both in the office and out in the community as part of their 'Telling Tales' project. The project involved working with youth dance community groups in the region exploring themes of heritage and identity through dance workshops and activities. As part of this work, the apprentice worked alongside dance artists from the company's education and outreach department, initially shadowing their work then independently leading groups of young people in dance activities, planning and delivering sessions and facilitating creative choreographic workshops.

In the office, the apprentice learned more about the input required to set up a dance project, including the practicalities of writing a budget, sending out marketing material and attending project planning meetings. The apprentice observed, in a post-project interview, that she did not have the opportunity to experience this aspect of dance administration and planning as part of her degree course and previous training and had limited opportunity to experience this in any of her previous work placements/employments. She suggested that '[my] lack of experience has held me back from reaching even the interview rounds of job opportunities. To gain in depth experience in such areas can only be of benefit in my future job applications.'

As part of the leadership project, apprentice B was also able to attend a dance symposium, which explored issues relating to the field of dance and disability. This provided her with an excellent opportunity to learn from established artists such as Wendy Hesketh from Wired Aerial Theatre and Louise Katerega from Foot in Hand Dance Company, and to network and build contacts with other people working in the field.

The apprentice's second placement was a mentoring opportunity working alongside an established community dance practitioner and choreographer. This second placement opportunity enabled the apprentice to reflect upon her experiences so far and align them with her previous work experiences in order to 'map' a pathway for future career progression. The apprentice was able to take time out from her daily routine and reflect on her facilitation and leadership skills and identify future opportunities for training and professional development. This was an extremely valuable part of the programme for this apprentice as she began to formulate ideas for establishing her own independent dance company working with disabled and able-bodied dancers. The apprentice had previous experience in this field of community dance practice but lacked the confidence and administrative experience required to apply for the necessary funding to facilitate the project. The mentor helped the apprentice to clarify her ideas and articulate her vision in preparation for the submission of a number of funding applications.

Post-project reflections

Throughout the project both apprentices were exposed to a range of community dance practices and processes and were able to develop a range of skills that will enable them to contribute to a field of practice that yields enormous benefits to the participants and facilitators engaging with this type of work and to the communities in which it takes place. In many ways, values such as the development of individual empowerment and community transformation underpinning this area of dance practice can be closely aligned to the University of Leeds' 'knowledge transfer' aspirations for influencing and improving communities outlined earlier.

The models of knowledge exchange between education providers and industry professionals and between mentors and apprentices employed within this project served not only to raise awareness of the employment needs of this particular sector of the dance industry but also developed the skills of two emerging dance artists who can contribute to the local provision of community dance practice in the future. However, as the project developed, tensions between approaches to the concept of 'lifelong learning' as perceived by conventional educational establishments and industry professionals became evident. For example, the acquisition of specific leadership and facilitation skills required for working with difficult or challenging groups of young people cannot be simply learned through the 'one-size-fits-all' approach favoured by higher education curricula. In this context, the experienced community dance artist becomes adept at monitoring and 'feeling' group responses and responding to developing group dynamics and less overt behavioural qualities manifested through body language, posture and energy levels. The less-experienced dance facilitator can develop these skills through observation and working alongside more experienced practitioners and mentors and through receiving feedback on their own attempts at leading groups in specific activities as they gradually begin to develop their own intuitive and embodied approaches. It inevitably requires real-time, real-life, situated learning for these skills to develop, a model that does not comfortably lend itself to more formalised and structured educational contexts.

One of the main outcomes of this project, therefore, has been an acknowledgement and affirmation from the participating dance industry partners of what work-based, lifelong learning and continuing professional development can actually consist of for this type of learner. The project deliberately targeted a particular type of learner profile; a learner with both established and emerging skills and a developing career trajectory. This profile is very different from conventional notions of 'work experience' programmes frequently operated in the UK, often aimed at 16–18-year-olds with a 'starter' profile, for whom work-based learning is a form of 'scoping' exercise in which they seek to get a 'flavour' of the world of work and to identify potential progression routes within it. Emerging from secondary school-based programmes, this 'starter' type of group is easily recognizable and quantifiable in many ways; however, the demographic represented by the two apprentices in this project is, perhaps, less visible and less easily served by a uniform approach to work experience. The project therefore raised my own awareness regarding the need for the identification and recognition of different 'strata' within the field of work-based learning and continued professional development. It also highlighted the need to adopt a flexible approach dictated by the individual's requirements, an approach that mirrors the aims and ethos of the community dance industry in which it sits with its emphasis on individual development, empowerment and inclusive practice.

The need for individualised work-based learning experiences is exemplified in the case studies presented here. Apprentice B, for example, participated in a more formal 'traditional' work-based learning template with Ascendance Rep Dance Company. However, the things that interested her most were project management, funding applications and administration processes, the less 'glamorous' yet essential side of the world of arts work, an experience that might not appeal to the less experienced practitioner who might still be concerned with skills acquisition. The apprentices participating in this project already had highly developed dance skills through their undergraduate studies. It was the articulation, management and application of these skills in a more entrepreneurial, strategic and sustainable manner that interested them both and provided a focus for development within this project.

As a result, both apprentices sought out individual mentoring type placements where they observed and worked with a solo/freelance-based practitioner who could essentially take the time to 'coach' them and discuss their skills in a holistic sense by asking questions such as 'Where do you see yourself and your work?', 'Where are your skills gaps?' and 'How do you see your work progressing?' in an advisory, critical friend capacity.

The 'model' of work-based learning and continuing professional development in this project was therefore more fluid and less quantifiable than I had been able to envision prior to embarking on it. Often, I came to a process of questioning – 'What is a placement?', 'How can it vary in frequency and duration?' 'What is needed here?' – with answers being provided by the individuals and their mentors or placement providers. Clearly a more fluid model was the most appropriate in this context.

Both apprentices interacted with community dance professionals either through observation/interviews and or mentoring experiences. Feedback from these 'providers' indicates that they also benefited from the opportunity to reflect upon their own practice and, through imparting their experiences and knowledge to less experienced practitioners, they gained a valuable opportunity to assess their work and their own working methods. In this sense the continuing professional development process developed a cyclical nature.

Both apprentices developed immensely as young professionals throughout the one-year project, though not all of this can be attributed to the West Yorkshire Dance Leadership project. Both benefited from a convergence of opportunities that created a critical mass of development opportunity in the region over the year. For example, both apprentices took part in additional career development advice, workshops and further mentoring provided by Yorkshire Dance as part of their ongoing professional development programme. Alongside this, their own creative work flourished. Drawing measurable outcomes from this experience is neither realistic nor desirable; however, all of these experiences appear to have contributed to the development of skills and, more importantly, to the retention of two increasingly skilled practitioners within the region as their work becomes more closely linked with West Yorkshire's dance infrastructure and networks.

Future developments in the UK

Following the completion of the project in April 2010 initiatives to regulate and validate qualifications and training for community dance practitioners have developed further, resulting in the validation of the Diploma in Dance Teaching and Leadership (validated by Trinity Laban) and the publication of new National Occupation Standards for dance in the UK.[1] The Diploma in Dance Teaching and Learning (Children and Young People) is the first step in providing a qualifications framework that sets benchmarks and provides quality assurance for practitioners and employers working with dance and young people in informal (outside education) contexts. The qualification was commissioned Youth Dance England and aims to contribute to the development of a professional accreditation framework for community dance leaders and freelance dance practitioners working in the community.

While the qualification only initially addresses work with a particular client group, it is hoped that this type of qualification will be expanded to include more areas of community and applied contexts and client groups in future years. The qualification is graded at level six on the UK's National Qualifications Framework, equivalent to the third year of an undergraduate degree programme, and consists of four modules that can be taken by individuals at any stage of their career. When completed, the four modules will comprise the final qualification.

During the development of the qualification, Yorkshire Dance was commissioned by the qualification's development team to pilot one module that focused on assessing an individual's teaching skills through class observation and portfolio evidence. The module was trialled by Yorkshire Dance's community and learning manager who worked with a group of local community dance artists and freelance teachers to assess the module's appropriateness, efficacy and relevance. The results of this pilot exercise were fed back to the qualification development team prior to the national rollout of the qualification in September 2010. Following this pilot, trial plans for the provision and 'hosting' of the DDTAL qualification locally within the West Yorkshire region began to develop. Having established a number of locally based dance networks, it is hoped that outcomes and knowledge emerging from the West Yorkshire Dance leadership project discussed in this chapter can be utilised to support the strategic plan to develop the qualification in the region. It is envisioned that the four modules covering aspects of dance activity delivery, planning and evaluation can be delivered in a collaborative manner between regionally based dance agencies, dance companies and higher education dance programmes. In this sense, the rollout of the qualification will draw upon a range of skills, resources and expertise currently existing in the region, providing several points of access for both graduate dance students and established community dance practitioners alike. This type of 'co-hosting' provision and flexible learning approach will help a wide range of individuals to validate and quantify their skills and expertise, enabling practitioners to demonstrate their experience and proficiency as community dance professionals to future employers, particularly those working with marginalised populations.

The West Yorkshire Dance Leadership project described in this chapter is an example of a particular type of higher education/industry collaboration. This project facilitated a valuable process of knowledge exchange that served to update and inform both partners of current developments and initiatives within the field of UK community dance practice. The project also facilitated an invaluable process of dialogue and network development between a broad range of higher education dance course providers, practising community dance artists and key industry stakeholders. On a national level, the outcome for the University of Leeds was to strengthen its portfolio of project partners and to demonstrate to the UK's Higher Education Funding Council its relevance as an industry partner with the potential to facilitate industry initiatives and provide knowledge and expertise to a particular sector of the cultural industries. Through a successful process of collaboration a valuable exchange of ideas and information occurred between the university dance programme and the local dance community. The enmeshment of ideas, practice and dialogue within the project created a strong link between both project partners and established firm foundations from which both parties could contribute collaboratively towards the development of further graduate and continuing professional development opportunities for community dance artists in the future.

Afterword

Since the writing of this chapter, the dance programme at the University of Leeds has ceased to exist as a discrete honours degree; movement, choreography and modules involving applied dance in community and industry-related contexts now feature within the School of Performance and Cultural Industries' Theatre and Performance degree programme. This development reflects a wider trend within the UK higher education sector towards an increasingly interdisciplinary approach to curriculum design that broadly covers a range of related subjects within a degree programme. While a breadth of knowledge and the development of a student's transferable skills is of course a desirable outcome for an under-graduate, the concern voiced here is that this process can result in a lack of disci-plinarity and a diminution of subject-specific skills. Additionally, this trend may well result in a progressive diluting of core discipline knowledge and skills that can only be acquired through the education system's continued investment in time, skills and resources, commodities that unfortunately appear increasingly endan-gered in the contemporary UK higher education environment.

References

Amans, D. (ed.) (2008), *An Introduction to Community Dance Practice*, London: Palgrave.

Burns, S. (ed.) (2006), *Mapping the Terrain: Entrepreneurship and Professional Practice in Dance Higher Education*, London: Palatine Publishing.

Burns. S. (ed.) (2008), *Making a Move: A Strategy for the Development of a Professional Framework for Community Dance*, Leeds: Foundation for Community Dance.

Department of Education and Science (2000), *Learning for Life: White Paper on Adult Education*, London: TSO.

Hall, T. (2007), *The Dance Review: A Report to Government on Dance Education*, London: Department for Children, Schools and Families.

Houston, S. (2005), 'Participation in community dance: a road to empowerment and transformation?', *New Theatre Quarterly*, 21(2): 20–35.

Notes

1 For further information on National Occupation Standards for dance see www.dtap.org.uk (accessed 16 September 2012).

Overlay:
messages, threads and tensions

Kathy Sanford and Darlene E. Clover

For me, aesthetics are about the capacity to really feel the world, to sense it without bodies, to be deeply aware ... For me, art is simply paying attention. (John Jordan, quoted in Kwakkenbos, 2011: 304)

At the heart of this volume is the belief that attention to the aesthetic dimension is a valuable response to Thompson's call for adult educators 'to make extraordinary sense of ... ordinary activity and experience' (2002: 23), and a means to challenge what Tracey and Allen in this volume refer to as problematic recurring distinctions enforced in today's neoliberal institutions of higher education. For the authors in this book, the arts and creativity are imaginative, embodied means of re-seeing, re-making, re-teaching and re-discovering the world in which we live. Equally importantly, arts-based work is paramount in helping to counter the harmful effects of racism, social exclusion and marginalisation, fear of 'the other', workplace stress, graduate student lack of confidence, disciplinary separations, and the rationalisation of learning and research and, even, community engagement.

The chapters take us on journeys in which art's social and aesthetic dimensions are polarities between which critical teaching, research and education can be done in and through the academy. But as with all roads, there are potholes, merging traffic and broken pavements along the way. This final chapter highlights some of the key messages scattered across this volume, providing a greater visualisation of interweaving themes within the various contributions. It follows threads of ideas, elaborates both articulated and tacit tensions and leaves you, the reader, with questions around teaching, learning, research, knowledge and community cultural engagement in the contemporary university to explore. Our discussion is not intended to be an exhaustive summary – and we ourselves do not always have the answers to our own questions – but rather to provide a sketchmap of query, reflection and meaning-making that interacts with the contributors' ideas and endeavours, as well as with past and contemporary aesthetic, adult education, lifelong learning and higher education discourses.

The wall of rationality, tradition and neoliberalism

Shukaitis, Graeber and Biddle once asked why it was that we 'assume creative and relevant ideas should be coming out of the universities in the first place?' (2005: 15). They go on to say that modern universities have only existed for a few hundred years and during this time have not really fostered much in terms of new ways of learning and understanding or engaging with the world.

Public universities are challenged by current socio-political changes in the epistemological landscape – the new knowledge economy – as well as market-oriented, competitive neoliberalism and its – as well as universities' – near deification of science and technology. Within this context, Sanford and Mimick and von Kotze and Small in Chapters 1 and 2 respectively speak of the tyranny of traditional classroom assessments and evaluations, of rational scholarly, text-based learning being privileged over embodied practices in higher education. Etmanski, Weigler and Wong-Sneddon in Chapter 9 refer to the 'unexamined ubiquity' of dominant traditional methods. To step outside this paradigm gives pause to professors, teachers and researchers within a university setting. What impact will using these 'extraordinary' arts-based methods have on their own evaluations, the continued support for or existence of their courses or even entire programmes?

Further, students and even community members take up these discourses of scholarly authority in problematic ways, as many authors in this volume note. Some fear they will neither learn nor be able to teach 'properly' if not immersed in slick academic 'professionalism' and made to measure up to the obsequious rationality of conventional academic ratings. Technical rationality has done its job well, disguising all that we cannot measure or prove in a discourse of scientific knowledge expertise at the expense of other discourses and ways of knowing, discouraging to the point of invisibility the aesthetic imagination. Lawrence and Cranton in Chapter 6 extend this to research courses, where they describe how students approach them both excited by the prospect of arts-based methods but fearful that this will take them away from learning what they identify as 'real' research methods. Community members, as Mark in Chapter 11 suggests, fret that in a non-formal education sphere already viewed as lacking credibility, using the arts will sink them further into the mire of frivolity and inadequacy. A case in point is Park's observation in Chapter 10 that her university's *Global Vision* for the future neither includes any reference to adult education nor to its own art museum. This leaves us to ponder the role of innovation in a university context but it also raises questions about the complex challenges of expanding community participation in the university.

The authors also draw attention to disciplinary silos and traditional aesthetic understandings in the academy with which many contend. With few notable exceptions, the adult educators and researchers contributing to this volume – many of whom work with or through continuing studies structures that are themselves often seen as marginal 'cash cows' in the university – speak little of connections to faculties of fine arts. Butterwick and Clover in Chapter 5 mention them simply to acknowledge how arts-based courses in the Faculty of Education are not always accepted for fine arts programmes. The reasons articulated range from their being too political or activist to their not sufficiently emphasising 'art'. This speaks to a narrow understanding of what art is, a misguided yet perpetual dismissal of art as a vehicle – the dreaded 'use-value' versus the prized 'art for art's sake' we spoke of in the Introduction – coupled with a total lack of understanding of the socio-political and cultural change potential of coupling aesthetics, politics, activism and learning (Clover, 2012; Lippard, 1983; Mullin, 2003). And yet nothing is as simple as it seems in a technically rational world theorised by Marx and Weber, and concretised in neoliberalism. Hunter, in the final chapter in this volume, while not asking for silos, is concerned that too much interdisciplinarity will diminish subject-specific skills and thereby weaken, in her case, dance in general and dance as vehicle for change in community in particular. Moreover, faculties of fine arts are often struggling for their existence. Schuller noted in 1996 how 'many universities [were] grappling with the sheer impossibility of maintaining a full range of subject provision' (1996: 5). The pressure to eliminate programmes, and particularly programmes not linked to the hard sciences and technology, has only increased. When fearing for one's existence in the academy, many retreat to traditionalism. Fine arts faculties' shelter under the theories and practices of High Art that they believe give them legitimacy. The problematic paradox is how this (re)action discourages linkages and partnerships with the authors in this volume who could potentially broaden their mandates and impact, thereby further legitimising their socio-educational value within the institution. One could also ask if it is the authors themselves who fear to engage with fine arts faculty, given that many may not see themselves as 'artists' in the professional sense of the term. However, one need only turn to the collaboration between Etmanski (adult educator in the Faculty of Education) and Weigler (theatre artist-educator in the Faculty of Fine Arts) to see the potential of such collaboration and the need to move beyond these fears.

(Re)imaging power

Underlying many of the discussions in this volume are issues of power, stemming from inequities created by hegemonic patriarchal structures foundational to traditional universities. Power struggles have significantly shaped how learning is perceived in society, and to date 'hard' sciences have triumphed over 'softer' arts-based disciplines. The power struggles engaged in by many of the authors are responses to the domination of science and rationality, but also, as Etmanski, Weigler and Wong-Sneddon and von Kotze and Small note, processes of colonisation and forms of 'apartheid', a strengthened conviction that the arts have something to contribute to our collective understanding and re-making of the world and a desire to redress the inequities inherent in the current university structure and society as a whole. The arboreal nature of universities and society has defined hierarchical power structures with strong roots, something arts-based education and research 'rhizomatically' resist (Deleuze and Guattari, 1987). Instead, as Jarvis and Williamson describe in Chapter 4, for example, arts-based forms embrace a multiplicity of modes, central to many initiatives but not control-ling the outcomes. Rhizomatic approaches to education cannot be contained and controlled, as the emergent nature of the projects described in this book have shown. Arts-based forms enable sharing and negotiating of power, challenging a binaristic view of the world in which 'truth' is sought through experimentation and theorising, in which power is maintained because of inequitable access to the creation of truth and knowledge. The arts enable multiple truths and perspectives to be acknowledged and valued, challenging traditional top-down power struc-tures. Herein lies the rub – lacking the ability to define and control, arts-based modes of knowing are dismissed and disparaged. As described by von Kotze and Small and Hunter in particular, there is an ongoing challenge to the existence and value of their programmes; programmes, as alluded to above, continue to cling tenuously to the margins of their institutions.

Men have traditionally held hierarchical institutional power over others. It is no accident in a volume addressing arts and community engagement – and focused on adult educators – that most of the authors are female, or that women play a significant role in developing arts-based and adult education programmes, or that arts-based 'non-scientific' ways of knowing are disparaged and dismissed, rejected as unscholarly and lacking academic rigour, as Lawrence and Cranton note so well. Yet this book argues that the use of collage, theatre and dance forges new paths that are often beyond the realm of patriarchal power and threaten its authority. Connecting mind with body and affect through artistic creation challenges accepted notions of valued ways of knowing, reshaping our under-standings of knowledge and truth. Rational abstraction, prized in the academy, is threatened with the messiness of sensory embodied presence, as Etmanski, Weigler and Wong-Sneddon, Lawrence and Cranton and Butterwick and Clover speak of so engagingly. Success in the academy, this volume asserts, cannot and should not continue to be measured in the traditional definitive ways, as imagi-nation and creativity vie for a legitimate place on the academic map. Alterna-tive systems of evaluation and recognition are imagined, created and recreated in the projects of Sanford and Mimick and Tracey and Allen as they attempt to develop new structures for valuing and recognising student learning, seeking ways to become more inclusive of multiple ways of exploring and representing diverse ways of knowing.

Imaginatively educate, creatively investigate

MacFarlane once argued, 'learning is an interactive and dynamic process, in which imagination drives action in exploring and interacting with an environ-ment. It requires dialogue between imagination and experience' (1996: 52). The arts, as recognised by Greene (1995), enable us to release the imagination – the very thing needed in the troubled times of the contemporary university, seeking more inclusivity and engagement of a broader range of professors, students and administrators. The power of the collective – well known to women – to challenge and reshape might well be what is needed to rescue the contemporary university, finding meaningful spaces for critical authentic pluralist engagement in multiple forms of knowing.

Against loneliness and violence, the arts offer community and connection (Mark). Against fragmentation, the arts bring a sense of wholeness (von Kotze and Small). Against racism and colonisation, the arts are means towards new understandings and a greater sense of power, as Etmanski, Weigler and Wong-Sneddon through *métissage* and von Kotze and Small through their community-based programme. Against workplace stress or the stupefactions of neoliberalism and traditionalism, the arts bring energy, vitality and renewal (Husted and Tofteng, Chapter 8).

The ideas and practices described in this book are pictorial representations of what some might refer to poetically as 'cracks'. These are small yet growing practices of resistance and change that challenge the defensive structures of a hyper-rationalist, neoliberal re-orientation whose roots are deeply embedded in Von Humboldt's idea of university study as non-purposeful and the pursuit of knowledge solely for knowledge's sake (or art's sake) or self-cultivation (Taylor, 2010). The arts themselves are indeed one of the 'cracks' that shed light for the type of work described in this volume, but another is the students and the community members themselves. As Hyland-Russell notes in Chapter 3: 'if the students could be courageous enough to cross the classroom's liminal threshold despite their profound anxiety, [I] could abandon the safety of a formal academic posture and could risk telling a story.' The students and community members embolden professors to jump into the fray, as described by Butterwick and Clover, and model artistic creation in all its imperfection, take aesthetic risks, challenge norms and seek out the voices that are silenced by encouraging what Wyman calls the defiant immigration. In turn, students and community members overcome their trepidation as they experience joy and meaningfulness through paint, music, glue, fabric, movement, crayons or the lens – the stuff of artistic/creative engagement.

There is no doubt that some students and community members' surrender for life to the imagination-crushing tactics of primary and elementary schools articulated poignantly by Butterwick and Clover. Moreover, for the reasons outlined in the Introduction to this volume, the arts have been aligned with mere entertainment, banished to an ontological homelessness. Yet the arts and research methods courses described in the first two sections of this volume are in fact filled to capacity, and often have waiting lists. Students do defy fine arts' warnings and they, along with others, as Tracey and Allen note, from a variety of faculties and departments, come in search of ways to use their talent as artists out of curiosity or out of need for a more socially, politically, academically and culturally meaningful engagement with ideas. Another crack of light, although often very faint, is the creative bridging of university and community illustrated particularly in the third section of this volume, inclusive of the work of artists. Today public higher education institutions are under increasing pressure from governments, taxpayers, civil society and even professors to connect with communities and to help them to develop solutions to major social and economic problems affecting contemporary society. This is now referred to as the socially responsive and responsible role of universities towards the communities surrounding the campus but, also, beyond university boundaries. This process can be problematic if universities design programmes and then simply 'deliver' them patronisingly in the 'best interests' of these communities. Moreover, these pressures to build strong university–community collaborations pose 'problems for the academy because they demand interdisciplinary cooperation, rejection of turf' (Fitzgerald et al., 2010: i). But for the authors of this volume, this push provides an opportunity for collaborative learning and working partnerships to produce purposeful knowledge and actions that creatively expand how, together, universities and communities can address the urgent needs of society today. These partnerships take various forms in this volume and they raise different kinds of questions and complexities.

One partnership illustrated in this book is a multi-university alliance with community organisations such as the one described by Mark. The collective goal is to play a more active role in peacebuilding initiatives by training literacy tutors to use artful and creative methods to more rapidly lift the shroud of silence and violence draped over Northern Ireland. A second type of partnership is university–cultural organisation collaborations as outlined in the chapters by Hunter, Park, and Hyland-Russell and Groen. In Hunter's case, the partnership aimed to challenge the bias in university instruction that produced dance graduates with expertise in performing and choreography (theory) but lacking the employability and managerial skills required for the UK dance industry (practice/praxis). Higher education scholars, however, share concerns about this, arguing that it may be an unwelcome professionalisation, a 'hypertrophy of pragmatic instruction and the disappearance of scholarly transcendence' (Palous, 1996: 177). Palous goes on to argue

> it is not the mission of universities to be 'professional' schools. Of course they must not allow themselves to fall behind in their professional standards and slip into dilettantism, but nevertheless their character as universities leads them to a broader perspective … For all the importance of professional qualifications, it is still basic scholarship and the original conceptualising of problems which again and again shatters the intellectual chains that hold mental life in closed caves. (1996: 177)

Smyth and Hattam concur, adding that we need 'to counteract a prevailing discourse which seeks to reduce the work of academics to that of a technical enterprise based on the needs of the market rather than scholarly practices informed by ethical frameworks' (2000: 159). While perhaps at first blush the work outlined by Mark in general and Hunter in particular seems to have slid down the slippery slope of 'professionalism', we would argue that a careful reading illuminates an ethos of transcendent scholarship that opens 'closed caves' and challenges mere employment training. In the case of Mark's work, the universities apply critical literacy theories as well as theories of imagination and creativity in learning to address the underlying elements of distrust and exclusion that perpetuate violence. Looking through critical aesthetic lenses in Hunter's chapter, we see learning dance 'skills' as a means to assisting more creatively with the work of organisations around disadvantaged individuals and communities such as street children and young gangsters. Yet, one must ponder, is it also this element that brings about the 'afterthought' in Hunter's chapter vis-à-vis the discontinuation of the programme? Or is it simply the contemporary drive towards 'research-intensity' and away from professionalism and practice under the guise, as noted above, of dismantling academic silos?

Cultural democracy

Hyland-Russell and Groen and Park speak to us of other types of university–cultural organisation collaborations, which provide complex discourses of the democratisation of culture versus cultural democracy. Allocated to the conservative end of the debate is the democratisation of culture – the process of bringing High Art to the masses that we spoke of in the Introduction. For some this is a hegemonic procedure aimed at cheating the mass of people of their right to create their own culture by actively disseminating elite classical ideas of art, thereby indoctrinating them into the established hierarchy of the art world. As we noted in the Introduction, this action was motivated by a moral, and what many would call patronising, commitment towards the 'betterment' of the lower classes. If this is the case then why would adult educators develop courses or promote the work of arts and cultural institutions? Of course there are counters to this, as illustrated in this volume. By denying the opportunity to engage with arts and cultural institutions, are we not simply creating a problematic elitism whereby adult educators have knowledge and a sense of their own right/ability to access the High Arts, but may patronisingly protect the lower masses or less educated from this sphere? Hyland-Russell and Groen illustrate how learning can become an interactive dynamic process in which, as MacFarlane argues, 'imagination drives action in exploring and interacting with an environment ... [Real learning] requires a dialogue between imagination and experience' (1996: 53). What we see in this volume through the interaction of learning and a public art environment is a growing capacity to question society's foundational principles about aesthetics, the role of the artist, the neutrality of the art establishment, as well as ways of understanding concepts of experimentation and how art is evaluated. Perhaps most importantly, this site-based learning develops in the adult a greater a sense of cultural agency, which includes the right to participate in the cultural making and re-making of society at all and any levels. This is referred to as cultural democracy, the demand to equal access, gaining greater control over and expanded opportunities to consume and produce or disseminate culture. An interesting bridge between the democratisation of culture and cultural democracy in this volume is in the research work described by Husted and Tofteng and Etmanski, Weigler and Wong-Sneddon, in which professional artists are used. Are the research participants the producers of culture (the theatre piece and the *metissage*), given that the performances mirrored information they provided on their lives to the artists? How much control do the participants have over the process of production? Clearly a great deal since they challenged the interpretation of their experiences at one point and changed the direction of the research in the case of Husted and

Tofteng. In both cases, cultural democratic principles enabled radical forms of critical pedagogy and challenging ways to give voice to and be of service to social change within and outside the academy.

Perhaps another twist to the notion of cultural democracy in this volume is around the artists, or 'Artists in Residence'. Risenhoover and Blackburn argued in 1976 that 'the institutionalisation of the arts within universities was not immediately paralleled by a move of … artists to the campuses' (1976: 8). Artists viewed universities as places with too many constraints to be viable sites for creative output. Yet back in 1536 in *Poetica*, Daniello wrote 'because of their power to delight, [artists] teach more pleasantly (and thus effectively) than any philosopher ever could'. Although this may not necessarily be totally true, 'artists' play key roles in the pages of this volume in a variety of ways.

First, as noted above in the chapters by Husted and Tofteng and Etmanski, Weigler, and Wong-Sneddon, there is the professional artist who assists with the research and then performs the findings to the audience of participants. The artists bring professionalism to the work but also provide anonymity. Although not always necessary, in the case of research where the group works together in one institution, or where the issues being raised are highly politically charged or could cause personal damage, anonymity ensures that voices and issues are heard without the speaker having to suffer any negative consequences. The actors also create the 'critical distance' that Besta (2007) argues is fundamental to educational research. Critical distance is what allows insights that may be troubling, that people would rather not hear or see but that, unless unearthed, will remain unresolved. Secondly, as demonstrated in and Jarvis and Williamson's chapter, there is the notion that 'we are all artists' or, at least, creative beings. In university classes, research and the community, students or community members become the creators of the art. Thirdly, we see the professional or community-based artist being brought into the classroom to teach. It is not easy to capture or specify exactly what comprises the power and potential of the artist in the classroom but there are several ways of speaking to this. Authors Butterwick and Clover, and Sanford and Mimick, for example, speak of how the artists encourage the artistry of art-making by encouraging people to take risks, add colour for emphasis, centre an image or seek balance, mindful that people have both affective and cognitive sides that require nurturing. The artists pay equal attention to the educative-community building process. What all of this says is that cultural meaning, expression and creativity reside within a community and collaborations between artists and others such as community members and students is central and necessary to the practice.

Whither technology?

MacFarlane argues that we need to challenge and re-examine many of the conventional teaching practices used in universities today. He believes that 'in particular, it is necessary to consider carefully how, and to what extent we make use of technology in improving the provision of teaching and the support of learning'

(1996: 54). Yet curiously there is little if any mention in this volume of technology as a useful tool. Rather, technology was one of the problematic issues being explored in Husted and Tofteng's chapter. Arts-based education, as described in the diverse chapters in this volume, offers ways of reconnecting cognitive, affective and physical holistically, weaving together the artificial Cartesian separation of mind and body. Technology as a set of tools has the potential to enable and support a wide range of creative endeavours, but in itself is somewhat of an abstraction – the physical body is removed from the experience. So, while participants in Tracey and Allen's project enjoyed creating collages with computers as well as with scissors and glue, it was the visceral characteristics of the creation that deeply connected their minds to the physical cutting and pasting. Although technology enables, for many students and community members, access to artefacts, ideas and experiences that were not open to them in earlier iterations, it does not replace – and does not need to replace – those moments of creation that engage us wholly. It is, perhaps, those mind/body/affect connections that prompted the authors of this volume to share their ideas. It is that 'being in the moment' with oneself and others, creating synergies that reconnect us to our emotions and our imaginations and speak to powerfully engaging educational practice. Technologies can create strong bridges between universities and community, but perhaps should not replace the relational aspects that resonate through embodied engagement with others.

That being said, many creative and imaginative learning experiences can be supported through diverse uses of technology, enabling greater access to ideas, community and formal university education. Tracey and Allen's initial attempt to use digital forms of collage can, using the ideas shared by their students, be reshaped into a more interactive experience. Moreover, although the technically produced collage is more thematic – the traditional way of analysing/displaying research – it does have an essence of symbolism and metaphor. Sanford and Mimick's use of interactive blogs, forums and websites enabled additional ways for students to connect with each other beyond the formal classroom space. The use of Moodle, a learning management system in which ongoing communication between students is facilitated and where artefacts (print as well as visual and aural) are shared, offers new possible uses of technologies that have previously not been considered. A creative fusion of traditional or historical forms with new technologies is demonstrated in these chapters and the potential for further connections might be seen through online storytelling, creation of art forms, and sharing of these forms across geographical distances.

Arts and the contemporary university: where to from here?

The twelve chapters in this volume offer examples of education drawing fundamentally on the arts to inspire, engage and educate – breathing new life into what can often be a dull process, as Lawrence and Cranton comment. In their struggles for legitimacy within the university, the authors have documented examples of creative ways forward. The need for lifelong learning has never before been so critical, and the need to provide access for all sectors of society is therefore self-evident. Access to education that enables future possibilities, as illustrated in Hunter's chapter, can in some ways improve conditions for individuals and their communities. For example, in Storefront 101, Hyland-Russell and Groen use storytelling to break down language barriers for their community participants, re-focusing on how language can enable rather than disable the learning process for the 'disenfranchised', providing hope as they seek to create new pathways for their students' future learning. Contemporary universities will need to continue bridging the gaping chasms between themselves and their existing and new communities.

Changing notions of organisational structures in networked communities can serve to break down the traditional disciplinary structures that have been upheld by universities for centuries, as suggested by the interdisciplinary skills training programme described by Tracey and Allen. Introducing a common arts-based course to students in a range of different programmes offers ways to increase communication across disciplines, see with new eyes and feel the power of arts-based exploration and creation. Thinking and problem solving with new tools opens our eyes to fresh perspectives that enrich all areas of study. As our human and ecological problems grow increasingly complex, we need to embrace new ways of engaging with ideas in order to find better solutions. As communication becomes enabled through cross-connections facilitated in part through arts-based interactions, stronger links are forged and the importance of relationship in the learning process is recognised. Contemporary universities will need to give more credence to interdisciplinary thinking supported by and through the arts, as it is arts-based engagements that will enable us to transcend language and discipline boundaries and create new synergies. These ideals are responses to the desires of community or students, but also expressions of what the educators, researchers and practitioners think an imaginatively empowering educational or research experience should be.

New relationships develop through arts-based expressions of ideas and serve to strengthen existing relationships, as Mark shows through the creative methodology of peacebuilding. Relationships across institutional, discipline and cultural lines become more established and acknowledged. The authors here have frequently drawn on existing relationships to write their chapters. They have written about relationships created through the needs of their learners, and have attempted to foster relationships within their classes and beyond.

Recognition of the value of relationships provides the foundation for different understandings of how learning happens. Instead of being understood as an individual pursuit, rich and powerful learning happens in relationship – with new ideas, new language, new communities. In aesthetic relationship, strong communities form around issues and people they truly care about, where there is responsibility for one another. Arts-based engagements nurture the creative and imaginative aspect of learners, supporting collaborative work in pleasurable ways. Once released from the confines of 'rigour' and 'scientific knowledge' that too often exemplify university learning, learners (students and professors) find enjoyment in shaping their ideas through drawing, dancing, role-playing, cutting and pasting. They enjoy sharing our artefacts and considering what they have learned through the creation process. Contemporary universities need to recognise both the power of relationship and the need to create more learning spaces that encourage relationships to form and grow.

Respect for diverse voices is created when learners are able to recognise each others' knowledge as demonstrated through a multiplicity of forms – storytelling, music-making, theatre, *métissage*, dance, quilts, online fora – to share insights, experiences and perspectives. Each member of the community has something of substance to contribute to the collective understanding and each voice is acknowledged and valued. Feminist pluralistic networks draw upon the arts to engage, connect and support the diversity of voices within and beyond existing communities. Diversity enables the evolution of ideas and the ability of institutions to respond to the wide-ranging needs of the communities within it. If contemporary universities are to thrive, they must adapt to meet the needs of the current population and seek to encourage new rhizomatic growth – including a legitimate space, beyond and within the fine arts, for arts-based education, research and community cultural engagement.

In spite of the challenges of the often excessively technocratic, standardised and individualised university that the authors draw attention to, it must be acknowledged that the university has always been, and will continue to be, a key player in the arts and cultural world. Indeed, Knox reminds us that universities play a key role in 'raising the consciousness of the general public about the nature and importance of creativity in various artistic, scientific, scholarly and professional domains' (2011: 108). The cultural impact of universities has in fact 'been the subject of a number of previous studies, and was a feature for example of work undertaken by the OECD' (Duke et al., in press). Moreover, Duke, Osborne and Wilson argue that 'at the most basic level this is achieved at universities by offering specific courses with a cultural content delivered for local audiences at all levels from non-accredited adult education to postgraduate'. The chapters by Hyland-Russell and Groen, Hunter and Park in particular reflect these links. But Zipsane (2011) adds another dimension. Speaking specifically of museums – though we would argue that this can be extended to many arts and cultural institutions – he argues that a gap has emerged between museums and universities. He believes that this is because museums do not always recognise that, in academia, disciplines such as history, archaeology, art and ethnology have long since lost their belief 'in the great narratives based upon unchallengeable interpretations of material and immaterial traces from the past' (Duke et al., in press). Based on this, Zipsane argues that arts and cultural institutions 'need' to collaborate with universities as it is they who can help break down silos and challenge problematic interpretations of the past and the present.

Conclusion

> Dreaming is involuntary and daydreaming is only vaguely intentional, but aesthetics involves consciousness and judgement. (Miles, 2012: 11)

The arts, Lippard argues, have both a 'social significance and a social function, which might be defined as the transformation of desire into reality, reality into dreams and change, and back again' (1983: 5). In this volume, the act of making, engaging in or connecting to or through the arts is essentially a creative process aimed at responding to the local, global, social, political, educational or cultural questions, issues and concerns that form the *mise-en-scène* of our time. Arts-based adult education, learning and research, as articulated in this volume, are imaginative, participatory and critical approaches to personal, political, economic, social and cultural transformation. They are based on working and learning collectively through artistic processes to develop new paradigms for comprehending and valuing culture and people's aesthetic selves; promoting consciousness and knowledge; stimulating imaginative critique; reconstructing and repositioning cultural identity; strengthening cultural democracy and community leadership; enhancing people's abilities to challenge processes and practices that exclude, marginalise and disempower; and fostering social action. Importantly, they bring us back to pleasure, meaningfulness and connecting socially, and thereby challenge individualistic teaching and evaluating.

Like Etmanski, Weigler and Wong-Sneddon, our hope in writing this book was that other scholars and practitioners would feel encouraged to use arts-based methods to create more imaginative, critical and holistic engagements within academic settings and communities or to reach out to arts and cultural institutions to develop new processes of visual literacy and ways to respond to a troubled world. If we did it, so can you.

References

Besta, B. (2007), 'Bridging the gap between educational research and educational practice: the need for critical distance', *Educational Research and Evaluation*, 13(3): 295–301.

Clover, D.E. (2012), 'Feminist artists and popular education: the creative turn', in L. Manicom and S. Walters (eds), *Feminist Popular Education in Transnational Debates: Building Pedagogies of Possibility*, New York: Palgrave Macmillan, 193–208.

Deleuze, G., and Guattari, F. (1987), *A Thousand Plateaus: Capitalism and Schizophrenia*, London: Athlone Press.

Duke, C., Osborne, M., and Wilson, B. (in press), *A New Imperative – Regions and Higher Education in Difficult Times*, Manchester: Manchester University Press.

Fitzgerald, H., Burack, C., and Seifer, S. (eds) (2010), *Engaged Scholarship: Contemporary Landscapes, Future Directions*, East Lansing: Michigan State University.

Greene, M. (1995), *Releasing the Imagination: Essays on Education, the Arts, and Social Change*, San Francisco: Jossey-Bass.

Knox, A. (2011), 'Creativity and learning', *Journal of Adult and Continuing Education*, 17(2): 96–111.

Kwakkenbos, L. (2011), 'The laboratory of insurrectionary imagination: art, activism and permaculture – an interview with Isa Fremeaux and John Jordan', in L. De Cauter, R. De Roo, and K. Vanhaesebrouck (eds), *Art and Activism in the Age of Globalization*, Rotterdam. NAi Publishers, 298–307.

Lippard, L. (1983), *Overlay: Contemporary Art and the Art of Prehistory*, New York: The New Press.

MacFarlane, A. (1996), 'Future patterns of teaching and learning', in T. Schuller (ed.), *The Changing University?*, Buckingham: Open University Press, 52–65.

Miles, M. (2012), *Herbert Marcuse: An Aesthetic of Liberation*, London: Pluto Press.

Mullin, A. (2003), 'Feminist art and the political imagination', *Hypatia*, 18(4): 190–213.

Palous, R. (1996), 'The social and political vocation of the university of the global age', in T. Schuller (ed.), *The Changing University?*, Buckingham: Open University Press, 176–78.

Risenhoover, M., and Blackburn, R.T (1976), *Artists as Professors: Conversations with Musicians, Painters and Sculptors*, Chicago: University of Illinois Press.

Schuller, T. (ed.) (1996), *The Changing University?*, Buckingham: Open University Press.

Shukaitis, S., Graeber, D., and Biddle, E. (eds) (2005), *Constituent Imagination: Militant Investigations/Collective Theorization*, Oakland: AK Press.

Smyth J., and Hattam R. (2000), 'Intellectual as hustler: researching against the grain of the market', *British Educational Research Journal*, 26(2): 157–75.

Taylor, M.C. (2010), *Crisis on Campus: A Bold Plan for Reforming Our Colleges and Universities*, New York: Random House.

Thompson, J. (2002), *Bread and Roses: Arts, Culture and Lifelong Learning*, Leicester: NIACE.

Zipsane, H. (2011), 'The changing roles of museums', http://pobs.cc/2r8l (accessed 3 October 2012).

Index